PLANTING GREEN ROOFS AND LIVING WALLS

PLANTING GREEN ROOFS AND LIVING WALLS

Nigel Dunnett and Noël Kingsbury

Timber Press
Portland • Cambridge

To my mother and father, for instilling in me a love of gardens and plants.

ND

Photographs on page ii: *left* Deeper substrates enable drought-tolerant subshrubs such as lavender to survive on green roofs ©ZinCo; *right* English ivy and Virginia creeper root freely into this modular, soil filled wall Photograph by Soil Retention Systems.

Published in 2004 by

Timber Press, Inc.
The Haseltine Building
133 S.W. Second Avenue, Suite 450
Portland, Oregon 97204-3527, U.S.A

www.timberpress.com

Timber Press
2 Station Road
Swavesey
Cambridge CB4 5QJ, U.K.

Reprinted 2004

Designed by Dick Malt
Printed through Colorcraft Ltd., Hong Kong

Library of Congress Cataloging-in-Publication Data

Dunnett, Nigel.
  Planting green roofs and living walls / Nigel Dunnett and Noël Kingsbury.
      p. cm.
  Includes bibliographical references (p.   ).
  ISBN 0-88192-640-X (hardcover)
  1. Green roofs (Gardening) 2. Ornamental climbing plants
  3. Vertical gardening. I. Kingsbury, Noël. II. Title.
SB419.5.D85 2004   635.9'671—dc22   2003024231

A catalogue record for this book is also available from the British Library.

CONTENTS

ACKNOWLEDGEMENTS

The writing of this book has been a personal journey of discovery that developed from a passionate interest in the innovative and ecological use of plants on and around buildings. Visits to Germany and Scandinavia opened my eyes to the small- and large-scale possibilities of roof greening, but it was the work of the North American organization Green Roofs for Healthy Cities that brought home the economic benefits of plants on buildings. I am grateful to Steven Peck from Green Roofs for Healthy Cities for the use of some of their material in the book. Particular thanks go to Heidi Eckert of ZinCo in Germany for supplying images. I am also very grateful to Tommy Porselius of VegTech, Sweden, Stephan Brenneisen, and Manfred Köhler for providing valuable images and to Andy Clayden for line drawings. Charlie Miller of Roofscapes, Inc., gave very helpful comments on the text. Thank you also to Anna Mumford from Timber Press for enabling this project to occur in the first place.

Special thanks go to my wife, Helen, for her love and encouragement and for allowing me to turn every available roof surface in our garden into an experimental planting site.

Nigel Dunnett

I'd like to thank all those people who have given so generously of their time in helping me understand this inspiring and hopeful group of technologies: Gunter Mann of Optigrün in Germany, Tom Liptan in Portland, Violetta Lindhqvist of Malmö in Sweden, and Fritz Wassmann in Switzerland. I'm also very grateful to Prof. Hans-Joachim Liesecke and Dr. Walter Kolb for their generosity in answering questions and providing me with extensive material on the history and background of roof greening.

I'm also grateful to Ian Huish, who was my German teacher at school, without whose efforts all those years ago much of this research would have been impossible. Finally, I thank my partner, Jo Eliot, for her love and support.

Noël Kingsbury

CHAPTER 1

Introduction

Planting on roofs and walls is one of the most innovative and quickly developing fields in the worlds of both horticulture and the built environment. To those not familiar with the concept, it may seem surprising and unexpected at first, even outlandish and difficult to accept. A little familiarity with the rationale and a closer look at some successful projects, however, soon win over sceptics. After all, even the Pentagon in Washington, D.C., has an area of planted roof. If the hard-headed soldiers of the U.S. military are convinced, then there must be a method behind the madness.

Visitors to central Europe may have noticed an increasing number of planted areas on roofs—not the roof gardens that are sometimes seen on luxury apartments, but areas of grass or other low plantings on flat or gently inclined roofs, often on commercial buildings where there can be little need for aesthetics or human use. In the southern German city of Stuttgart, there is a small and very beautiful Chinese garden. At the rear is a spot with a particularly spectacular view over the city, where it is possible to see the rooftops below. The observant visitor can use this vantage point to appreciate how many of them have some kind of vegetative covering. Visitors to modern buildings such as colleges, apartment blocks, schools, and industrial plants can see a great number of these roofs at closer proximity.

In neighbouring Switzerland in the city of Zürich, anyone coming out of the northern exit of the central railway station can see the national museum with its striking tower, some six storeys high, on two corners of which are wisteria plants, clambering up cables almost to the very top. Having seen a few spectacular examples like this, the attentive visitor starts to look out for others and becomes increasingly aware that

All the available roofs in this commercial development in Stuttgart, Germany, support vegetation.

© ZinCo

1

not only do people in this part of the world like covering their roofs with greenery, they seem to be quite happy to let plant life loose on their walls, too. For those who are used to the idea that buildings and plants somehow do not mix, it is all a bit much to come to terms with! The sense of surprise becomes even deeper when one learns that in some countries and regions it is a legal requirement to build green roofs.

Elsewhere in the world, examples are fewer but seen increasingly often, usually on new and innovative buildings. An idea and technology that started in the German-speaking countries of central Europe is spreading to other countries in northern and north-western Europe and to North America. No doubt the concept and the techniques will soon begin to be adapted for other regions of the globe as well.

The contemporary use of plants on roofs and walls is distinguished from previous uses by the integration of planting and its supporting structures with the construction of the buildings themselves, as well as the use of modern materials. The result is a dovetailing of living plants, the building, and its human users, a closeness and integration not easy to achieve with older construction technologies. It is important to appreciate the distinction between older technologies of plant use and the new.

Old-style roof gardens either restricted the planting to containers and planters or used a layer of ordinary soil spread onto a roof surface, which had to be massively stronger than would otherwise need to be the case. New-style roof greening recognizes two distinct approaches, intensive and extensive.

Intensive roof greening is similar to the old-style roof gardens, where it is expected that people would use the area much as a conventional garden. Plants are maintained on an individual basis in the same way as they would in a garden at ground level. Soil depth is generally at least 15 cm (6 in) deep, but now may be composed of lightweight growing media, and is thus more correctly known as *substrate*. Simple intensive green roofs are covered with lawns or ground covering plants that still require regular maintenance, but have thinner substrates and are therefore less costly to install. Access may be possible, but generally these roofs are intended to be overlooked (English Nature 2003).

Extensive roof greening is not intended for regular human usage and may not even be intended to be seen on a regular basis. Plants are treated

Intensive green roofs can support diverse vegetation. This roof garden, constructed over a car park (a ventilation outlet is visible), contains trees and shrubs as well as stone paving. ING Bank Corporate Building, Amsterdam.

Contemporary approaches to greening buildings are characterized by the integration of planting and its supporting structures with the construction of the building itself.

Photograph by Fritz Wassmann

This grass-covered roof links the building with the surrounding park but also enables people to walk and sunbathe on top of the building.

Extensive green roofs are lightweight and thin compared to intensive roofs and generally more naturalistic in appearance.

en masse, rather as grass plants are in a lawn. Any maintenance operation is carried out on them all simultaneously, such as mowing. In any case, maintenance is generally designed to be minimal. Substrate depth can be between 2 and 15 cm (0.8 and 6 in), which reduces the amount of extra loading that must be built into the roof construction.

Ecoroof is a term used in some places as a substitute for *green roof*. Some people use the name to describe vegetated extensive roofs as a way to distinguish them from other types of roof that may have an ecological function (such as roofs covered with photovoltaic cells) that can also be called green roofs (using the word green in its popular ecological or environmental sense). Ecoroof has also been taken up as a descriptive term for extensive green roofs in climates that experience very dry periods that cause vegetation to brown or ripen. For example, extensive green roofs in the city of Portland, Oregon, are referred to as ecoroofs because they are not green but brown for much of the growing season and therefore the term green is seen as a misnomer.

Brown roof is a term to describe roofs that have been covered with substrate or loose material but have not been purposefully planted. Brown roofs are created primarily for biodiversity purposes and aim to recreate typical brownfield conditions through the use of by-products of the development of urban sites: brick rubble, crushed concrete, and subsoils. Such roofs may colonize spontaneously with vegetation but the unvegetated loose substrates can also provide habitat for a range of invertebrates and birds.

This book is largely concerned with extensive rather than intensive roof-greening techniques; the latter is a subject that has already received coverage in several books (for instance, Osmundson 1999). However, the simple classification of intensive versus extensive is not so clear-cut. A more recent concept has begun to emerge, the semi-extensive green roof, that holds much potential for the creative extension of roof planting (Dunnett 2002). Semi-extensive roofs have the same low or no-input philosophy of the extensive roof and use similarly lightweight substrates and modern green-roof construction technologies, but they have slightly deeper layers of growing medium (10–20 cm, 4–8 in) and therefore enable a wider and more diverse range of plants to be grown.

There is also no reason why ecologically informed approaches should be restricted to inaccessible, extensive green roofs. There is great scope

for using extensive and semi-extensive techniques on accessible roofs, combined perhaps with larger herbaceous and woody plant material in strategically placed containers or planters to create contemporary roof gardens that are much more sustainable than the roof gardens of the past. The ecological theme can be extended still further through water recycling, water storage, and harnessing the solar and wind energy that is available in abundance at roof level.

FAÇADE GREENING

While it has been common practice to grow climbers on the exterior walls of buildings for many centuries, they rarely reached more than two storeys high, with the exception of self-clinging species such as Virginia creeper (*Parthenocissus tricuspidata*), and their use tended to be very localized to particular geographical regions. Modern *façade greening* refers to the application of modern technologies to support a much wider range of climbing plants to much greater heights.

Left: Semi-extensive roofs use the same lightweight technology and growing media as extensive roofs, but their slightly greater depth enables a wider range of plants to be grown. Planting design by Nigel Dunnett.

Intensive and extensive roof greening techniques can be combined on the same roof. Green roof atop Chicago City Hall.

Green roofs and climbers cover virtually all available surfaces on this building, improving both its visual quality and its environmental functioning.

Photograph by Manfred Köhler

There are several other modern and highly innovative approaches to the use of plants that we examine in this book. Some of these concern the use of plants in hydroponic systems of vertical or non-horizontal surfaces, either for decorative effect or as part of a water-purification process. Others involve using plants growing in the ground, as a living alternative to hard construction materials or mechanical water-filtration systems. *Bioengineering* is a useful term that covers these novel techniques.

Integrating living plants with the built environment has many advantages, and outlining these is an important part of this book. Those who wish to promote any new technology almost invariably face an uphill struggle in convincing clients, policy makers, the media, and the general public to take their ideas seriously. This is especially the case with something like growing plants on roofs and walls, the advantages of which can seem quite counter-intuitive. Setting out the case for using plants on buildings is also an important part of this book. While the advantages are discussed in more detail in their relevant sections, it is worthwhile summarizing them here.

Greenery improves the visual and aesthetic aspects of urban areas. More fundamentally it is widely recognized as therapeutic, with a number of research studies illustrating this, for example, hospital patients who can see a tree out of the nearest window recover more quickly than those who cannot (Ulrich 1984). Plants also can provide habitat for urban wildlife. A great many animal species are happy to live in urban areas if they can find the habitat.

All green plants help to ameliorate the effects of pollution: absorbing noise, trapping dust, recycling carbon dioxide, and absorbing and breaking down many gaseous pollutants. Plants help to reduce the negative climatic effects of urbanization, for example, by absorbing some of the heat generated in city environments and absorbing the rainfall that runs off hard surfaces. They can thus contribute to improved urban climates at the microclimatic scale but also at the larger scale, helping to ameliorate the effect of the urban heat island, combat urban flooding, and reduce energy costs associated with keeping buildings cool in hot climates. Plants can help to regulate the interior climates of buildings by insulating them against extremes of heat and cold, and they can play a part in air-conditioning systems.

While these points apply to all plants, the great advantage of planting on roofs and walls is that it is a way of getting greenery into places where conventional tree and shrub planting is not feasible, and so bringing these positive aspects into many more places.

This book aims to be a general introduction to the topic, looking at both the reasons for working with plants on buildings and the essentials of the techniques involved, with a strong focus on the plants used. Only

Even the most rudimentary of vegetation layers on a roof can confer a wide range of benefits compared to bare roof surfaces.

a limited amount of detailed construction information is given, partly for reasons of space. Also, the technologies involved are young and are developing rapidly, and technical details will rapidly change as new materials come onto the market and new ways of doing things are developed. Instead we aim to discuss the basic principles, so that anyone interested in applying them can discuss their application with relevant specialists in an informed way. The actual business of large-scale roof and façade greening and bioengineering can often involve the specialist knowledge of several professions: structural engineers, surveyors, builders, architects, and water engineers. Even the professional installer of green roofs is often dependent upon giving these people a brief, and leaving the technical details to their expertise. However, keen amateurs will be able to find enough information here to enable them to carry out small-scale projects themselves. Potential readers of this book include:

Professionals involved in architecture, construction, horticulture, landscape, town planning, environmental management, ecology, and nature conservation.
Keen amateur gardeners looking for exciting and innovative ways of growing plants.
Environmental and community activists looking for ways to improve their local environment.
Decision and policy makers concerned with environment.
Horticultural professionals who work with the landscape and construction business, for example, owners and managers of nurseries and garden designers.
Do-it-yourself and self-build enthusiasts, particularly those interested in the ecological building movement.

Having set out the basic principles, we also aim to provide readers with the tools to discover more about the technical details and more particular applications of bioengineering technologies and to keep up to date with the latest developments. This is the role of the sources section at the end, listing the technical literature, consultants, journals, websites, installation companies, and some places where examples of good practice may be seen.

In the field of garden and landscape design it is customary to talk about the *hard* and *soft* aspects, the former being the use of non-living materials such as paving and stone, the latter the plants. Likewise in the use of plants on buildings, this is also a useful distinction to make. Whereas the hard elements used, such as geotextiles, substrate materials, and cabling will be similar all over the world, the soft elements used will depend very much on climate and region. This is an area where appropriate species will need to be tested afresh in every region, which, together with the fact that it is the plants that are the visible end result, means that plant selection is a particularly exciting area. While the plant selection we discuss in detail is one that has been used successfully in the realm of bioengineering, we also discuss the general principles of plant selection, providing practitioners with the tools to start making appropriate choices in other parts of the world.

BACKGROUND AND HISTORY

Ornamental roof gardens appear to have been developed initially by the ancient civilizations of the Tigris and Euphrates River valleys (the most famous examples of which were the hanging gardens of Babylon in the seventh and eighth centuries B.C.) and by the Romans. However, it was only the development of modern building materials and techniques that allowed the more extensive creation of rooftop gardens. In particular, with the development of concrete as a roofing material in the mid-1800s, flat-roofed buildings began to be constructed in major cities throughout Europe and America. The 1868 World Exhibition in Paris included a planted concrete "nature roof," the first of several such experimental projects in western Europe. Among these was the construction of a block of apartments built with planted terraces and a roof garden in Paris in 1903, a restaurant with a roof garden in Chicago in 1914 designed by Frank Lloyd Wright, and a similar project by Walter Gropius in Cologne in the same year. The architect Le Corbusier was perhaps the first to use roof gardens more systematically from the 1920s onwards, but only within the context of elite buildings for wealthy clients. The most famous roof garden, which still exists, was that built for the London department store Derry and Toms in the 1930s. Containing a variety of themed gardens spread over 6000 square metres (64,560 square feet), more than any other example it introduced a wide range of people to the idea.

It wasn't until the twentieth century, however, that improved building techniques promoted the dominance of flat roofs in new urban development. The widespread construction of flat roofs that could carry relatively large weight loads led to the development and expansion of roof gardens or intensive green roofs. These were primarily installed for aesthetic reasons, and, as discussed above, required solid and expensive materials and intensive garden maintenance (Herman 2003). Indeed, in the second half of the twentieth century, technology enabled the construction of urban plazas that were in effect huge roof landscapes, but in a form that would be unrecognized by the general public, over underground car parks, roads, subways, and so on.

As we noted earlier, this book is not primarily focused on the high-input intensive green roof. Instead we have to look to a different tradition for the roots of the low-input extensive green roof: the grass, turf, or sod roof. Grass roofs have been a feature of the vernacular architecture of certain geographic regions for centuries, and probably millennia, notably Scandinavia and Kurdistan—the areas of Turkey, Iraq, Iran, and neighbouring countries occupied by Kurdish-speaking peoples. Mud or earth is a traditional building material in this region. Flat, mud-covered roofs often become colonized with grasses, producing the turf-roof effect. The combined soil and grass on Scandinavian roofs helped reduce heat loss during the long, dark winters. Traditional Kurdish turf roofs serve to keep in heat in winter and keep out the burning sun in summer. Scandinavian immigrants to the United States and Canada took the idea with them, and for some time grass roofs were used on settler cabins.

In Scandinavia, turf grass was basically seen as a readily available and cheap building material. Together with layers of birch bark and twigs or straw, it functioned well in keeping the rain on the outside of the small houses and cottages. Built over closely fitting wooden boards, the construction of these roofs in some way resembled that of the modern extensive green roof. The birch bark functioned as the sealing membrane, the twig layer as drainage, and the turf cut from a meadow was

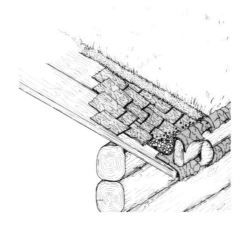

used as insulation for the house and to protect the lower roof layers from wind and sunlight that otherwise would have reduced the life span of the bark. Different species of *Sedum*, *Sempervivum*, and *Jovibarba* were sometimes planted on the roofs because their roots had a reinforcing effect on the soil layer. Documents show that even rye (*Secale cereale*) was deliberately sown to reinforce the soil layer. However, grass roofs needed regular maintenance; the grass vegetation had to be cut and spontaneously established trees had to be removed. Vegetated roofs with a high organic content and dense grass vegetation were also highly flammable. Their lifetime was limited, and they needed to be changed after twenty years, mainly due to decomposition of the sealing birch-bark layer (Emilsson 2003).

Diagram of a traditional Scandinavian turf roof, with sections of birch bark forming a waterproof layer.

Drawing © Eugen Ulmer GmbH & Co, Stuttgart

The Norwegian Folkcenter in Oslo consists of historic wooden structures with living roofs using turf and a membrane of birch bark.

Photograph by Catherine Waneck

The development of modern building materials greatly reduced the number of green roofs being built in Scandinavia. The building materials supplied by industry required less maintenance, were affordable, and were available in places where there was no turf grass. Traditional sod roofs or peat roofs are still being built in some Scandinavian countries, but mainly for aesthetic reasons.

It is to the German-speaking European countries that we must look for the origins of what we would recognize as the contemporary green roof. Here, a combination of an environmentally aware public, radical ecological pressure groups, and scientific research produced not only the technology and means for green-roof development, but also a social and political climate that fostered and promoted their widespread implementation. The 1960s and 1970s saw a number of projects in Germany and Switzerland which experimented with new ways of integrating plants with buildings. *Terrassenhäuser* (not to be confused with the British terraced houses) were constructed where houses are built on a steep gradient, the roof of the lower being the garden of the upper. Underground garages, covered with earth and vegetation were another location for such work. Until the 1980s, however, there were considerable technical difficulties in constructing buildings sufficiently well sealed against water leakage or the penetration of tree roots.

In the early 1970s several books and articles on roof greening were published in Germany which did much to promote the idea, in particular by encouraging architects and designers to go beyond the elite roof garden. Particularly seminal was an article by the influential landscape architect Professor Hans Luz, titled "Roofgreening—luxury or necessity?" in which he made the case for roof greening as part of a strategy of improving the urban environment.

The Austrian architect and artist Friedensreich Hundertwasser built what has become perhaps the most influential green roof in Vienna, the Hundertwasser-Haus with 900 tonnes (992 tons) of soil and 250 trees and shrubs. Hundertwasser's colourful and eccentric style was part of the counter-culture of the 1960s and early 1970s, instrumental in combining several radical critiques and bringing them to the attention of a very large number of mainly young people. From the late 1960s onwards some involved in the counter-culture movement began to experiment with new ways of living, part of which could be described as "greening

The opening of Vienna's Hundertwasser-Haus in 1986 was the turning point in bringing an awareness of the possibilities of roof greening to a wider audience in central Europe.

Photograph by Hundertwasser Archive

A German ecohouse complete with green roof and solar power.

Photograph by Fritz Wassmann

the city." Squatter settlements inspired by a variety of libertarian philosophies took over whole blocks of some European cities, notably former West Berlin: plants in containers made from reused industrial containers sprouted on every flat surface, vegetables were grown in planters on roofs, huge climbers were encouraged up walls, while areas of waste ground were given over to community gardens. At the same time, ecologists as well as writers and artists began to imagine what cities of the future could look like; unlike futurists elsewhere, German visions featured enormous amounts of greenery: tower blocks bedecked with greenery, every flat surface planted, and swags of trailing plants hanging from balconies and rooftops.

While the research and the technological developments that made roof greening more technically feasible was not a part of the counter-culture movement, there is little doubt that the movement has done much to popularize the concept. Key to contemporary work is the development of extensive roof greening, closer in spirit to the Scandinavian or Kurdish grass roof than the roof gardens of the wealthy apartment dweller. Since the formulation of the distinction between the extensive and intensive styles in the mid-1970s, extensive roof greening has been the focus of most research. An important development was the creation, in 1977, of a green-roof study group within the FLL (Forschungsgesellschaft Landschaftsentwicklung Landschaftsbau:

the society for research into the development of landscape and landscape construction), a German-based body which acts as an umbrella organization for research into landscape construction and the definition of specifications and the setting of industry-wide standards.

Green-roof research began in Germany in the 1950s as part of a wider movement that recognized the ecological and environmental value of urban habitats, and in particular the benefits to plants and wildlife of what many people still regard as wasteland or derelict sites (so-called brownfield sites). One of the urban habitats that received attention was the spontaneous flora that developed on gravel- or ballast-covered flat roofs. Later work in the 1960s investigated the techniques and practicalities of growing plants in thin substrate layers on roofs. From the late 1970s on, research, primarily by Professor Hans-Joachim Liesecke at the Institute for Green Planning and Garden Architecture at the University of Hannover and by Dr. Walter Kolb at the Bavarian Institute for Viticulture and Horticulture at Veitshöchheim, established that roof greening has a great many benefits, particularly for energy conservation and minimizing water runoff. At the same time a number of companies began to offer specialist roof-greening services, undertake product development, and establish their own research programmes, notably ZinCo and Optigrün. Both these companies are based near Stuttgart, in southern Germany.

So, the growing of plants on roofs and walls has moved out of a marginal social position. As many of the ideas of the counter-culture and the environmentalist movement were taken up by mainstream society, the practical advantages of what at first had seemed like the ideas of a few crazy hippies were increasingly appreciated and subjected to rigorous scientific and economic evaluation. One of the ways in which environmentalist ideas have moved into mainstream thinking is in the area of environmental costs, the idea that pollution and other damage to the environment is not just damaging to nature, but to the economy as well, as usable resources are adversely affected. As we shall see, the use of plants in urban areas can do much to reduce some of the costs that urban areas impose on the environment.

Green roofs make an unobtrusive alternative to standard roofing solutions in this housing development.

CONTEMPORARY GREEN ROOFS
AROUND THE WORLD

Green roofs are now being taken up to a greater or lesser extent in many regions of the world. It is fascinating that the motivating factors for green-roof implementation in these different regions can be quite different, according to climatic, cultural, and political factors, and as a result, the level and type of incentives to promote their use can also vary. For example, in Germany the driving force for green-roof installation was primarily environmental, and in particular as mitigation for the loss of habitat or landscape as a result of built development. In contrast, in North America green roofs have largely been installed for economic reasons, as a more cost-effective method than standard engineering techniques of tackling environmental problems at the city level and as a mechanism to save on the long-term costs of buildings at the level of the individual owner or developer. In Norway green roofs are seen as part of the national heritage and are linked to deep romantic feelings of closeness to nature, whereas in Britain contemporary green roofs are viewed more as imported and somewhat alien technologies. These differences reflect the political, cultural, and economic structures of the various countries and regions. Similarly, the primary benefit of green roofs may change geographically, with storm-water management being a prime concern in more temperate climates and reduction of urban temperatures a motivating factor in hot or tropical climates.

Europe

There is no doubt that Germany is the current centre of green-roof activity throughout the world. The rapid expansion of green roofs in Germany has been made possible by laws that promote their implementation. The Federal Nature Protection Act, the Federal Building Code, and state-level nature protection statutes ensure that development should avoid any unnecessary damage to nature or the landscape and that any unavoidable damage should be compensated for within a fixed time period. Green-roof installation is one such measure. By 2002 one in every ten flat-roofed buildings in the country had a green roof (Stender 2002). Stuttgart was one of the first cities to give official support to roof greening, as early as 1980, when a Green Programme for Urban Renewal was instituted, giving subsidies for the costs of materials and installation and free technical advice from various city departments. Berlin instituted measures to encourage green roofs in 1988, requiring that if a new building takes up too much ground space, permission for construction is given only if a green roof is constructed. Support for green roofs in Germany comes from all government levels, frequently linking the granting of permission for construction to the ability of new roofs to limit the amount of runoff. Consequently, it is not just the scale of new green roofs that is regarded as important but the thickness of the substrate and other details of construction that affect water-holding capacity. Around 43 per cent of all German cities offer some form of incentive for green-roof installation. Green roofs are also frequently encountered in Austria and Switzerland, where similar incentives to those in Germany are available. For example, Swiss federal law requires all federal agencies to apply the Swiss Landscape Concept, which states that facilities must be compatible with natural settings and landscape and that 25 per cent of all new commercial developments are greened in an attempt to maintain favourable microclimates (English Nature 2003).

Britain and The Netherlands and other countries of north-western Europe lag far behind the German-speaking European countries. In Britain, for example, green roofs are regarded as a new concept and are restricted to a limited number of high-profile buildings or environmental centres (English Nature 2003), purpose-built sustainable housing schemes, and on the houses and garden buildings of some committed amateurs. The Scandinavian countries, as discussed above, have a tradition of grass-covered buildings, although in most countries these are regarded as historical features and contemporary extensive green roofs are again fairly rare. The exception is Norway, where turf roofed buildings are relatively commonplace and the idea of the green roof is imbued with romantic notions of nature (Simone Abram, personal communication).

In southern Europe (that is, Greece, Italy, Spain, and Portugal) there has been much less development of the green-roof concept. This is perhaps partly because the hot, dry summer climate means that the typical German-style sedum roof is not so successful. Also, the reduced summer rainfall compared to central and northern Europe means that the German concentration on rainwater retention is perhaps less applicable. Instead, in these climates the greatest benefit of green roofs may be reducing the surface temperature of buildings (Köhler et al. 2001). Great difficulty has been encountered by proponents of extensive green roofs in Greece because of a general attitude that if additional money is being spent on a green roof then it should be accessible for recreational use. The Greek company Green Hellas has installed a demonstration green roof on a school that uses tough, drought-tolerant perennials and shrubs, but irrigation is needed to combat severe summer heat. Trials are also being undertaken into appropriate, well-adapted Greek native species.

Further east, there is little in the way of current roof greening. A notable exception is the ongoing movement to produce rooftop food in St. Petersburg in Russia as a response to food shortages and basic hardships over the past decade. Rooftops are seen as offering great potential for food production by urban apartment dwellers who have no access to land either in or outside the city.

North America

The concept of the contemporary extensive green roof has become well established in certain cities in the United States. This happened partly as a result of researchers, designers, and horticulturists among others travelling to Germany and other European countries, seeing the extent of roof greening there, and wishing to promote the same in the United States. It is also a result of European green-roof manufacturers expanding their activities and markets into North America. Two cities in the United States in particular have established a strong reputation in green-roof implementation: Chicago, Illinois, and Portland, Oregon. In Chicago, green roofs are an important component of an overall strategy to make the city the greenest city in the United States. Other aspects of the strategy include street tree planting, provision of numerous small-scale urban gardens and pocket parks, and high standards for the urban parks of the city. The city has established a high-profile demonstration green roof on top of City Hall. In Chicago all new and replaced roofs must meet minimum standards of solar reflectance and emissivity, and green roofs are one way of achieving this. In Portland, green roofs (or ecoroofs) have been utilized as part of a wider strategy to reduce or prevent polluted urban runoff reaching rivers, thus damaging salmon stocks and an important local industry. Developers are encouraged to install green roofs by being given opportunities to increase the permitted floor space of their development according to the area of green roof they put onto a building.

The installation of a green roof for a new assembly plant of the Ford Motor Company at their complex in Dearborn, Michigan, is in many ways a sign that green-roof technology is not only here to stay but commercially respectable. At the time of its completion in 2003 it was the largest green roof on an industrial complex in the world. Ford chairman, Bill Ford, declared that "this is what I think sustainability is about, and this new facility lays the groundwork for a model of sustainable manufacturing . . . this is not environmental philanthropy; it is sound business" *Green Roofs Infrastructure Monitor* (2001a).

In Canada there is also significant green-roof activity, centred in particular around the city of Toronto, home of Green Roofs for Healthy Cities, a subscription organization dedicated to expanding the market for green roofs in North America. Much research activity centres around developing cost-benefit scenarios for the city of Toronto, with a particular focus on the benefit of green roofs and other techniques for reducing the urban heat island effect of the city. As with Chicago, a well-known demonstration green roof has been constructed on Toronto City Hall.

Asia, South America, and Australia

Hot and humid tropical regions of South-east Asia and parts of South America present a different set of opportunities for roof greening. Rainfall is high and so are evapotranspiration rates. Flooding and water erosion can be major problems, causing regular destruction and death. Despite costly drainage schemes in South American cities such as Rio de Janeiro, even massive sewer and canalization schemes are overloaded as a result of peak storm rainfall—what is seen as a hundred year event in temperate climates is a yearly event in the tropics (Köhler et al. 2001). Here, green roofs could be very useful in reducing peak water flows. However, a number of points must be borne in mind: erosion and damage of newly planted roofs is likely; substrates may be saturated over long periods (drought-tolerance may not be such an important characteristic in the plants used); plant growth is quicker than in temperate climates; and there is a possibility of roof vegetation harbouring mosquitoes, bringing a danger of malaria (Köhler et al. 2001).

There is currently active interest in Singapore in the use of roof gardens and vertical greening as a means of combating the urban heat island effect. Singapore is a country the size of many typical Western cities and has a major problem with space for new development. Roof gardens are seen as a means of providing access for significant proportions of the population to green space. Interest in green-roof technology in Japan is also rising. Tokyo's municipal government is particularly interested in green roofs again as a means of mitigating the urban heat island effect. In 2001 the government introduced a requirement that all new buildings with more than 1000 square metres (10,760 square feet) of floor space cover 20 per cent of their roofs with vegetation. The aim is to establish at least 1200 ha of green roofs by 2011, reducing the city centre temperature by 1°C (1.7°F). There is also a growing interest in façade greening as part of this strategy (*Green Roofs Infrastructure Monitor* 2001b).

In Australia, green-roof implementation is at a similar stage to Britain and much of the United States: much interest, increasing awareness, but little ready information available and few examples. The current centre of activity is Melbourne, where a number of demonstration projects have sprung up around the city.

Despite the increasing interest in green-roof installation there remain many barriers to the wider implementation of green roofs. These include a general lack of awareness of the benefits of green-roof technologies, lack of incentives for their implementation, and risks associated with the uncertainties of relatively new technologies (Peck et al. 1999). Apart from this natural resistance to new concepts, the main obstacle to overcome is in convincing people that the additional costs associated with green roofs give worthwhile paybacks. These costs may include the additional strengthening required for the roof to support vegetation and substrate, the cost of the components of the green roof, and additional construction costs as well as costs involved in actually getting the materials on to the roof. There are then ongoing maintenance costs. Chapter 2 is intended to provide hard evidence of the many and varied benefits that the additional resources required for the installation and maintenance of a green roof can bring.

CHAPTER 2

Why Build Green Roofs?

Many claims are made about the benefits of green roofs, often with little direct evidence to back up the various assertions. There is no doubt that roof greening has substantial and wide-ranging advantages over traditional roof surfaces. Until recently, however, it has been difficult to make strong arguments for their use outside of the German-speaking countries because most of the research into the performance of green roofs has been published in German. However, since the mid-1990s research has also been undertaken and published in North America and some of the German work has been published in English. In this chapter we explore the benefits of roof greening and, as much as possible, provide sound evidence for the various claims.

The benefits of green roofs operate at a range of scales. Some will only work if relatively large numbers of green roofs are implemented in any particular area and their benefits will only be apparent at the larger neighbourhood or city scale. Others will operate directly on an individual building. Most can be related in some way to the domestic or garden scale as well as larger-scale commercial or industrial applications. We can classify the various advantages into three main areas: the amenity and aesthetic, the environmental, and the economic, although there is a great deal of cross-over between these categories. These advantages can also be divided in private and public benefits that can be used to sell or promote the idea depending upon the intended audience (Peck and Kuhn 2000). Private benefits (such as savings in energy costs, extension of the life of the roof, aesthetic improvements) are likely to promote the use of green roofs by giving financial or personal advantage to individual building owners and developers, while public benefits (such as storm-water management, urban climate mitigation, promotion of biodiversity and habitat) will

Some benefits of green roofs will only be apparent if roof greening is carried out on a large scale; others can operate at a much smaller scale.

© ZinCo

23

foster the adoption of planning regulations by local and city authorities to encourage green-roof construction for a better quality of life and environment.

AMENITY AND AESTHETIC BENEFITS

The amenity value of green roofs

Roofs are an enormously underutilized resource in urban and suburban areas. If the load-bearing capacity of the roof is sufficient and the construction of the green roof is planned for recreational use, green roofs can play an important part in the provision of recreational areas in neighbourhoods where there is little ground-level green space. Recreational space at roof level has the advantage that access can be controlled, thereby making an environment safer from vandalism, assault, and the other social problems which tend to plague public green space at ground level. Because the fear of crime or strangers is often even greater than the reality, having a secure green space adds considerably to feelings of security for users. Observations from one green roof on top of an apartment block in Portland, Oregon, revealed many activities taking place, from clothes drying, barbecuing, eating and drinking, dog exercising, and even letting off fireworks (Hutchison et al. 2003). There is no need for these recreational spaces to be small: golf courses and playing fields have been constructed on top of buildings.

Areas of flat roof that are not designed for heavy recreational use may still be strong enough for limited personal use: sunbathing or a few containerized plants, for example. In many urban areas this may be the only possibility for people to personalize the exterior of their living space. With the move towards ever more compact and high-density towns and cities there is increasing pressure on green space at ground level. Roof spaces therefore have enormous potential in providing urban dwellers with the amenity and recreational space essential for healthy living. The provision of attractive communal gardens, filled with lush greenery rather than stark hard surfaces, is also likely to be a positive selling point to developers wishing to sell space in city apartment blocks.

Provision of roof gardens may not only be desirable, they may become a necessity. Certainly in the United States, where the overall population demographic is aging, larger numbers of older people are moving back into cities and are demanding and requiring higher quality living environments. This is mirrored in the trend in the United Kingdom for new, high-quality, and high-density inner city apartment developments attracting younger professional dwellers.

In high-density areas, roof planting can provide much needed recreational space.

Food production

Concern has increased over the quality of food and how it is produced. One particular issue concerns the distance that food may have travelled to reach its destination—out of season vegetables and fruit being shipped from the other side of the world is a commonly given example—but in many instances it is difficult to source local food in shops and supermarkets. Transporting food over long distances has many implications in terms of the energy used and pollution caused by its transport, while the nutritional quality of fruit and vegetables deteriorates with increasing time after harvest. Roof surfaces offer one opportunity for growing healthy food, particularly in high-density urban areas or where garden space may be small or restricted. While food-producing plants can be substituted for ornamental plants in conventional roof garden situations, extensive or thin roof coverings can also be productive. Many herb species, for example, perform best in free-draining soils in sunny situations. Alpine strawberries will grow in shady areas or in the damper areas at the base of a sloping roof. Food production on roofs is perhaps not such a far-fetched concept. In some countries (for instance, Haiti, Colombia, Thailand, Russia) rooftops and balconies have been used to produce a range of marketable products from fruit and vegetables to orchids (Garnett 1997). Meaningful cropping will require some depth of soil (30–45 cm, 12–18 in) and irrigation. Clearly, the weight-bearing capacity of the roof will have to be considered. However, use of lightweight media, rooftop green houses, and hydroponic techniques will widen the potential use. One of the best examples of roof food production is the Fairmount Hotel in Vancouver, Canada. This roof garden covers 195 square metres (2098 square feet) and the soil depth is 45 cm (18 in). The garden provides all the herbs used in the hotel, at an estimated yearly cost saving of 25,000–30,000 Canadian dollars. It also provides amenity space for hotel guests and gives rise to higher room rates for those located adjacent to it. Similarly, the organization Earth Pledge in New York City is dedicated to promoting environmentally friendly living in the city. The urban agriculture green roof on top of its building in New York provides food for use in Earth Pledge's sustainable cuisine cooking classes, while organic waste from the building is composted and used on the green roof (Cheney 2002).

Roof space can be leased for food production or other amenity benefit, opening up commercial possibilities for an as yet untapped resource. This is all the more attractive because in most instances the release of space on the rooftop for productive use does not entail any additional land purchase cost for the owner.

Green roofs can integrate a building into its surroundings.

© ZinCo

Green roofs can have a purely aesthetic purpose on a wide range of buildings and structures.

Photograph by VegTech

Green roofs can go on any structure, however small.

Small-scale roof greening on a porch.

Right: The meadow roof on this shed enables a whole new set of plants to be used in this garden.

Aesthetic value of green roofs

The view of the majority of urban roofscapes can be far from pleasant. While the skyline profile of well-known buildings or the massed skyscrapers of an urban metropolis can be dramatic, the smaller scale reality is often of a hotchpotch of ugly surfaces and structures. This is perhaps particularly true of large flat-roofed industrial or commercial developments. Unattractive views are not restricted to the city: anyone who has a garden shed or outbuilding garage, porch, or flat-roof extension to their house will almost certainly be looking out over an expanse of dark asphalt or bitumen. These situations all represent untapped potential for greening. For a garden-loving culture, domestic- and garden-roof surfaces represent one of the last horticultural challenges. In a garden setting, where roof spaces may be accessible and irrigation can be given in dry periods, roof spaces offer opportunities for growing a wide range of plant species.

Even where roofs are inaccessible but clearly visible, attractive planting can be beneficial. The therapeutic effects of having green plants and nature around one are known to be considerable and include stress reduction, lowering of blood pressure, relief of muscle tension, and increase in positive feelings (Ulrich and Simmons 1986). Higher therapeutic values appear to accrue to properties with roof or façade greening (Ulrich 1986). The financial advantages can also extend to surrounding properties which have a view of green-roof planting (Köhler et al. 2001).

ECONOMIC BENEFITS

Increased roof life

The initial reaction of many people to green roofs, from both laypeople and those professionally involved in construction, is that because they hold water they will increase the likelihood of leaks and damp penetration to the building. In actual fact, if an appropriate method of construction is used, green roofs will last longer than conventional ones, with obvious cost benefits.

Heat exposure can accelerate aging in bituminous material, thus reducing its durability. Ultraviolet radiation can change the chemical composition and degrade the mechanical properties of the bituminous materials. An exposed roof membrane absorbs solar radiation during the day and its temperature rises. The extent of the temperature increase depends on the colour of the membrane. Light-coloured membranes are cooler because they reflect solar radiation, and dark membranes are hotter because they absorb much of the solar radiation. Results from many studies show that exposed roofs experience much higher temperatures than that of green roofs. For example, in a study of greened and ungreened systems on a roof in Toronto, Canada, the membrane on the ungreened roof absorbed solar radiation and reached close to 70°C (158°F) in the afternoon. However, the membrane on the green roof remained around 25°C (77°F) (Liu and Baskaran 2003). Table 2.1 compares the number of days out of the observation period (a total of 660 days) when the maximum roof membrane temperature exceeded various levels.

There are 219 days of the 660 days (that is 33 per cent of the days) observed that the membrane on the ungreened roof reached a temperature above 50°C (122°F). While the ambient temperature exceeded 30°C

Roof planting that is visible from inside a building, but not necessarily directly accessible, can still be of great value to the general well-being of building users.

© ZinCo

Temperature greater than	Ungreened roof		Greened roof		Ambient	
	Number of days	Per cent of days	Number of days	Per cent of days	Number of days	Per cent of days
30°C (86°F)	342	52	18	3	63	10
40°C (104°F)	291	44	0	0	0	0
50°C (122°F)	219	33	0	0	0	0
60°C (140°F)	89	13	0	0	0	0
70°C (158°F)	2	0.3	0	0	0	0

Table 2.1 Statistics of daily maximum temperatures on an ungreened and a greened roof in Toronto, Canada, over a period of 660 days.

From Liu and Baskaran (2003)

(86°F) for 10 per cent of the days during the 22-month observation period, the membrane temperature of the ungreened roof went above 30°c (86°F) over half of the time, compared to only 3 per cent for the green roof. The colour of the membrane in this instance was light grey, the temperature of a dark membrane would be likely to be even higher.

An exposed membrane absorbs solar radiation during the day and its surface temperature rises. It reradiates the absorbed heat at night and its surface temperature drops. Diurnal (daily) temperature fluctuations create thermal stresses in the membrane, affecting its long-term performance and its ability to protect a building from water infiltration. Roofing materials are degraded over time by a variety of natural processes: by ultraviolet light and the constant expansion and contraction caused by extremes of temperature and freeze-thaw action. Disintegration of materials, cracking, delamination, and splitting are the end result. For example, Graph 2.1 shows the daily membrane temperature fluctuation (daily maximum temperature minus daily minimum temperature) of the greened and ungreened roofs in the same Canadian study. The green roof significantly moderated the daily temperature fluctuations experienced by the roof membrane during the spring and summer (snow cover in winter on both roofs evened out the differences). The daily membrane temperature fluctuations of the green roof were consistently lower than the diurnal ambient temperature fluctuations.

German researchers found that reductions of diurnal temperature variations of up to 94 per cent could be achieved, with an average diminution of 12°c (54°F) in temperature extremes between day and night, but that the level of reduction was heavily dependent upon the type of vegetation used. This high figure was achieved with a wide

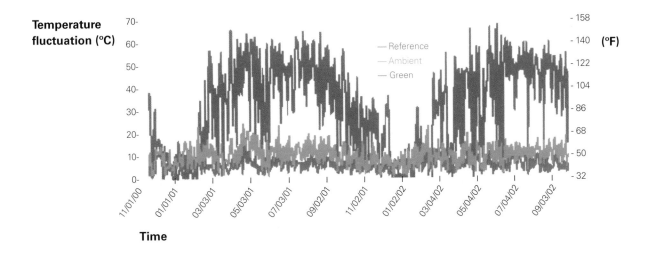

Temperature fluctuation (°C) ... (°F)

— Reference
— Ambient
— Green

Time

variety of grasses and forbs, based on that found in a typical central European wildflower meadow. With this vegetation, the actual summer maximum temperature on the control roof with no vegetation was 67 per cent higher than on the vegetated roof. However, less biodiverse plant communities, such as grasses with no forbs, achieved lower reductions, down to only 32 per cent in some cases. As well as grass-based mixtures, a variety of ground cover perennials were trialled. Again the most biodiverse mixture was the most effective, with a reduction of in temperature variation of 90 per cent. Speculating on the reasons for the mixtures being more successful than the monocultures, the researchers suggested that their greater height and complexity trapped more air cushions thereby producing a greater insulating effect (Kolb and Schwarz 1986a).

Green roofs are not the only roofing solution to reduce heat transfer into a building. Highly reflective roofs, or white roofs, also achieve this function, reducing energy needs for cooling by up to 40 per cent (but of course white roofs lack many of the other advantages of green roofs). For both green and white roofs, any energy reduction will greatly depend on the form and design of the building itself. The greatest effect is achieved with single-storey or low buildings with large roof surfaces, or on older buildings with poor insulation.

Green roofs need to be built to a higher standard than conventional roofs, partly because of their greater weight but also because they need to be 100 per cent leak proof. This inevitably means greater costs, but the resulting roof will last longer because it is better made and as a result of the protection given by the substrate and vegetation. Conventional roofing (in the United States, at 2002 prices) costs $4.00 to $8.50 per square foot, the lower figure being for a system that lasts no more than fifteen to twenty years before widespread repairs are necessary, the latter for a system that should last thirty to fifty years. An extensive green roof, which should last fifty to a hundred years, costs $10–20 per square foot. For comparison, an intensive green roof costs around $20–40 per square foot (Broili 2002). European research suggests that a green roof at least doubles the life span of the roof membrane (Peck and Kuhn 2000) and pays for itself in the long term. The protective properties of green roofs have been an important factor in the survival of the older generation of roof gardens, for example, Derry and Toms department store in central London which has had a roof garden since 1938 and with a roof membrane still in good condition (Peck et al. 1999).

A major problem with conventional flat roofs is that water tends to pool rather than run off, so allowing the water time to exploit any weakness in the covering. Green roofs will greatly reduce this as the substrate and plant layer will hold much of the water falling onto the roof. Maintenance of ungreened roofs is itself a factor in the degradation of materials, as maintenance crews often damage surfaces as they walk across, as do other personnel who work on the roof such as ventilation or air-conditioning engineers. Plants and soil provide a naturally regenerating protective layer between human traffic and the roof. In addition, one of the ongoing maintenance concerns of the drainage systems of roofs is the build-up of organic matter such as dead leaves, in guttering, leading to overflows, flooding, or even blocked pipes. Green roofs can trap some of this debris, eventually incorporating it into the substrate as humus.

Insulation and energy efficiency

A major part of the *raison d'être* of the green-roof concept is the contribution it can make to both building insulation and the control of runoff; these areas were an important part of the early research into green roofs conducted in Germany. Many of the other benefits of green roofs manifest themselves at the larger neighbourhood or city scale and developers or owners need to have an altruistic sense of wider environmental benefit to be persuaded of the value of their installation (unless there are legal or financial incentives in place). However, the insulating effect of green roofs in reducing heating or air-conditioning costs represents direct economic benefit for the individual building and, if clearly demonstrated, can be one of the strongest arguments for their wider installation. For this reason it is important to collect real data on their energy performance in a wide range of climatic situations.

Several properties of green roofs contribute to their thermal characteristics: direct shading of the roof, evaporative cooling from the plants and the growing medium, additional insulation values from both the plants and the growing medium, and the thermal mass effects of the growing medium (Liu and Baskaran 2003). Differences in these factors can have important effects on the roof's performance. For example, if the vegetation is not predominantly evergreen, then the insulating and evaporative function of the roof may be diminished. Climatic differences may also be important: prolonged winter freezing or snow cover may also eliminate any energy benefits on thin extensive roofs with short vegetation cover.

Reductions of up to 90 per cent in solar energy gain on plant-shaded as opposed to unshaded locations can be achieved, while indoor temperatures have been shown to be 3–4°C (6–8°F) lower under a green roof when outdoor temperatures are between 25 and 30°C (77 and 86°F; Peck et al. 1999). In climates where air-conditioning is regarded as essential for creating decent indoor working conditions, this could be a major reason for considering roof greening: every reduction in internal air temperatures of 0.5°C (1°F) can reduce electricity use for air-conditioning by up to 8 per cent. In Canada, Environment Canada found that a typical one-storey building in Toronto with a grass roof and 10 cm (4 in) of substrate brought about a 25 per cent reduction in summer cooling needs (Peck 2003a), compared with an unvegetated reference roof. In spring and summer, the unvegetated roof absorbed solar radiation during the day, resulting in positive heat flow into the building while at night the absorbed energy was reradiated back into the air, resulting in heat loss from the building. This resulted in high energy demand in the building, both in air-conditioning requirements from

Graph 2.2 The average daily heat flow through a vegetated and unvegetated roof in Toronto, Canada, between January 2001 and December 2001.

Redrawn from Liu and Baskaran (2003).

Graph 2.3 Surface temperature measured under vegetation, bare soil, and exposed paved surface, on 3 November 2001.

Redrawn from Tan et al. (2003)

midday into the afternoon, but also in the need for heating in the morning. Graph 2.2 shows the energy demand to maintain a comfortable internal environment due to the heat flow under both the reference and green roofs. In this situation the green roof was effective from April to September, resulting in much reduced energy demand for cooling, but in the cold continental Toronto winter with permanently frozen growing medium and periodic snow cover there was little significant additional benefit from the green roof (Liu and Baskaran 2003).

Similar findings arose from a study in the tropical climate of Singapore. Surface temperatures were measured on an intensive green roof in the city over a range of materials and vegetation. The results, shown in Graph 2.3, for a typical 48-hour period show that with an exposed paved surface, the surface temperatures reached a peak of around 57°C (135°F) by mid-afternoon. The maximum diurnal fluctuation in temperature was around 30°C (86°F). In contrast, maximum surface temperature measured under *Raphis* species (a palm) was only 27°C (81°F) and the maximum diurnal fluctuation in temperature was under 3°C (6°F). The surface temperatures measured above bare soil or under *Ophiopogon*, a plant with less dense foliage, were in between the two extremes presented by the exposed paved surface and under *Raphis*.

The net heat gain or heat loss was also calculated from a room beneath the different surfaces. Under the unvegetated surfaces the room beneath the roof experienced a net heat gain over the period of a day: even during the night heat was still entering the building because of the absorbed heat energy of the roof. However, under the vegetated surfaces there was a net heat loss from the room. Interestingly, the rate of heat loss from the room at night was the same under the vegetated surfaces as from the bare soil. This indicates that in this situation there was little additional insulating benefit from the presence of vegetation and that the main effect of plants is to reduce solar heat gain through shading during the day. The shading effect of vegetation works even with low-growing plants such as sedums. Because green roofs reduce temperatures in buildings partly through shading and partly through evapotranspiration, the plants have to be actively growing, rather than in a state of heat-induced dormancy for the roof to be fully effective. For this reason effective cooling by green roofs necessitates some irrigation to keep the plants alive and green.

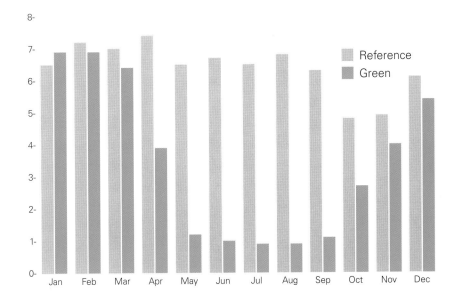

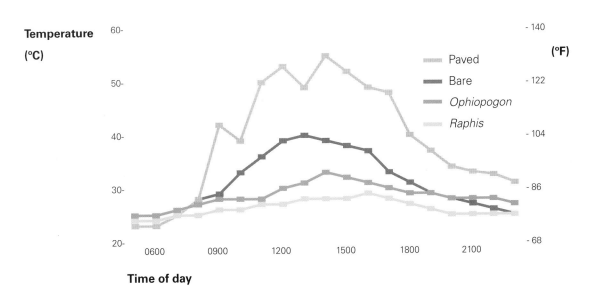

Research in Germany also indicates variation in the winter insulating value of different types of vegetation, with uniform evergreen vegetation appearing to be better than mixed vegetation such as a wildflower meadow that collapses to form a mat of dead stems and leaves with few air pockets, whereas, for example, a lawn of fine turf grasses forms a more continuous cover, better trapping a mass of air pockets. Among ground cover perennials, *Vinca minor* was the most effective, its evergreen leaves and arrangement of stems trapping extensive air pockets (Kolb and Schwarz 1986b). The effects of different vegetation types on insulation in winter and summer can be inconsistent (see page 31). The insulating effect of green roofs is the combined result of the plants and the substrate, and it should be clear that thicker layers of both will increase the insulation effect. Measurements have shown that a 20- to 40-cm (8- to 16-in) layer of grass growing on a 20-cm (8-in) substrate layer is equivalent to 15 cm (6 in) of mineral wool insulation (Peck et al. 1999). Green roofs and façade greening have the ability not just to reduce the costs of heating and cooling buildings, but to reduce construction costs too, as they will reduce the amount of insulation needed or the size of air-conditioning equipment required.

Green building assessment and public relations

Green roofs can gain points in various assessment and rating schemes for sustainable or green building. For example, under the U.S. LEED (Leadership in Energy and Environmental Design) programme which rates the environmental performance of a building, green roofs gain one point for landscape to reduce heat islands if the roof covers at least 50 per cent of the building and one point for storm-water management (Oberlander et al. 2002). Gaining high scores under these schemes can make economic sense. For example, new housing gaining high scores may attract environmentally conscious sections of the public. The potential to gain certain positive credit ratings may aid planning consent. And there is considerable public relations value in using a green roof to project an environmentally aware image for a building or organization; a visible green roof is probably the single most effective way that a building can express differences in environmental attitude.

ENVIRONMENTAL BENEFITS

Biodiversity and wildlife value of green roofs

The enhancement of biodiversity through the use of green roofs is closely linked to the plant species and the habitat or vegetation type that is being used as a model for the green roof. Given that the rooftop as a habitat is so similar to that of many seasonally dry environments with shallow soil, it is clear that these environments will be very important models for green roofs. They are also habitats that for a variety of reasons are often at risk, whether in urban or rural areas. Therefore the construction of similar habitats featuring species that may be rare or endangered in the wild may be valuable in their conservation. Extensive green roofs, which are not designed to be walked on and are therefore isolated from people, can be potentially very good undisturbed habitat for plants, birds, and insects. Roofs and other building surfaces do not need to be intentionally planted to support plant growth: simple observation of older buildings and other surfaces such as old walls and pavements will usually reveal a good deal of spontaneous colonization of lichens, mosses, and flowering plants and grasses, varying enormously depending upon the size, aspect, materials, and accessibility of the surface in question. Similarly, a range of bird species, usually those favouring cliff habitats or open grassy or stony habitats in the wild, have nested successfully on urban roofs, whether greened or not.

Indeed as time goes on the biodiversity value of green roofs may prove to become more and more important. It is a fundamental fact of plant ecology that relatively infertile habitats support a large number of plant species, because the vigorous aggressive plants that can dominate and outcompete more delicate species in fertile soils are unable to gain a toe hold, thereby enabling a much greater diversity of plant species to co-exist (Grime 2002). In turn, a greater diversity of plant species tends to support a greater diversity of animal species.

Green roofs may also be valuable in conserving or restoring endangered habitats and vegetation types. For example, the award-winning green roof on an office building at the corporate campus for The Gap at Cherry Hill, California, utilized native grasses of relict coastal grasslands and prairie of the region, linking the building with the surrounding landscape, visually changing with the seasons as the native grasses flower and ripen, and extending the distribution of natural plant communities into an urban setting (Burke 2003).

The spontaneous flora and fauna of green roofs tends to be limited to more mobile species, although plants and animals can be introduced inadvertently as weeds in containers of plant material, on the shoes and clothes of visitors, or on the feet of birds. Further limitations are placed on their fauna by the fact that in continental climates the entire substrate may freeze, making it impossible for insects to overwinter on them. However during the growing season they may offer valuable ecological islands where both flying insects and birds may rest, feed, and breed. Surveys of wildlife have found many insect species at twenty storeys and above (Peck et al. 1999).

One of the most detailed studies to date of the biodiversity value of green roofs has been carried out in Basel, Switzerland (Brenneisen

The green roof on this pavilion at the Oase Garden, near Arnhem, The Netherlands, gives additional ecological benefit to a garden already rich in wildlife value.

Photograph by Jane Sebire

2003). Seventeen green roofs were monitored, including turf roofs, sedum roofs, and specially designed roofs with landscaped surfaces created using local waste material substrates and rubble which were either left to colonize spontaneously or capped with thin layers of regionally distinctive topsoils (brown roofs). Two groups of invertebrates that are good indicators of vegetation structure were monitored: ground beetles and spiders. In the first three-year period of the study, 78 spider and 254 beetle species was found. Fourteen (18 per cent) of the spider species and 27 (11 per cent) of the beetle species were classified as rare or endangered. Older green roofs tended to support more species than younger ones. In a comparison of the fauna of these roofs with similar brownfield habitats on the ground (for instance, railway sidings or demolition sites) which are very important in terms of urban biodiversity, little difference was found between the numbers of spiders and beetles on the roof or on the ground.

The Swiss researchers also studied bird activity on the roofs. The principal reason for birds visiting the green roofs was to look for food.

Orchids growing on an old green roof in Basel, Switzerland.

Photograph by Elias Landolt

The most frequently recorded species were black redstarts (*Phoenicurus ochruros*), wagtails (*Motacilla* species), rock doves (*Columba livia*), and house sparrows (*Passer domesticus*), species naturally occurring in open landscapes such as higher mountain areas, on river banks, or in steppes with grasslands and bare stony ground and patchy vegetated areas. Green roofs in the suburbs, located closer to agricultural land, were less frequently visited and used than in the city. Seemingly, the lack of green spaces and food in densely built-up areas resulted in more frequent use here of the new habitats on the roofs.

The key message to come out of this research is that diversity in the planning and construction of a green roof leads to diversity in plants and animals. Having a variety of heights and slopes, open stony unvegetated areas, a variety of vegetation types, and freely and poorly drained areas maximizes their ecological value. It is also apparent that the standard (some would say monotonous) extensive sedum-mat based green roof has rather limited biodiversity value compared to other types. Alternatively, the use of locally derived waste materials and the promotion of spontaneous colonization, as well as seeding or planting native plant communities, as a means of vegetating roofs appears to offer planners and developers real opportunities for substituting valuable brownfield habitat lost on the ground as a result of new buildings in urban areas with new habitat at roof level.

In fact, this approach has been the driver behind a new generation of green roofs in London which have been given planning permission (and have been a requirement of that permission) because of their value in conserving the habitat of the black redstart, a rare and protected bird restricted to industrial and post-industrial sites in several British cities. Urban regeneration initiatives tend to clean up and eliminate these sites, threatening the existence of the bird. In response, the Black Redstart Action Plan has initiated a green-roof programme in London to provide this endangered bird with breeding habitat (Wieditz 2003). New developments on sites where the bird is demonstrated to be breeding must include measures to protect against loss of habitat for the bird. This is being achieved by creating brown roofs that re-create the original footprint of the building prior to development by utilizing the waste material and subsoils excavated from the base of the building as the substrate for the roof, thereby eliminating transport costs for the roofing material. To date, around 15,000 square metres (161,400 square feet) of green and brown roofs have been planned for London (Gedge 2003). In the United Kingdom, where no central or local support is given for green-roof implementation, biodiversity and the mitigation for loss of brownfield land is one of the few levers that can be used to promote their wider use.

Green roofs may be thought of as one of the elements in creating functioning habitat and green space networks in cities. Vegetated roofs can function as stepping stones, creating links between larger habitat patches: parks, gardens, derelict sites, and railway embankments, for example. Because built development usually disrupts any existing networks of links of green spaces, green roofs have as yet unrealized potential in minimizing this disruption (English Nature 2003), but of course this is only for the more mobile species. Similarly, green roofs also aid visual green space continuity through urban areas. More extensive information on the benefit of urban green roofs to wildlife is given in English Nature (2003).

Specially created green roofs in Basel, Switzerland, using a range of substrates and vegetation establishment techniques, to monitor the value of green roofs to urban wildlife.

Photograph by Stephan Brenneisen

41

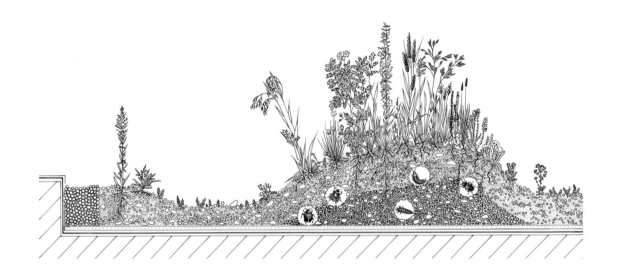

Above: Section through a green roof designed for wildlife benefit, showing a variety of substrate types and depths.

Drawing by Sibylle Erni (originally published by Hochschule Wädenswil)

Below: The green roofs on this house provide additional wildlife value to complement the meadow plantings at ground level.

A brown roof with spontaneously colonized substrates and dead wood.

Photograph by Pia Zanetti

Green roofs integrate the houses with native tree and shrub planting around this development.

Green roofs and water management

The fate of water falling as rain on land covered in vegetation and on the hard surfaces of built-up areas is very different. The vast majority of precipitation on vegetation is absorbed by the soil and goes on to join the water table; some is absorbed by plants and through them is transpired back to the atmosphere. However, on man-made hard surfaces (asphalt, concrete, roof tiles), water cannot be absorbed and runs off, through drainage systems, into rivers. Indeed, the main aim of these drainage systems is to remove the maximum amount of water from an area as quickly as possible. As a result, around 75 per cent of rainfall on towns and cities is lost directly as surface runoff compared to around 5 per cent for a forested area (Scholz-Barth 2001). Research indicates a direct link between runoff from impervious surfaces and degradation of water quality in streams—even relatively low levels (10–15 per cent of total land area) of impervious surfaces can have an effect.

Consequently, in built-up areas, where impervious cover resulting from development ranges from 10 per cent for residential development to 71 to 95 per cent for industrial and shopping centres (Ferguson 1998), river systems are quickly inundated with water. Moreover, high rainfall is rapidly reflected in river level peaks, and flooding is often the consequence if river banks cannot cope. The major flooding witnessed in many English towns and cities in 2000 and 2001 has been attributed, in part, to increased built development in river catchments and flood plains and the consequent disruption to natural drainage patterns. The associated loss of water to the water table can result in the reduction of the availability of water for trees, crops, streams, and boreholes. Groundwater acts as a vast reservoir for both nature and humanity, and its reduction is a major blow to the ability of both to cope successfully with drought. Table 2.2 shows the relative runoff characteristics for a range of urban land uses. The ability of green space to reduce runoff is clear, with reduced building densities and/or increased open space being associated with increased water holding capacity. In the case of a park, all rainfall which falls on the site is potentially absorbed, used, or evaporated back in to the atmosphere rather than leaving the site. It is, in effect, runoff neutral.

Heavy runoff brings with it a host of problems. Heavy surges of storm water can overflow into sewage and other wastewater disposal systems, resulting in overloading of wastewater treatment works and drainage infrastructure and culminating in discharges of raw sewage into rivers. This is a relatively frequent occurrence in older sewage treatment systems. Storm water running off urban surfaces is also likely to be contaminated with particulates, oil and other synthetic hydrocarbons, heavy metals, road salt, pesticides, and animal waste. High levels of runoff also create erosion problems.

Nearly all the rainfall hitting a non-living roof runs directly off into the drainage system, potentially contributing to flooding problems. In contrast a living, green roof can absorb much of the rainfall that hits it.

Drawing by Andy Clayden

To combat these problems an alternative view of dealing with rainfall and drainage is emerging that aims to dramatically reduce the amount of water leaving a site, either through capturing it and reusing the water for irrigation or domestic use, or encouraging it to infiltrate into the soil or evaporate back into the area. There are many advantages to this: reducing pressure on urban drainage systems, enabling groundwater to be replenished, providing areas of habitat and amenity wetlands, reducing flood risk and, importantly, reducing the cost of drainage schemes because using smaller bore pipes is possible. Because roofs represent approximately 40–50 per cent of the impermeable surfaces in urban areas, green roofs have an important role in such integrated or sustainable urban drainage systems. Other components of these systems may be the use of bioswales (open vegetated drainage channels) as an alternative to buried drainage pipes, allowing water to soak away as well as evaporate back to the air; rain gardens and storm-water planters that intercept runoff at ground level; storm-water management ponds and drainage basins; the use of sumps to direct water from roof drainage systems into the water table; and porous road and pavement surfaces, which again promote infiltration rather than runoff (Liptan and Murase 2002). In most cases these measures are cheaper and more sustainable than the end-of-pipe solutions traditionally favoured by engineers, planners, and the construction industry.

Land use	Coefficient of runoff
High-density housing	0.7–0.9
Medium-density housing	0.5–0.7
Low-density housing with large gardens	0.2–0.3
Sports grounds	0.1–0.3
Parks	0.0–0.1

Table 2.2 The runoff characteristics of different urban land uses. The coefficient of runoff is a relative figure indicating comparative water shedding potential rather than absolute values.

From Meiss (1979)

Governments are increasingly setting standards for both the reduction of storm-water runoff and the quality of any that does occur, providing powerful reasons for green roofs to be taken seriously by policy makers at local government level. In Portland, Oregon, the city has drawn up building codes that give bonuses for developers who include green roofs in their buildings, so that for example, for every 0.09 square metres (1 square foot) of green roof created they are allowed an extra 0.27 square metres (3 square feet) of floor space. In one case under this code, a developer was allowed to build an extra six condominiums, worth $1.5 million (Liptan 2002). In Portland the issue of runoff is closely associated with the pollution of salmon spawning grounds in the Columbia River, which has certainly given extra impetus to the city's water management strategy. Both state and city governments in the United States are increasingly charging fees for connection to storm-water systems or allowing developers tax breaks if they use systems to reduce runoff. Indeed in some counties in the arid western states, new developments need to demonstrate zero runoff from the areas they occupy.

As well as reducing run-off quantity, extensive green roofs may also have value in improving the quality of runoff, by reducing pollutant release. For example, recent German research has shown that green roofs on the buildings of Potsdamer Platz in Berlin (specifically designed for water quality improvement through the use of coarse media and drought-tolerant sedum varieties) have been highly effective. The purpose of the roofs is to reduce nutrient loading in runoff which results in algal blooms in the River Spree which runs through Berlin (Charlie Miller, personal communication).

Investigating the reduction and management of runoff is the most important research area currently in the roof-greening world, with both state-funded research institutes and commercial bodies actively involved. Techniques typically include the construction of experimental roofs, where test beds using different combinations of materials and planting are constructed, often incorporating both level and inclined areas. Such experimental facilities may be sited on top of existing or purpose-built buildings, but often take the form of flat tables or containers at ground level with no direct connection to an actual building. Comparisons with conventional ungreened areas are always a vital part of these test areas. Flow meters with an electronic rain gauge are typically connected to each individual test bed are linked to a central computer, so that exact measurements of runoff and precipitation can be taken and then plotted against time.

Green roofs influence roof water runoff in a number of ways. Water that falls on the roof can be absorbed into pore spaces in the substrate or taken up by absorbent materials in the substrate. It can also be taken up by the plants and either stored in plant tissues or transpired back to the atmosphere. Some water may lodge on plant surfaces and subsequently evaporate away. Water may also be stored and retained by the drainage system of the roof. By absorbing water and returning it to the atmosphere, the roof reduces the amount of water available for runoff, and by storing it for a period before it runs off, it acts as a buffer between the weather and drainage systems. Water stored by the green roof is released over a period of time, so that the peaks of heavy rainfall characteristic of storms, especially summer storms, are evened out, with the result that drainage systems have to deal with moderately increased flow over relatively long periods instead of massively increased flow over very short periods.

Graph 2.4 Runoff from a conventional flat roof and an extensive green roof over a 22-hour period.

Redrawn and adapted from Köhler et al. (2001)

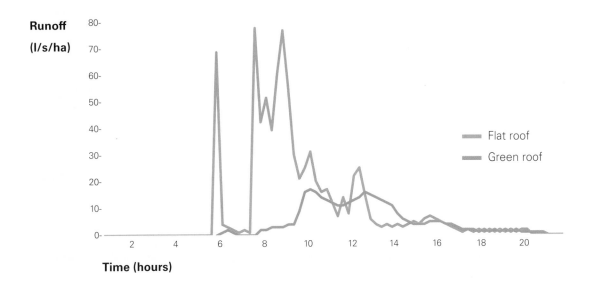

Graph 2.4 illustrates the typical effect of a green roof on rainfall runoff. The runoff from the flat roof mirrors closely the amount of rain falling on the roof and its intensity (not shown) over the period of recording. The comparison of runoff from a typical conventional flat roof with an extensive green roof shows that not only is the total amount of runoff reduced (and the peak runoff reduced considerably), but the there is a delay in water draining from the roof, and the rate of runoff is relatively constant after the initial surge. This pattern is found consistently from experimental roofs across the world.

The storage capacity of a green roof varies with the season of the year, the depth of substrate, the number and type of layers used in its construction, angle of slope of the roof, the physical properties of the growing media, the type of plants incorporated in the roof, and intensity of rainfall. It is therefore dangerous to generalize from results of research studies, particularly if they were conducted in a different climate regime. Here we give the results of a number of studies to indicate the general properties of green roofs. However, most research indicates yearly reductions in runoff of between 60 and 80 per cent.

The presence of vegetation and substrate invariably significantly reduces runoff from flat roofs. For example, Rowe et al. (2003) recorded runoff from experimental roofs in Michigan over a six-week period in late summer and autumn. The roofs were covered by either a 12-cm (4.8-in) layer of gravel or a layer of green-roof plant growing substrate, with or without a vegetation covering of sedums. The study revealed consistent reductions in runoff with the presence of growing media compared to the simple gravel-covered roof. The presence of vegetation achieved additional runoff reduction following heavier precipitation. Similar results come from a study in Belgium that indicated increasing water retention benefits with increasing substrate depth and presence of vegetation (Table 2.3).

Table 2.3 The influence of substrate depth and vegetation on the percentage of total rainfall running off a roof.

From Mentens et al. (2003)

Roof type	Runoff (mm)	Runoff (in)	Runoff (per cent)
Standard	665	26	81
Standard with 5 cm (2 in) of gravel	636	25	77
Green roof with 5 cm (2 in) of substrate	409	16	50
Green roof with 10 cm (4 in) of substrate	369	14.5	45
Green roof with 15 cm (6 in) of substrate	329	13	40

A study in Portland, Oregon, showed that over two years, an extensive green roof measuring around 10 cm (4 in) in depth absorbed 69 per cent of all rainfall falling on it, with 100 per cent retention for most warm-weather storms (Hutchison et al. 2003). Retention differs according to the existing roof moisture content—less rainfall is likely to be retained if there has been recent rainfall because the substrate is likely to be near its water holding capacity (Rowe et al. 2003). There is a considerable difference between the amount of water retained in summer and in winter, due to the much greater amount of water that can be returned to the atmosphere in summer through evaporation and transpiration: retention rates in summer can be between 70 and 100 per cent but in winter only 40 to 50 per cent (Peck et al. 1999). German research agrees, with extensive roofs with 10 cm (4 in) of substrate absorbing 90 per cent of precipitation in summer and 75 per cent in winter (Köhler et al. 2001). However, it is summer rain that is more likely to involve the heavy downpours that overload drainage systems. The work of Optigrün (2002) in Germany indicates that roof gradients of up to 15 degrees make little difference to runoff quantity. The company's work also suggests that the effect on runoff begins to tail off with substrates deeper than 15 cm (6 in), with little advantage to constructing deeper layers.

Water management on vegetated green roofs offers great design potential. Cisterns and wells can store water for later use, and storage pools and ponds can be attractive features in themselves. Where rain water or recycled grey water from the building is being filtered through planted wetland vegetation (either on the roof or at ground level) there is much opportunity to be creative with both the planting and the design of containers, planters, and pools.

Excess water is collected from the green roof of the Peggy Notebaert Nature Museum, Chicago, creating an ornamental pond, with associated wetland planting and additional wildlife benefit. The pond receives water from the surrounding green roof, but is also kept topped up to a standard level. A solar-powered pump gently recirculates the water to prevent build up of algae. Design by Conservation Design Forum, Inc., Chicago.

Green roofs and air pollution

There are several problems associated with urban air pollution. Particulate matter, primarily from vehicle (particularly diesel) engines, has been linked to increased respiratory disease and breathing difficulties. Heavy metals, again in vehicle and factory emissions, are toxic in relatively low concentration. Ozone, the main aggravating component of smog, is produced on hot sunny days (enhanced temperatures being a major side-effect of urbanization, as discussed below). Both ozone and particulates are associated with increased death rates from respiratory-related complaints during hot weather. Generally, these are not seen as direct causes of death, but as agents that cause fatalities where respiratory problems are already present. Nevertheless, the numbers of premature fatalities as a result of air pollution can be large—an estimated 24,000 per year in the United Kingdom (English Nature 2003).

Vegetation in urban areas can filter out fine airborne particles as the air passes over the plants, settling on to leaf and stem surfaces. This material will then be washed off into the soil through the movement of rainwater. Foliage can also absorb gaseous pollutants, sequestering the material in their tissues. Most of these benefits are associated with trees and larger vegetation. It must be admitted that some extravagant claims are made about the ability of roofs to aid this process. There has been little direct experimental work to investigate the role of green roofs in this regard, and most claims are made by inference from the results of tests on other types of vegetation. The ability of extensive roofs with low-growing sedum-based vegetation is probably rather small in this regard. It will also be necessary for a high density of green roofs to be present in an area rather than a few isolated individuals.

Heavy metals are a particular pollution problem in urban areas, but green roofs can play a major role in trapping them, studies have shown that they can trap up to 95 per cent of cadmium, copper, and lead and 16 per cent of zinc (Peck et al. 1999). Lead, zinc, and copper are used in roof construction themselves, and green roofs can help to limit the extent to which dissolved salts of these metals can contaminate water supplies.

Green roofs and the urban heat island effect

Beneficial effects of roof greening and other uses of vegetation on buildings can act at the individual building level and can accumulate to improve the whole environment of a city. The increase in the concentration of buildings and paved areas in cities leads to the formation of a specific urban climate, characterized in particular by higher night-time temperatures, increased humidity, and, because of the restriction of airflows, polluted air and increased concentrations of particulates. Increased temperatures also increase the likelihood of smog formation and associated higher risk of asthma and other respiratory problems. This is a result of many factors, such as the large number of built structures with heat absorbing properties, the reduction in evaporating surfaces, lack of vegetation cover and increasing surface runoff, increase in air pollutants (mainly from vehicles), heat production from buildings, and less cooling from wind because of the shelter of buildings. As a result urban air temperatures can be significantly higher than in the surrounding countryside. For example, the centre of Berlin on clear windless nights can be up to 9°C (16°F) higher than the outskirts (von Stulpnagel et al. 1990). This so-called urban heat island effect may also increase convection currents which can generate more rainfall over cities, often in the form of more violent weather events such as thunderstorms (yet cities, as discussed previously, are much less able than rural areas to absorb this rainfall.) Convection currents generated by hot surfaces have the strength to raise dust, adding to that already put into the atmosphere through air pollution, industrial processes, and traffic. Convection currents that develop over vegetated surfaces are much weaker or non-existent (Peck et al. 1999). In human terms these factors can all lead to urban inhabitants suffering heat stress and general discomfort as well as respiratory and circulation problems as a result of poor air quality.

The effect of urban green spaces in general on urban climate has received little attention. The main function of urban vegetation in this context (apart from creating favourable microclimates at the smaller scale) is to use heat energy to power the process of evapotranspiration from vegetation, thereby achieving a general cooling effect. Evapotranspiration is the combined effect of transpiration (the movement of water through the plant from the roots to its release to the atmosphere from the leaves as water vapour) and the evaporation of water from the soil and vegetation surfaces. Both processes are powered by solar energy. As a result this energy is retained within the water vapour and is prevented from being converted into heat at the surface (Bass 2001). In this regard, the climatic quality of a town is directly related to the proportion of open and vegetated spaces in the total area (Meiss 1979).

What little research there is on vegetation and urban climate tends to suggest that the larger the individual green areas are, the greater is the range of temperature moderation within them. The effect of open areas of vegetation is generally reduced if the area lies lower than the land around it or if it is surrounded by walls or peripheral vegetation—in these cases the barriers prevent cool air draining from the site to influence adjacent areas (the so-called urban park cool island effect; Spronken-Smith and Oke 1998). Where green areas are small (such as roofs), they will only be beneficial if there are many of them interspersed with other types of urban green (gardens, pocket parks, street trees) that serve to connect them into a wider network. Indeed it has been proposed that, from a climatological point of view, the optimal arrangement is to have a limited number of major open spaces (parks) supplemented by a large number of smaller well-vegetated spaces evenly distributed throughout the town or city (Miess 1979). It should also be noted here that of all land surface types open water has the most beneficial properties in terms of climate moderation. Combining shallow pools or water collecting basins with vegetated areas on roofs will therefore maximize their benefits.

Vegetation can also contribute to reducing urban night-time temperatures by reducing the amount of heat radiated at night from dark or hard surfaces. While not as effective as the white roofs which are painted white to reflect maximum sunlight, vegetation is more effective at reflecting solar radiation and reducing heat absorption than the majority of conventional roofing products.

Of all the benefits of green roofs, the diminution of the urban heat island effect is the one of the most difficult to quantify. There have been a few attempts to mathematically model the effect of urban vegetation on the urban heat island effect. For example, Bass et al. (2002) modelled the influence of green roofs on Toronto's urban heat island. A theoretical figure of 50 per cent of the buildings in the downtown area receiving green roofs had negligible effect on the heat island, reducing mean temperatures only by around 0.5°C (0.9°F). The addition of irrigation in the computer model to these roofs to ensure effective evapotranspiration even during severe dry periods had a much more dramatic effect, reducing temperatures by up to 2°C (4°F) and increasing the area of the city affected by the cooling. This initially appears to be rather contradictory: moderating one undesirable environmental factor through the addition of water, when water management and conservation is promoted as one of the main advantages of green roofs. However, the irrigation in question could be delivered through stored or recycled rainwater or from wastewater from the building (or indeed may be the result of summer rainfall). Other workers support this conclusion: von Stulpnagel et al. (1990) state that vegetated roofs will only achieve evaporative cooling in summer if they are watered. Nevertheless even dried-out roofs will alter the reflection and absorption qualities of the roof surface compared with unvegetated surfaces.

Noise pollution

The hard surfaces of urban areas tend to reflect sound rather than absorb it. Green roofs can absorb sound, however, with both substrate and plants making a contribution, the former tending to block lower sound frequencies and the latter higher ones. Some extravagant claims are made about the ability of green roofs to reduce noise. For example, it has been stated that a green roof with a 12 cm (4.8 in) substrate layer can reduce sound by 40 decibels while a 20 cm (8 in) layer can reduce by 46–50 decibels (Peck 2003a). However, there is little published scientific evidence to back these claims. German researchers have investigated noise reduction using green roofs at Frankfurt airport. A 10-cm (4-in) green roof was shown to reduce sound transmission into buildings by a minimum of 5 decibels. Because the level of sound damping increases with media depth, deep intensive systems may attain the sort of noise reduction hinted at above (Charlie Miller, personal communication).

Acoustic insulation was one of the main reasons for the installation of the green roof at the award-winning Gap's 901 Cherry Hill office in California, situated next to a noisy freeway and on the flight path of San Francisco International Airport. The roof aimed to dampen sound transmission by as much as 50 decibels (Burke 2003).

Fire prevention and risks

There is some evidence from Europe that green roofs can help slow the spread of a fire to and from the building through the roof, particularly when the growing medium is saturated (Peck and Kuhn 2000). Of course, very dry vegetation on a roof can also be a fire hazard, although the amount of dry vegetation on an extensive green roof is unlikely to be sufficient to cause anything more than a flash fire with little intensity. German building codes require lightning rods and stone or cement pathways of 60 cm (2 ft) wide every 40 m (131 ft) in order to minimize risk (White 2001). Where fire is a concern, integrate fire breaks such as gravel or concrete pavers at regular intervals, use fire-retardant plants with high water content such as sedums, and install a sprinkler irrigation system fitted to the fire alarm (Peck and Kuhn 2000).

CONCLUSION

The benefits of green roofs are many and varied. In fact they deliver so many benefits that it is often difficult to evaluate their potential in an integrated manner (Peck 2003b), because individual researchers or professionals tend to be concerned with their own area of expertise, whether it be storm-water management, temperature profiling, biodiversity, and so on.

Integrated cost-benefit analysis enables an overall picture to be built of the effect of roof greening in any given area. One of the most wide-ranging investigations has been conducted for Toronto by a partnership of the Toronto City Authority, Environment Canada, Green Roofs for Healthy Cities, and the Canadian National Research Council Institute for Research in Construction. They worked with a modest scenario of 6 per cent of Toronto's roofs to be greened over the next 10 years (representing 1 per cent of Toronto's total land area: around 6 million square metres, 65 million square feet). The average roof type was proposed to be 15 cm (6 in) thick, with a thick layer of grass vegetation. The benefits of this level of green-roof implementation are *conservatively* estimated as follows:

Direct and indirect job creation: 1350 person years/year

Reduction in the urban heat island of 1–2°C (2–4°F)

Annual greenhouse gas emission reductions from buildings of 1.56 megatonnes (1714 tons) and 0.62 megatonnes (681 tons) indirectly from heat island reduction

Reduction in the number of serious smog incidents by 5–10 per cent

Amount of particulate matter captured by plants: 30 tonnes (29.5 tons) per year

Storm-water retention capability: over 3.6 million cubic metres (127 million cubic feet) per year (the cost of constructing a storm-water retention tanks to attain similar results: $60 million)

Urban food production, assuming 10 per cent coverage, 4.7 million kg (10.4 million lb) per year

Annual energy cost savings: more than $1 million per year

Potential recreational space, public and private: 650,000 square metres (7 million square feet).

These figures are, almost by definition, far from perfect but they do provide an overall picture of the immense benefits that may result from the wider uptake of green roofs.

Perhaps the last word should be left to the Austrian artist and philosopher, Friedensreich Hundertwasser, quoted by Herman (2003):

> Everything under the heavens that is horizontal, belongs to nature. One must be persistent in the quest to green, or forest, all rooftops so that from a bird's-eye view, one would only recognize a natural, green landscape. When one creates green roofs, one doesn't need to fear the so-called paving of the landscape: the houses themselves become part of the landscape. People must use the roofs to return to nature what we unlawfully took from her by constructing our homes and buildings—the layer of earth for grasses and trees.

This green roof, as well as being much more attractive than adjacent roofs, has much greater potential benefit to wildlife and functions in a significantly different manner in terms of water and energy management.

© ZinCo

CHAPTER 3

Components of Green Roofs

A green roof is a green space created by adding layers of growing medium and plants on top of a traditional roofing system. This is not the same as a traditional roof garden in which planting is done in free-standing containers and planters located on an accessible roof terrace or deck (Peck and Kuhn 2000). In very simple terms, to achieve this all green roofs are composed of at least two layers: the vegetation itself and the media or substrate within which the plants are growing. In addition most commercial green-roof systems will also have a drainage layer, and in all cases there must be a mechanism by which the building below is protected from the twin dangers of damage from plant roots and leaking of water from above.

Within these parameters there is a myriad of possibilities depending upon the exact requirements of the roof and the system that is chosen, with many commercial systems being composed of many additional layers, each fulfilling a specific technical function. In this chapter we intend to steer a clear path through these various options to build a picture of how green roofs are put together. Although we will concentrate on the components of typical commercial systems, we will also look at alternative approaches to green-roof construction and planting and consider the basic components of more rudimentary do-it-yourself systems that might be used on a smaller or domestic scale. But before doing so we must examine a number of technical and structural considerations that will determine what sort of green roof may be possible, and if, indeed, such a roof is feasible in the first place.

The green roof on this curved and sloping roof is being installed as a series of self-contained fixed units.

© ZinCo

STRUCTURAL CONSIDERATIONS

In chapter 1 we discussed the difference between the so-called intensive and extensive green roofs. While the differences between the two types manifest themselves in their visual appearance and in the amount of maintenance they may require, fundamentally, the division exists because of their relative overall weights. Extensive roofs being relatively lightweight and generally within the normal load-bearing capacity of modern roof structures, and intensive roofs have more serious weight and structural implications. The choice as to what type of roof is possible, therefore, relates directly to the load-bearing capacity of the roof structure of the building. Where green roofs are to be included on a new building this is not so much of a problem because supporting requirements can be factored in at the design stage. Retrofitting a green roof onto an existing building will mean that either the roof must fit the existing carrying capacity of the roof or the owner must be prepared to upgrade the structure, perhaps at some significant financial cost (Peck and Kuhn 2000). Lightweight extensive systems with substrate depths of 5–15 cm (2–6 in) increase the loading on a roof by between approximately 70 and 170 kg per square metre (14 and 35 lb per square foot). Intensive green roofs with soil-based substrates will impose additional weight of between 290 and 970 kg per square metre (59 and 199 lb per square foot).

Each country or region will have its own building standards that determine the minimum load-bearing capacity of a roof. This will normally take account of the need for access, the weight of snow cover or storm water, and the ability to support a protective layer of gravel or ballast. For example, in Ontario, Canada, roofs must be designed to support a loading of at least 195 kg per square metre (40 lb per square foot). This takes into account a typical winter snow loading of 107 kg per square metre (22 lb per square foot). This then leaves 88 kg per square metre (18 lb per square foot) spare capacity—enough for a simple extensive system (Peck and Kuhn 2000). In Britain the standards for the load-bearing capacity of roofs are given in BS 6399 which set out the minimum standards necessary to meet the requirements of the weight of the roof deck itself; dead loads, that is, green-roof materials, snow, and ice; live loads, people; and the effects of wind shear.

As noted in the British standards, if the green roof is accessible the additional weight of people much be accounted for, as well as estimating the additional weight of the green-roof components themselves. This live load will also relate to amount and frequency of intended use. Where snowfall is a regular winter occurrence, this must also be accounted for.

When calculating loading, it must be remembered that the weight of green-roof materials will vary greatly depending on how compacted and how moist they are. Saturated weights of materials will indicate their maximum loading. In Germany the term *saturated weight* of green roof substrate materials has a clear meaning. A standard test is applied by the German green-roof industry that involves moistening a sample of the material, compressing it into a mould, soaking for twenty-four hours, draining for one hour, and then weighing. This saturated moisture content is usually around twice as high as normal field capacity, but gives a clear indication of the maximum weight of the material. There are currently no similar measures outside of Germany (Charlie Miller, personal communication).

When working with existing roofs the following measures can be taken to give additional support if necessary. Strengthen the roof with strategically placed additional structural components such as columns, beams, and braces. Place the heaviest components of the roof on or near column heads and over beams. Finally, consider systems that attach the green roof to a wall or parapet or on small structures, such as a domestic garage or outbuilding, or consider constructing a framework around the building that enables the green roof to sit clear of the existing roof. Where a green roof is to be installed on a new building (or if there is doubt about the suitability of an existing roof) a structural engineer should be consulted.

As a general rule of thumb, a flat roof on which stone chippings have been spread will impose a weight loading of 200 kg per square metre (41 lb per square foot) for every 10 cm (4 in) depth of chippings. Replacing this with an extensive green roof with a substrate depth of 4 cm (1.6 in) will impose no additional weight—such a system will have a loading of around 40–60 kg per square metre (8–12 lb per square foot) However,

Substrate materials	Weight of a 1-cm layer (kg per square metre)	Weight of a 1-in layer (lb per square foot)
Gravel	16–19	3.3–3.9
Pebbles	19	3.9
Pumice	6.5	1.3
Brick (solid with mortar)	18	3.7
Sand	18–22	3.7–4.5
Sand and gravel mixed	18	3.7
Topsoil	17–20	3.5–4.1
Water	10	2.1
Lava	8	1.6
Perlite	5	1.0
Vermiculite	1	0.2
Light expanded clay granules (LECA)	3–4	0.6–0.8

Material	Weight (kg per cubic metre)	Weight (lb per cubic foot)
Stone (granite, sandstone, limestone)	2300–3000	144–187
Concrete (precast)	2100	131
Concrete (reinforced)	2400	150
Concrete (lightweight)	1300–1600	81–100
Hardwood timber	730	46
Softwood timber	570	35
Cast iron	7300	456
Steel	8000	499

where there has been no previous protective layer of gravel or paving, a structural engineer should again be consulted.

Table 3.1 indicates the typical loading of a range of green-roof materials. The weight of the material when saturated, if appropriate, is shown. Table 3.2 shows typical weights of a range of roof garden construction materials. Note that the units in Table 3.1 are for a 1-cm (0.4-in) layer of the material and the units in Table 3.2 are for a cubic metre of material. It is important to realize that when mixing media using a variety of materials, shrinkage caused by the intermingling of particles of different sizes will tend to make final weights and moisture capacities of the resulting mix unpredictable. The values in the following tables should be used with caution, therefore (Charlie Miller, personal communication).

The typical loadings of extensive green-roof systems range from 80 to 150 kg per square metre (16 to 31 lb per square foot). This is in contrast to typical intensive green-roof loadings of 300 to 1000 kg per square metre (61 to 205 lb per square foot) or more. Although partly related to vegetation type, these differences in weight are largely a result of substrate and construction materials. For example, relatively shallow substrates of 10–15 cm (4–6 in) topsoil supporting turf roofs weigh around 500 kg per square metre (103 lb per square foot; Kingsbury 2001).

Table 3.1 The weight of a variety of green-roof materials. Where appropriate, saturated weights only are listed.

Adapted from Osmundson (1999) and Johnson and Newton (1993)

Roof slope

The major problem associated with sloped green roofs is slippage. The maximum possible slope is controlled by the friction coefficient between the two slipperiest materials in the green-roof profile. Virtually no green roofs avoid having a fabric-membrane or membrane-membrane interface (for example, at root barriers and sheet drains). These are the planes along which slope movement will occur. Without additional slope

Table 3.2 Weights of various construction materials.

From Osmundson (1999)

Green roofs can be installed on sloping roofs, although they will be subject to greater moisture stress than on flat or gently sloping roofs.

Battens are placed underneath a waterproofing layer on this sloping roof of a garden building to prevent slippage of substrate.

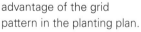

A wooden grid on the same roof provides further stabilization as well as a template for planting patterns.

The finished roof takes advantage of the grid pattern in the planting plan.

Photographs by Andy Clayden

stabilization measures, it is unwise to design green roofs for slopes steeper than 2:12 (which equals around 9.5 degrees or 17 per cent).

Slipping and slumping can be combated by the use of horizontal strapping, laths, battens, or grids. Using these methods and others, green roofs can readily be constructed on pitches up to 7:12 (which equals 30 degrees or 58 per cent). This is the angle of repose for most granular materials. To build on steeper pitches it is necessary to use special media mixes and specialized devices.

Wind

Structures on roofs have to withstand high wind uplift because of their exposed positions. This pressure varies across the surface of a flat roof, being relatively low in the centre and at its most extreme near the edges and corners. The layers of a green roof are therefore vulnerable to wind shear, particularly if the waterproofing layer is not bonded to the roof beneath and the green roof itself is acting as ballast to hold it down. A strip of gravel, stones, or pavers around the edge of the roof can prevent such wind damage. Such strips are also often used as vegetation barriers, preventing damage by plants to the edges of the roof where the waterproofing layer rises above the surface of the growing medium.

Irrigation

If green roofs are carefully designed, with an appropriate plant mix and substrate, and if the plants have been properly established, there should be no need for irrigation except in the most arid climates. Indeed it is a tenet of the ecological or sustainable approach to landscape management that inputs of resources, such as water or fertilizers, should be reduced to the absolute minimum, or be eliminated completely, apart from those which naturally enter the system. The traditional roof garden or intensive green roof which needs constant irrigation for plant survival is, on these terms, unsustainable. It is possible, through plant selection, to achieve equally rich effects without the need for continuous water input, even in intensive situations.

Having said this, there are good arguments for *controlled* and limited irrigation of green roofs in certain circumstances. Where aesthetic value is important, then irrigation in particularly dry periods may be necessary to maintain growth. Research indicates that strategically applied irrigation has significant benefit in semi-extensive green roofs (N. Dunnett and A. Nolan, unpublished data), being more important than increasing substrate depth in promoting the growth of a diversity of plant species. If the full benefits of green roofs are to be achieved with regard to temperature amelioration, biodiversity, and rainwater storage, it is necessary to have plants green and growing (that is, transpiring) rather than desiccated and dead—again judicious irrigation may be beneficial. In very arid climates irrigation can reduce the fire hazard of green roofs. Rainwater storage and recycling systems should be actively considered as the basis of irrigation systems. There are also promising developments with regard to the use of recycled grey water from domestic use as irrigation for green-roof systems (see chapter 2).

Four main irrigation methods are used on green roofs:

1. Surface spray with traditional sprinkler systems. These are wasteful of water and can also encourage surface rooting which is vulnerable to extreme temperatures and moisture stress.
2. Drip and tube systems. These can either be pegged to the surface or buried in the substrate. Subirrigation systems direct the water only to plant roots, lose less water to evaporation, and are not visible. Weed seeds are less likely to germinate if the substrate surface is kept dry. Buried pipes are more efficient than surface pipes.
3. Capillary systems. Porous mats deliver water to the base of the substrate and are ideal for shallower systems, that is, 20 cm (8 in) or less. At depths greater than this water will not infiltrate through the full substrate profile. Water introduced at just a few locations can be distributed evenly through the use of a capillary mat.
4. Standing-water systems. These systems maintain a layer of water at the base of the roof. These systems can be self-regulating, being filled by percolating rainfall, but can also be maintained by float-control devices (Miller 2003).

GREEN-ROOF CONSTRUCTION

Green roofs can be constructed over any properly designed and constructed roof deck, whether steel, wood or concrete, plastic or composite, so long as the structural considerations discussed above are met. Of course, roofs differ greatly in their construction. A roof on an architect-designed building will need to meet certain structural and other requirements such as building insulation, while that on a domestic garage or garden outbuilding may be minimal in its construction. In

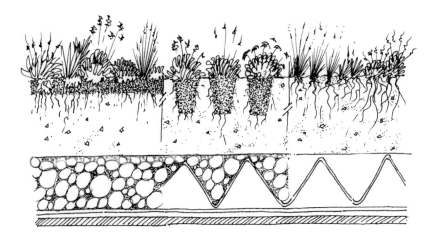

A section of a typical extensive green roof. The vegetation layer may be established using a pregrown vegetation mat, through pot or plug plants, or by sowing seed and/or spontaneous colonization. A filter mat separates the growing medium from the drainage layer to prevent clogging of the layer with the medium above. The drainage layer may consist of an aggregate material or preformed plastic drainage units, with or without a filling of aggregate. Finally, a root barrier prevents plant damage to the roof surface, and a fully waterproof membrane provides a watertight seal to the building below. Modified from an original by Blackdown Horticultural Consultants.

Drawing by Andy Clayden

both cases, the same starting point for a green roof will be required: a weatherproof, even surface capable of withstanding the load of whatever type of green roof is proposed.

The construction of green roofs, as supplied by the main manufacturers, has moved on considerably from the earliest examples of what we would recognize as modern-day green roofs: those developed in the second half of the twentieth century in Germany. Contemporary systems can be very complex, with many product options and many different layers. This complexity has arisen partly from the very existence of green-roof suppliers and manufacturers, with each company developing its own patented systems. But also, as the concept of green roofs gained wider application in Germany there was a need to ensure uniformity and dependability of the product, resulting in the application of technology and research to maximize the reliability of the products. While most roof greening systems used around the world are based upon the original German models, we will also mention some examples of a different approach.

Rather than trying to account for all the different systems that are available, we will instead look at the main *functions* that the components or layers of green roof have to perform and then discuss various ways in which this can be achieved. These functions include: weatherproofing of the roof, protecting the roof surface from root penetration and damage, drainage, and the support and growth of the vegetation layer.

Drainage units being laid over the waterproof and root protection layers.

© ZinCo

A vegetation mat is laid over a thin layer of growing medium, with a granular drainage layer and metal roof surface.

Weatherproof membrane

An effective waterproof seal to the roof is an essential prerequisite for all green roofs, and the importance of making sure this is effective and durable cannot be overstated. The layer on the roof that performs this function is the weatherproof or waterproof membrane. There are three main types of membrane: the built-up roof, the single-ply membrane, and the fluid-applied membrane (Osmundson 1999).

Built-up roofs are the most commonly encountered and are composed of the familiar bitumen/asphalt roofing felt or bitumized fabrics. These roofing materials generally have a limited life span of fifteen to twenty years and are susceptible to degradation from temperature extremes and ultraviolet radiation—both of which cause cracking and leakage, although a layer of substrate and vegetation will reduce this (see Increased

Roof Life section in chapter 2). Equally important in the green-roof context is their susceptibility to plant root growth; for this reason, a root protection barrier must always be used with such membranes. However, this type of roof is not ideal as a base for a green roof. There are other types of built-up roofing systems that are entirely different in material and performance than conventional asphalt/felt built-up systems. These much more robust systems are more suitable for green roofs and include SBS modified bitumous membrane sheets set in SEBS polymer modified bitumen and coal tar pitch/polyester built-up systems.

Single-ply roof membranes are rolled sheets of inorganic plastic or synthetic rubber material that are overlapped at the joints and sealed with heat, in the case of thermoplastic materials such as PVC, or adhesive, in the case of butyl rubber or EPDM (Osmundson 1999). They may also be available as tiles (sometimes composed of recycled rubber). These membranes can be very effective if properly applied. However, the seams or bonds between the sheets and tiles can be weak points that may be exploited by plant roots and become the basis for leaks—seals around drainage points and any exposed parts of the liner are also prone. PVC and butyl rubber sheets are also susceptible to degradation from ultraviolet rays. For this reason it is essential that all parts of the liner are covered in some way to protect it from sunlight. Green-roof suppliers and consultants can advise on roof membranes that provide both weatherproofing and protection from damage by plant roots: these membranes may contain root-deterring chemicals or metal foil between the membrane layers and at the seam lines to prevent damage (Peck and Kuhn 2000).

Fluid applied membranes are available in hot or cold liquid form that is sprayed or painted on to the surface of the roof and forms a complete seal when set, eliminating the problem of joints (Osmundson 1999). They are also easier to apply to vertical or awkwardly shaped surfaces.

There may be further layers. A protection board may be laid directly over the membrane to protect this layer from anything above and also construction operations—the most lightweight approach is to use a PVC sheet or expanded polystyrene. There may also be an insulation layer of a material such as Styrofoam. On flat roofs a layer of gravel, concrete slabs, or sand may be spread to protect the roof membrane from temperature fluctuations and ultraviolet radiation. (In fact it was the observation of plants spontaneously colonizing these loose substrates that led to the initial research on extensive roof greening in Germany.) Because an extensive green roof will achieve the same protective function as such a layer of gravel, the most lightweight systems can be used as substitutes for this layer with no additional loading on the roof.

Root protection barrier

If the membrane on a roof upon which a green roof is to be installed contains bitumen, asphalt, or any other organic material, it is crucial that a continuous separation is maintained between the membrane and the plant layer because the membrane will be susceptible to root penetration and the activity of micro-organisms—these organic oil-based materials are not rot proof. If the roof is not completely flat, then any pockets of collecting water can also form the basis of plant growth on a roof—again there must be protection from root damage.

Root protection membranes are usually composed of rolls of PVC (varying in thickness from 0.8 mm [0.03 in] to more than 1.0 mm [0.04 in] in thickness) and laid out over the weatherproofed roof deck or surface. Although claims are made about the environmental implications of the manufacture of PVC, it performs multiple functions, is long-lasting (thus eliminating waste), can be easily recycled, eliminates the need for additional materials and costs, and because it can be heat-seamed, PVC reduces the risk of potential leaks (Scholz-Barth 2001). As with many ecological issues, the decision to use particular materials is a balancing act of costs and benefits. Some commercial systems are based upon metal or plastic base plates that form a complete underlying structure to the green roof and isolate and raise the green roof completely from the underlying roof structure (for example, the Kalzip Nature Roof®). These systems automatically result in a root-proof barrier between the green roof and the building.

The membrane must be raised up beyond the surface of the planting medium at the edges and around all projections such as chimneys and vents. The membrane sheets are welded together to form a complete seal—it is essential that the welding is effective because any gaps or weaknesses will be exploited by the plant roots.

Drainage layer

Maintaining proper drainage on a green roof is extremely important for several reasons. First is the protection of the waterproof roof membrane. Without greening, flat roofs are 50 per cent more susceptible to damage after five years than slightly sloped roofs (that is, those with a fall of greater than 5 degrees) as a result of water collecting and pooling rather than running off the roof (Peck et al. 1999). If drainage is inadequate on a flat green roof, then damage to the roof membrane may ensue because of continuous contact with water or wet soil. Because green-roof vegetation, particularly of the extensive type, is selected to be drought-resistant and tolerant of dry, free-draining soils, prolonged saturation of the soil is likely to cause plant failure, rotting, and sour, anaerobic conditions. A permanently wet green roof also will lose its thermal insulating properties.

Precipitation falling onto a green roof has several fates. It may evaporate directly off the substrate or plant surfaces. It may be taken up into plants through leaves or roots. It may be stored within the substrate, either through adhering to particles or by filling pore spaces and voids. Any excess water will percolate away. All of these components of green-roof water management are essential to the functioning of a green roof. For small rainfall events there will be little runoff and most of the moisture will be retained within the roof and returned to the atmosphere as water vapour. However, as discussed in chapter 2, during heavy rainfall green roofs can significantly delay and reduce the amount of runoff from the roof.

Green roofs turn our normal interpretation of rainfall runoff on its head. The water that escapes a green roof is actually underflow, or percolated water. Surface runoff should not occur at all on a well-designed green roof (Miller 2003). The function of the drainage layer is to remove excess water or underflow as rapidly as possible to prevent over-long saturation. Note the term *excess*—drainage is only necessary if the growing medium is already saturated. The drainage layer in some instances may also double up as a means of introducing irrigation.

Drainage can be achieved in several ways. These techniques relate mainly to flat or very slightly sloping roofs. Where there is a more definite slope, that is, 5 degrees or greater, drainage may be effective without specific drainage layers (Johnson and Newton 1993). In fact on sloping sites, addition of additional drainage may mean that the roof drains too effectively, producing overly harsh conditions for plant growth and eliminating the storm-water management benefits of the roof. In some cases the drainage layer may also provide the means of irrigating the green roof and providing additional nutrients or fertilizer.

From the late 1980s onwards much research in Germany was put into developing roof-greening systems that used several construction layers to both drain and store water. Combining a drainage layer with a water-storage layer below it not only further reduces runoff compared to roof-greening systems without such a layer, by 11 to 17 per cent, but acts as a reservoir for plants to draw upon in dry weather (Kolb et al. 1989). The three main types of drainage materials are discussed below.

Granular materials—Coarse granular materials such as gravel, stone chips, broken clay tiles, clinker, scoria (lava rock), pumice, expanded shale, or expanded clay granules contain large amounts of air or pore space between them when packed together in a layer or space. This pore space is available for water to move into from the vegetation and substrate layers above. The principle is the same as crocking, placing course material at the base of plant pots and containers to promote drainage. This is the most low-tech and simple form of drainage mentioned here. A thin layer of granular material may be all that is required to spread over a roof to lift the main area of substrate and vegetation above any puddles or water pockets that may collect in uneven areas of the roof. Many of the materials mentioned above are actually lighter than the overlying growth media. Therefore, one strategy for reducing the overall green roof weight is actually to increase the relative proportion of drainage layer in the green roof profile. A great advantage of granular materials is that they convert this zone into additional root space. The roots of most plants will readily infiltrate through the separation fabric into the drainage layer. A drainage layer that consists of granular material is particularly hospitable, offering an aerated environment with more stable moisture and temperature conditions than the overlying growth media. In fact, a system with, for example, 6 cm (2 in) of granular drainage media and 6 cm (2 in) of growth media will always outperform a system with 12 cm (4.8 in) of a single general-purpose media (Charlie Miller, personal communication).

Porous mats—These mats, which operate in a similar way to horticultural capillary matting, act like sponges, absorbing water into their structure. They are constructed from a range of materials, including recycled materials such as clothing and car seats. There is a danger that some of these mats can be too absorbent, sucking moisture from the growing substrate and thus negatively affecting plant growth (Tobias Emilsson, personal communication).

Lightweight plastic or polystyrene drainage modules—These modules vary tremendously in design and appearance. Most sheets are thinner than 25 mm (1 in). Some include the capacity to retain water and others do not; some can be filled with granular media. These interlocking modules have several functions. They are rigid enough to support the growing medium and vegetation, enabling these layers to sit clear of the immediate roof surface. They provide a permanent free-flowing lightweight drainage layer beneath the planting medium. In some instances, they will also store water, providing reservoirs from which plants can derive moisture during excessively dry periods. Some types of module also enable irrigation water to be introduced to the roof from the base.

Sloping roofs may produce significant variability in the moisture regime of the substrate, with relatively dry medium at the top of the roof and moist medium at the base where the water drains away. These differences can be exploited in terms of plant choices.

Drainage outlets must be kept free of planting substrate at all times so that they can fulfil their function. There are several potential drainage outlet options—of course, an existing roof will already have drainage points installed. Where a drainage layer is included a filter mat (semi-permeable polypropylene fabric) is laid loosely over the drainage layer and prevents fine material from the growing medium being washed into the drainage layer, thereby blocking pore space. These particles may also cause blockage to drainage outlets. The edges of the filter mat should again be taken up over the edge of the planting medium. The matting is supplied in rolls, each roll can be overlapped by around 20 cm (8 in) when laid out.

Growing medium or substrate

The ideal substrate has to achieve the seemingly miraculous combination of being highly efficient at absorbing and retaining water while at the same time having free-draining properties. It should also be able to absorb and supply nutrients and retain its volume over time, as well as provide anchorage for the plants of the green roof. This is generally achieved by granular mineral materials that absorb water and create pore space, mixed with fine particles (in relatively small proportion) to which water will cling (Miller 2003). In addition, unless the roof is of the intensive type, the substrate must be lightweight so that the weight imposed on the roof is kept to a minimum. German research indicates that the ideal growing medium will comprise 30–40 per cent substrate and 60–70 per cent pore space. This will ensure good moisture retention capacity as well as aeration to the roots of the plants. If the pore space is saturated on a long-term basis, that is, continuously less than 15 per cent of the substrate containing air-filled pore space, then poor plant growth will result (Hitchmough 1994).

General garden soil or topsoil is not suitable for non-intensive green roofs because it is both too heavy and too fertile. High fertility is not desirable because it encourages vigorous lush growth that is susceptible to environmental stress, whether this be from extreme cold or drought. Medium to low fertility is also a precursor to the development of more diverse meadow vegetation, preventing dominance by vigorous aggressive species.

Clay has good moisture-holding capacity and also provides surfaces that attract and bind nutrients in the soil, but tends to clog up drainage layers and fabric. Therefore, clay or silt should be present in small proportions in green-roof substrates (Miller 2003). Organic matter, such as peat, compost, and coir tends to oxidize over time, leading to shrinkage of the substrate. Although it is valuable in terms of water retention and nutrient availability, organic matter should be used in low proportion, if at all on extensive green roofs. It must also be borne in mind that unless the organic matter is completely decomposed it will rob the substrate of nitrogen as it completes its decomposition—this must be compensated for when using substrates that are already very low in fertility. Most commercial green-roof substrates are based upon non-organic mineral components that have moisture holding capacity, mimicking the function that organic material may achieve in conventional soils. In many cases these materials fulfil the same purpose as the minerals in a hydroponic (no soil) horticultural growing system.

For plant growth artificial soils can be superior to many natural soils (Hitchmough 1994) provided they are tailored for the specific type of vegetation they are to support. Examples of natural mineral materials include sand and lava. Artificially produced materials that have been used include vermiculite and perlite—both forms of heated and

Table 3.3 Some materials used as a basis for green-roof substrates.

Materials	Comments
Natural minerals	
Sand	Fine texture can result in lack of pore space and problems of saturation of the substrate if drainage is poor. Conversely, coarse sands can be so free-draining as to require constant irrigation.
Lava (scoria) and pumice	Lightweight and valuable if locally available.
Gravel	Relatively heavy.
Artificial minerals	
Perlite	Particles tend to collapse over time (Hitchmough 1994).
Vermiculite	Very lightweight, but has no water- or nutrient-holding capacity and again may disintegrate over time (Hitchmough 1994).
Light expanded clay granules (LECA) Expanded shale	Lightweight, produce large amounts of pore space because of their size, and absorb water because of their porous nature.
Rockwool	Very lightweight but energy-intensive production and no nutrient-holding capacity
Recycled or waste materials	
Crushed clay brick or tiles, brick rubble	Stable and uniform, some nutrient and moisture retention. Brick rubble may contain mortar and cement, which will raise the pH of the substrate.
Crushed concrete	Limited moisture retention and nutrient availability, alkaline. However, cheap and available in quantity as a demolition material.
Subsoil	Heavy, low fertility, readily available as by-product of construction.

expanded minerals formed into granules. These are both extremely lightweight but have disadvantages in that they must be mixed with other materials because they cannot store nutrients and water and the particles of vermiculite tend to collapse over time (Hitchmough 1994).

Table 3.3 lists some materials that have been used as the basis for green-roof substrates. Natural minerals are a good choice if locally available. Although sand has been used it is rarely satisfactory on its own, and should be used in combination with other materials that will provide pore space and retain water (Osmundson 1999). Artificial minerals can be very useful. Light expanded clay granules (LECA) are widely used on their own or in combination with other materials, and in many ways fulfil all the requirements of an ideal base for a green-roof substrate, being lightweight and having some moisture and nutrient storage capability. The material is created by kiln-firing clay, shale or slate to extremely high temperatures (1150°C, 2102°F) until the parts expand, forming round pellets. The air spaces formed by the expansion can retain liquid and reduce the material's weight (Osmundson 1999). The material can absorb 35 per cent of its volume in water and retain 28 per cent of its volume in water for slow release to plant roots. It is also very resistant to break down and decay. It can be used on its own as a base for extensive green roofs the lightweight nature of the material can be a problem in plant anchorage and the large pore space can prevent water retention: it is therefore desirable to mix in other materials of finer texture, such as a silt-free sand: (Osmundson 1999).

All these and similar artificial inorganic materials can be criticized on ecological grounds because of the energy inputs required for their production. As always, the situation is not clear cut—when does it become permissible to use an energy-intensive product if there are wider environmental benefits to using that product?

The most ecologically sound materials are those that are derived from waste or recycled products. One common material is crushed clay bricks, made from the unusable waste bricks or tiles from brick factories. Where waste or recycled materials are available locally then the energy used in their transport to a site is minimized (with accompanying cost reductions). In this respect, where available, demolition materials or by products of the building development (brick rubbles and crushed concrete, or subsoils from building foundations) represent the most environmentally beneficial option. However, such materials may not be available in all locations.

In most cases, then, a mix of materials may be used—perhaps with a low percentage of organic matter for nutrient and moisture retention. Green-roof companies generally supply their own substrate formulations, which in some cases may run to a very extensive range; one German company, for instance, has formulations for different types of vegetation (perennials, woody plants, calciphobe species), different levels of water-holding capacity, and different types of construction (lightweight and heavyweight; Optigrün 2002).

The depth of the substrate is directly related to the sort of vegetation that may be supported by it. A simple community of sedums and mosses is feasible with a substrate depth of as little as 2–3 cm (0.8–1.2 in). Depths of 5–8 cm (2–3.2 in) allow taller sedum species and grasses to grow as well as hardy, low-growing, drought-tolerant herbaceous species and alpines. Depths greater than 10 cm (4 in) for extensive roofs begin to cause structural problems because they result in loadings of greater than 120 kg per square metre (25 lb per square foot). The depth and type of green-roof substrate and vegetation also have a direct influence on its moisture-retention characteristics. German research indicates that a 3-cm (1.2-in) growth media layer over a 6-cm (2.4-in) drainage substrate retains around 58 per cent of water; a 6-cm (2.4-in) vegetation layer has around 67 per cent retention; and a 12-cm (4.8-in) growth media layer of mixed grass and herbaceous vegetation has around 70 per cent retention (Scholz-Barth 2001).

Some differentiation of the substrate layer into sublayers may be possible, in a manner that resembles natural soil profiles. For example, a thin layer of clay, sand, or organic matter may be placed above the typical mineral substrate. This is useful if vegetation is to be established from direct-sown seed. In fact some green-roof companies supply preseeded soil which is spread as a layer over the underlying substrate. In Germany mulching with 20 mm (0.8 in) of crushed brick, lava, or gravel is often used on a newly planted roof to deter establishment of wind-blown weeds and to conserve moisture (Johnson and Newton 1993).

Hessian or jute netting can be spread over the substrate surface to prevent erosion prior to vegetation establishment (Johnson and

Newton 1993). Again, this is primarily used as erosion control following seeding but is also useful to stabilize substrates on sloping roofs.

ALTERNATIVE GREEN-ROOF CONSTRUCTION SYSTEMS

Modular systems

Modular systems are based on interlocking units which contain the growing substrate, a drainage system, and the plants. They have the advantage of great flexibility and ease of installation. In effect the standard layers of a green roof are replaced with a fully planted module (Valazquez 2003) which can be taken to the roof via lift or crane and laid directly over the waterproof membrane to give an instant effect. One of their greatest benefits is that they easily allow access to the roof membrane if repair is needed, and they also enable the appearance of the roof to be changed rapidly, either through rearranging existing modules or replacing with new modules containing different vegetation.

Modular systems have not been in existence for as long as the layer-based green-roof systems. It is therefore too soon to be precise about their long-term performance. Because they are, in effect, shallow plant containers, they will be subject to some of the problems of growing plants in pots or planters on roofs—these include restricted space for lateral root spread, resulting in severe nutrient and water stress and possible long-term souring of the growing medium. Success will therefore depend upon plant selection and maintenance.

Wall mounted systems

Much discussion in this chapter has centred on the weight and load implications of the various green-roof components, and the point has been made that it is these considerations that limit what is possible in terms of substrate depth and therefore vegetation possibilities. The

RoofForest® system represents an alternative approach by which a self-supporting durable membrane structure is attached to the surrounding walls or parapet of the roof. The load is therefore transferred to the outside walls of the building and down to its foundations. The membrane is held clear of the roof by simple supports. This system has no need of a root protection barrier, and substrate and drainage layers can be placed directly on top. The manufacturers claim that the system supports soil depths of more than 1 m (3.3 ft) without any loading implications on the roof and will also support human traffic.

The system would appear to be very attractive, particularly where accessible intensive-type roof gardens are desired on roofs that would otherwise not support their weight, or to enable more diverse vegetation in visible and accessible extensive applications as a result of increased substrate depth. There would appear to be little advantage in using the system on typical inaccessible and invisible extensive applications or on structures such as steel-frame industrial warehouses and sheds where there is no walling in the traditional sense.

Much of this chapter has dealt with the components of commercial systems. The products have been developed to make sure that the systems work—if they don't the manufacturers may be liable for the failure. On a small garden or domestic scale there is less need to work with overly complex approaches or to use a ready-made system. Where the green roof is going on a garden shed, outbuilding, or extension and where access is possible, it is important to bear in mind only the underlying important principles: work within the load-bearing capacity of the roof, ensure that excess water is able to drain away, and, above all else, make sure that the roof is waterproof and that this waterproof layer won't be damaged by the green roof. Within these parameters there are any number of possibilities for the use of different substrates and vegetations. In particular simple, easily available materials can be used. PVC or butyl rubber pond liners can form the basis of root protection membranes and additional waterproofing. It may be possible to increase soil depths or to use more organic material than usual because of the possibility of replacement, or to use simple granular drainage layers or no drainage layer at all.

As with many other landscape situations, the planting of green roofs is often the most neglected aspect of the whole installation process. This may be a result of budget limitations. Often, however, green roofs are specified by professionals with limited plant knowledge, whether they be architects or engineers. Green roofs, as with the majority of other planted or designed vegetation types, require some maintenance. Again, this can be overlooked or neglected in the long term. The majority of guides to green roofs and roof greening concentrate on the technical and construction aspects but have relatively little to say about planting opportunities—mainly because most authors are not plant specialists. Suffice to say that the wide range of planting opportunities, even on relatively thin substrates, are little appreciated. Chapter 4 is devoted entirely to this important subject.

CHAPTER 4

Planting on Green Roofs

We were talking recently with an engineer, who is very active in the world of sustainable water management and green roofs, about the need to investigate the wide possibilities of planting on extensive green roofs and, in particular, how to go beyond the ubiquitous use of sedum species in Britain. To which she replied, "What's wrong with sedums?" The answer to which is, of course, nothing—they do their job brilliantly. There is, however, a tendency to think that the range of plants that can be grown on green roofs is rather limited. This is partly a result of necessity: on shallow extensive roofs which are subject to the most extreme environmental conditions, only a restricted range of specialized species will survive. Indeed, all roofs present a unique set of challenges for successful vegetation establishment and growth. These include:

Drought: thin, free-draining growing medium layers, elevated temperatures, and wind combine to make roof substrates excessively dry. Plants should ideally be drought tolerant. Conversely, plants must also be able to withstand periods of saturated substrate.

High temperatures: roof surfaces generally receive more sun than areas on the ground because there are no trees or shrubs nearby that can provide shade or evaporative cooling. Concrete or stone buildings absorb and hold significant amounts of heat in their walls and reradiate this heat at night. Parapet walls (perimeter roof walls used for safety) can block wind but, if composed of brick or concrete, also absorb heat during the day and reradiate it at night. Steel and wood deck buildings may not be insulated, thus heat from the interior of the building will be transmitted through the roof. Hot or cold air may come through the roof from hvac vents and exhaust onto nearby plants (White and Snodgrass 2003).

Wind: high wind speeds and eddies can desiccate vegetation and substrate and cause physical damage to plants.

Not only does the shallow substrate on a roof limit the ability of deep-rooted plants to extract moisture from deep sources, it also means that the entire root system will be subject to the extremes of temperature that are rapidly moderated by soil depth. During winter it is quite possible that some species regarded as hardy may be damaged by very low temperatures. Testing species for cold tolerance is therefore advisable before widespread use. So far, little information on the cold hardiness of plants on roofs is available in English (but see Boivin et al. 2001).

Plants will also be exposed to high summer temperatures, a problem that is inevitably linked to the severity and length of droughts. So far roof greening is in an early stage of its development in climates where both summer temperatures and droughts are more severe than in central Europe, and only extensive trialling will reveal how well plants cope.

Unfortunately, there is also a limited range of research into widening the planting possibilities on roofs: while many of the German green-roof companies carried out their own research into suitable species for low-input green roofs, they are now doing very little additional research. The result is that tried-and-tested plants are used regularly. In parts of the world where green roofs are a new phenomenon, there is a tendency to repeat the use of these species. In the United States, for example, there has been very little exploitation of native American species for green roofs. Where the function of a green roof is to go beyond the efficient fulfilment of engineering requirements (water management and thermal regulation, for example) to embrace aesthetics and biodiversity, it is worth considering carefully the options that are available. In this chapter we look at how plants may be established and managed on green roofs and attempt to indicate the wide range of unexploited opportunities for planting on roofs.

Plants colonize walls and suitable roofs spontaneously. Such plants can be used in designed roofs.

PLANT SELECTION FOR
ROOF ENVIRONMENTS

Whereas the construction materials used for roof greening will be largely similar the world over, the plants chosen will have to be selected for the climatic conditions prevailing at the site. This means that successful roof greening depends very much on a sound knowledge about what plant species will thrive in extreme local conditions. Plants selected will have to be able to not just survive the worst frosts, wind chill, and droughts that local conditions may throw at them, but positively flourish. Maintaining a good coverage of the substrate is vitally important if it is not to be exposed and possibly eroded. Good substrate coverage is also important for visual appearance.

As with plant selection for a garden, there are two main sets of criteria to consider. First and most importantly, plants will have to be chosen that will thrive in the conditions expected to prevail at the site. Second, visual appearance may be important, if the roof is to be seen and is regarded as an important part of an overall design concept. Plant selection for roof greening is very different to choosing plants for a garden, however, largely because the balance between the functional and the aesthetic is weighted much more towards the former. An analogy with hedging is perhaps appropriate—a hedge is primarily functional, and the first priority in choosing hedging plants is to look at such aspects as eventual height, speed of growth, and suitability for the site conditions. Only after a short list of species is produced are aesthetic criteria looked at. But hedges vary in how important the aesthetic criteria for plant selection are; simple screening may be entirely functional and plant selection may not involve any aesthetic criteria; the best plant for the job is chosen, whereas as for a key position in a garden or landscape the visual appearance will be very important.

To achieve its function, rooftop vegetation must be able to:

cover and anchor the substrate surface within a reasonable time after planting,

form a self-repairing mat, so that new growth will be able to fill any areas that become damaged, for example, through drought,

take up and transpire the volumes of water that is planned for the water balance of the structure, and

survive the climatic conditions prevailing at the rooftop, with particular attention to cold hardiness and drought tolerance; worst-case weather scenarios should be assumed.

Plants suitable for roof greening tend to share certain characteristics, for the simple reason that adaptation to certain environments favours the development of a certain growth form. Drought-tolerant plants the world over will therefore tend to share these characteristics, which means that for our purposes they are often well matched aesthetically. Plants of dry habitats are able to survive through a variety of adaptations to their form and physiology, not all of which make them suitable for roof greening. Sedums reign supreme in the roof-greening world because they store water in their leaves and are shallow-rooted, whereas many plants of dry habitats are able to grow where they do because of having immensely deep root systems. Many plants seemingly rooted in nothing but rock fragments in fact have roots metres long that penetrate fissures in the bedrock. But this deep rooting will be of no use to them on a roof with a 10-cm (4-in) substrate. In other words, the simple presence of plants in dry environments does not indicate their suitability for roof greening.

The combination of drought- and exposure-tolerant characteristics relevant to rooftops and the aesthetic qualities of appropriate plants come together to suggest that the following are features that should be looked for:

Low mat-forming or cushion-forming growth. Stems that root into the substrate as they grow are arguably more useful than those that root only from a central point, as this allows the plant to maintain good coverage of the surface after damage. Low, carpeting or mounded plants will be less susceptible to wind damage and uprooting than taller plants. Many ground-hugging and mat forming plants are also well adapted to drought conditions.

Succulent leaves or other water-storage capacity.

Compact twiggy growth and small evergreen leaves held close to the stem on ground-hugging plants. These characteristics are typical of a wide range of subshrubs from habitats that experience either heat- or wind-induced water shortages.

Grey or silver foliage. This colouring is due to either minute hairs on the leaf surface or a waxy coating, both adaptations that reduce water loss. These characteristics are also visually attractive.

Geophytes, species which die down to bulbs or tubers during winter or during a hot and dry season, are often visually striking and can play an important secondary role in roof-greening vegetation.

A seasonally dry natural habitat with shallow soil. Generally, plants that are able to survive under such regimes require full sun.

Shallow rooting. Except in the deeper soils, tap-rooted species will be less successful than species with spreading root systems. Such plants are known as "shelf plants" because of their ability to grow in very thin layers of substrate.

Evergreen foliage. For green roofs to work year-round, plants must be also be functioning year-round. This is particularly true in terms of water management—evapotranspiration only being effective when plants are actively photosynthesizing. Having said this, the cooling benefits associated with evapotranspiration are going to be most effective during the warmer months of the year when most plants will be in active growth. The insulating effect of vegetation can also be achieved partly by a mix of forbs and dead winter skeletons of plants, providing this doesn't disintegrate into a sodden dense mass of dead plant material.

Short life-cycles and effective reproduction will result in gaps in the vegetation being effectively filled, promoting the maintenance of long-term vegetation cover.

Attractive characteristics. Where roofs are visible and actively used, the species, as well as promoting the functioning of the roof, should also be visually attractive.

While it is unlikely that all these characteristics will be present in any one plant, mixtures of different species can easily fulfil these requirements.

PLANTING OPTIONS FOR GREEN ROOFS

Before going further, it is useful to remind ourselves of some points made in the introduction to this book and to state again our main focus. We are not concentrating on the traditional roof garden that demands relatively deep layers of growing media, containerized plants, and regular feeding and irrigation. Even where roofs are designed and constructed to withstand the greater weight loading of intensive green roofs, we argue strongly that the plantings on these roof gardens should also be sustainable, that is, be able to grow without the need for regular and prolonged irrigation (unless using recycled water) and feeding. Our focus is on the creative use of plants and vegetation in more shallow and lightweight layers of growing medium: this is the only way in which the practice of roof greening can achieve wider acceptance.

There is little point in using the same vegetation mixes everywhere, even on extensive green roofs. The most appropriate plantings for any given situation depend on the specific factors unique to that situation. Climate plays a large role here—it has been argued that green roofs are only suitable for certain climatic regimes and that in hot, arid climates there are far more efficient means of achieving the ecological and environmental (although perhaps not aesthetic) benefits of roof vegetation. In cooler, moist maritime climates such as the western British Isles there are opportunities for a different range of plant species than in warm continental climates such as central Europe. Moreover, different limiting factors come into play. For many, the ability to withstand summer drought will be the main factor deciding plant choice, whereas in regions with prolonged severe winters, cold hardiness will play a pivotal role. In non-seasonal wet tropical climates, ability to withstand prolonged saturated conditions may be the paramount consideration and drought tolerance a minor factor. However, in tropical and subtropical climates with seasonal rainfall (such as the south-eastern United States)

Table 4.1 Relationship between substrate depth and the accessibility and visibility of a roof in determining the appropriate character of planting. These are general indications only, and one should assume minimal additional irrigation and a temperate climate.

Depth	Accessibility/visibility of the roof			
	Inaccessible/ invisible	Inaccessible/visible from a far distance	Inaccessible/visible from a close distance	Accessible
0–5 cm (0–2 in)	simple sedum/moss communities	simple sedum/moss communities	simple sedum/moss communities	simple sedum/moss communities
5–10 cm (2–4 in)		dry meadow communities, low-growing drought-tolerant perennials, grasses and alpines, small bulbs	dry meadow communities, low-growing drought-tolerant perennials, grasses and alpines, small bulbs	dry meadow communities, low-growing drought-tolerant perennials, grasses and alpines, small bulbs
10–20 cm (4–8 in)			semi-extensive mixtures of low to medium dry habitat perennials, grasses and annuals; small shrubs; lawn, turf grass	semi-extensive mixtures of low to medium dry habitat perennials, grasses and annuals; hardy subshrubs
20–50 cm (8–20 in)				medium shrubs, edible plants, generalist perennials and grasses
50+ cm (20+ in)				small deciduous trees and conifers

green-roof plants may need to withstand high humidity with alternating periods of very wet and very dry substrates.

Leaving aside issues of climate, there are basic economic considerations that dictate the appropriate choice of vegetation: what is the most cost-effective means of achieving the aims of the roof planting. We propose that there are two main sets of factors that interact to determine the character of vegetation on any given site (Table 4.1). One set of factors relate to environmental severity (that is, depth of growing substrate and availability of irrigation and/or nutrients). The other relates to the intended function and use of the roof—is it accessible and is it visible?

Soil depth and environmental stress

As a rule, as soil depths decrease so does the list of viable plants that are suitable for roof planting, and these plants become increasingly specialized and adapted to the particular conditions of the roof environment. As discussed in chapter 3, the very thinnest substrates of 2–3 cm (0.8–1.2 in) will support simple communities of sedums and mosses. Because of the extreme conditions on shallow substrates, plants must be able to survive on a long-term basis with minimal reserves of moisture and nutrients—substrates generally don't have high moisture and nutrient storage capacity because of the low proportion of organic matter contained in them.

Succulent plants are very well adapted to these conditions: the lack of storage capacity in the soil is compensated for by the plants through the storage of water in above- or below-ground organs. Their nutrient requirements are met partly by dust falling from the atmosphere and partly by the decomposition of dead plant material. Many succulents, as well as other specialized plants, can metabolize differently in extreme heat and dryness through possessing Crassulacean acid metabolism (CAM). CAM enables plants to avoid transpiration. Non-CAM plants, which take in air through pores on the leafs (stomata) during the day, use the energy of the sun to convert carbon dioxide into sugars through photosynthesis. As a result they can lose large amounts of water during the heat of the day or under windy conditions

On very thin depths of substrate only a limited range of plants are suitable, such as these sedum-dominated roofs on 4 cm (1.6 in) of growing medium.

Increased substrate depth enables greater diversity in planting. This mixed vegetation including grasses and the mauve sea lavender (*Limonium latifolium*) is growing on 10 cm (4 in) of growing medium.

(Stephenson 1994). CAM is an alternative mechanism by which certain plants produce sugars by photosynthesis. CAM plants open their stomata at night and therefore minimize the amount of water lost per amount of carbon dioxide absorbed. Such plants are generally well adapted to survive in arid environments.

Substrate depths of 5–8 cm (2–3.2 in) support a wider range of succulent species, grasses, and herbaceous plants. Depths of 10–20 cm (4–8 in) will enable a wide range of drought-tolerant perennials and grasses to be grown, as well as tough subshrubs. These depths will also support turf grass and lawns. Depths of 30–50 cm (12–20 in) will enable many perennials and shrubs to be grown, while trees will grow in depths of 80–130 cm (32–52 in; Johnson and Newton 1993).

Plants will survive in shallower substrates, if there are frequent soaking rains, heavy mist, or dewfall or if irrigation is provided when necessary. In an experiment where a range of drought-tolerant herbaceous perennials with different structural characteristics (low growing, medium height, and taller emergents) were grown in two depths of lightweight substrate (10 and 20 cm, 4 and 8 in) and with or without limited supplementary watering, increasing substrate depth without supplementary watering produced relatively few significant improvements in plant performance. However, supplementary watering at both depths promoted growth in the majority of species. Low-growing species (those typical of standard extensive green roofs) performed less well under the irrigated conditions. This may be a negative physiological response to increased moisture supply at the roots. However, the reason for the reduced performance of these species may be linked to competition: the increased growth and vigour of the larger species under the more productive conditions of greater moisture supply meant that competitive exclusion, both above and below ground, reduced the growth potential of such species compared to conditions where the biomass of tall species is more sparse (Dunnett and Nolan 2004).

Function and use of the roof: visual criteria

Installing a green roof entails additional expense compared to a traditional roof. In many instances, the benefits of the roof will need to be justified in economic terms. The vegetation layer is one aspect where the cost of plant material and maintenance is in proportion to the complexity of the plantings. It is therefore wise to ensure that the plant mixes chosen are appropriate to the location and context. Where roofs are invisible (for example, on top of warehouses, factories, and tall buildings where there is no access to the roof), then it makes sense to use the most straightforward green-roof systems composed of thin layers of substrate and simple sedum and moss communities. In Sweden, for example, the main interest in green roofs is currently as materials to control storm-water runoff from the large areas of light-industrial and retail warehouses that spring up on the edges of towns and cities. Most of these roofs are invisible from the ground and are ugly when viewed from surrounding high-rise apartments. Very thin extensive green-roof systems are used, because of the possibility of applying them to buildings without adding large extra costs and almost no structural adjustments to the building. The most common roof-greening technique in Sweden has been the use of thin, prefabricated vegetation mats. These mats have a soil substrate layer of about 4 cm (1.6 in) and weigh around 50–60 kg per square metre (10–12 kg per square foot; Emilsson 2003).

As noted above, there are good reasons for going beyond such simple systems. Thin substrates and sedum-dominated communities probably have limited biodiversity value: wildlife and habitat considerations may well be an important consideration in the future implementation of green roofs. Different vegetation mixes may offer significant benefits in terms of environmental functioning, although there has been relatively little research to date on the functional attributes of different vegetation types in different climates. Varying the plant components can have greatest influence on visual appearance. It is surprising what effect the simple addition of a single upright or vertical species (such as a short fescue grass, *Festuca*, or chives, *Allium schoenoprasum*) among sedums can have in terms of visual diversity.

Rate of growth and ultimate shoot height are important plant selection criteria because the fewer plants needed to fill a given roof area the less expensive it costs to install (White and Snodgrass 2003). In extensive systems growth up 30 cm (12 in) tall is possible if maximum dead weight load allows sufficient soil depth for deeper roots. However, because some fast-growing plants are short lived, there may need to be a mixture of fast-, moderate-, and slow growing plants. Plants that are short at maturity are more resistant to wind damage and easier to maintain. Plants with tall stems or flower stalks are more likely to tiller (blow over). However, if the roof is surrounded by a solid parapet, it will be possible to grow taller plants in the increased shelter—although wind eddies will be a problem adjacent to the parapet—even on shallow substrates.

Again, the degree of complexity of the vegetation should be matched with the function and use of the site. Where roofs are visible from afar but inaccessible to users, then simple patterns of monocultural blocks of different species can be very effective. Where meadow vegetation is used in these situations, it can pay to limit the number of constituent species so that dramatic large-scale flowering effects are achieved rather than the diluted blooming of a mass of species. Where roofs are inaccessible but clearly visible from closer distances (from office windows, hospital wards, or housing developments, for example) more detail can be included, with the degree of complexity relating to the proximity of view. Only where roofs are directly accessible to users is it worth spending great effort in more formal or involved designs. Usually, such plantings are found on intensive roof gardens. We suggest, however, that high-quality plantings can be achieved with extensive and semi-extensive techniques on accessible roofs, perhaps in combination with areas of deeper soils or containerized plants where appropriate. The importance of visual criteria can therefore be summarized on a gradient:

Purely functional: where the visual appearance is of no importance.

Limited overview: the area will be viewed at a distance. Bold patterns involving simple contrasts in foliage colour are particularly appropriate.

Frequent overview: an area that is frequently seen and at relatively close quarters. Here, a strongly visual planting may not be strictly necessary but it would add to the amenity value of the site.

Ornamental: areas where the visual appearance is very important, usually because it is adjacent to a terrace or balcony or because the roof is accessible.

Visual criteria for rooftop plants may include the following:

Winter or dormant-season interest: evergreen foliage or grasses with an attractive form and texture or dead foliage colour.

Flowers during the growing season.

Variety of form, for example, a large area of grasses or other low vegetation can be made more interesting with variations in height, form, and texture through the use of occasional dwarf shrubs.

Variety of foliage: even areas with a shallow substrate can be made much more visually exciting through contrasting foliage colours, textures, and forms.

METHODS OF VEGETATION ESTABLISHMENT

There are four main approaches to establishing vegetation on green roofs: direct application of seed or cuttings, planting of pot-grown plants or plugs, laying of pregrown vegetation mats (including turf), and spontaneous colonization. We shall take each in turn and outline the main advantages and disadvantages of each.

Species	Per cent by weight
Achillea millefolium	2
Allium schoenoprasum	4
Anthemis tinctoria	6
Anthoxanthum odoratum	2
Briza media	7
Campanula rotundifolia	2
Dianthus carthusianorum	6
Dianthus deltoides	6
Festuca ovina	10
Geranium robertianum	4
Leucanthemum vulgare	4
Petrorhagia saxifraga	4
Pilosella officinarum	3
Plantago lanceolata	4
Poa compressa	2
Potentilla argentea	2
Prunella grandiflora	5
Ranunculus bulbosus	6
Sanguisorba minor	5
Sesleria albicans	10
Thymus pulegioides	3
Thymus serpyllum	3

Table 4.2 An example of a meadowlike seed mix for extensive green roofs.

From Kolb and Schwarz (1999)

Direct application of seed and cuttings

Directly sowing seed mixtures is a useful and cost-effective technique for establishing plants on roofs larger than 20 square metres (215 square feet). It is particularly appropriate for seeding turf grasses or meadow-type vegetation, where a whole plant community is being established (see Table 4.2). Alkaline substrates, with a pH of between 8.0 and 8.5 are best, as these will offer optimum conditions for a large number of stress-tolerant grasses and forbs.

Disadvantages of direct sowing include the longer period of time that plants take to develop from sowing. If sowing is carried out at a higher rate to try to overcome this problem, in the case of complex mixtures there is a chance that competition will result in stronger growing species eliminating weaker growing ones, with poor diversity as a result. Whereas a large particle size for the substrate, up to 16 mm (0.6 in) helps to reduce the ability of unwanted weedy species to establish, it is too large for good seed germination. A layer of finer particles over the top helps seed germination and seedling establishment. Lighter coloured materials heat up less than darker, which leads to less drying out in sunshine and therefore generally better seedling establishment (Kolb and Trunk 1993). Sowing rates depends on the type of vegetation being established, with supplier guidelines being the best guidance. Seed is best sown in spring, as there is the danger of erosion if it is done at a time when seedling growth may be slowed down by cold or drought.

Seed mixtures that comprise forbs and grasses, or forbs only, can be difficult to distribute evenly, and given the importance of eliminating gaps and thus any danger of substrate erosion, it is vital that this is achieved. This task can be made easier if seed is mixed with sharp sand prior to distribution, and in the case of large areas, the roof divided up into sectors of equal area and the seed-sand mixture divided up appropriately, too. To further ensure even distribution, each seed batch can be split into two, with one batch being sown first by walking in one direction and the second by walking at 90 degrees. Seed should be lightly covered after being sown: 3–5 mm (0.1–0.2 in) deep in the substrate is ideal. Hitting the ground with the back of a flat shovel is a good way of achieving this, the action serving to knock seed downwards into the interstices of the substrate. Watering with a fine droplet size will then further settle the seed into the substrate as well as provide moisture.

Seed can also be introduced through the technique of hydroseeding, whereby a mixture of seeds, water, and gel are sprayed onto the substrate. It is a useful technique for large areas, the glue holding fine seeds onto the substrate and making it easier for moisture to be kept in the vicinity of the seed. Hydroseeding is also very useful for sloping sites, where both substrate and seeds are liable to be washed off by rain or irrigation until fixed in place by roots.

Those plants that root very easily from small cuttings, chiefly sedums, can be distributed through shoot spreading, where 3- to 5-cm (1.2- to 2-in) long cuttings are distributed through hand-throwing, much as seed might be hand-distributed. Species which produce small bulbs such *Allium schoenoprasum* or *Allium insubricum* may also be distributed this way. Alternatively, hydrosprigging is the process by which cuttings are applied in a liquid slurry in a manner analogous to hydroseeding. The use of sedum shoots allows the vegetation to develop from a larger number of growth tips than through the use of plug or pot plants. However, the use of shoots might be more sensitive to climatic conditions at the time following the establishment, particularly in dry periods.

A good distribution of shoots is vital, as is the timing of spreading to coincide with rain and, if necessary, irrigation during the establishment phase. Any time between spring and midsummer is suitable. Ideally, a distribution of 60–80 shoots per square metre is wanted, with care taken to ensure that after spreading, no gaps or heaps of shoots are left behind. For rapid cover, however, densities of 200–250 shoots per square metre can be used. Rain or irrigation is needed immediately after spreading to ensure a good contact is made between the shoots and the substrate. Rooting should take place within six to eight weeks, with rooting being significantly advanced after two weeks. Sixty per cent of surface coverage is possible after this six to eight weeks. Birds may cause problems during the establishment phase, so it may be wise to consider using netting as protection or using scaring techniques. Once rooted in, the shoots will benefit from a thin coating of hydromulch.

Planting pot-grown plants or plugs

Direct planting is the best way to plant up small-scale roof-greening projects and allows the planting to be designed so that naturalistic or artistic effects can be incorporated. In evaluations of green roofs, planted areas generally score higher than sown, especially in the early years (Kolb and Trunk 1993).

Plants bought from conventional garden centres or nurseries are not always a good option though: for one thing, costs can rapidly escalate if plants are not bought at wholesale prices. Also, the size of the root ball may be too large for the more shallow types of project. The best option is to propagate plants in plug trays, the cellular units widely used in the nursery trade to grow large numbers of small plants. It may be worthwhile asking a nursery for a quotation on the production of plants in plug trays, or alternatively obtaining some second-hand trays from a nursery (vast numbers are discarded at the end of the spring) and propagating plants yourself. The trays come in a large variety of sizes, but for our purposes those with cells around 2.5 cm (1 in) across and 3–5 cm (1.2–2 in) deep are ideal. Plug plants are usually very efficient when establishing vegetation because they have a well-developed root system and canopy. They can start growing directly after being transplanted to the field, but a large number of plants are needed to achieve a rapid cover because the development of the vegetation only takes place from a limited number of plants or growth tips. For a tight mat of vegetation, planting is normally carried out at ten plants per square metre. Higher densities are recommended where the species do not cover rapidly or the client is interested in a quick establishment. Because of their small size and lack of anchorage roots, plug plants may be susceptible to being pulled out of the substrate by birds searching for food (Emilsson 2003).

Planting should be done in spring or early summer and organized so that the areas furthest from the access point are planted first. Sharp tools should not be used, as they may damage membranes. Watering after planting will not only provide moisture but also help settle plants. A mineral-based mulch applied after planting will help to conserve moisture. Coloured mulches, such as light coloured limestone, reddish chippings, or dark slate, to set off the plants can be considered.

Green roof plug plant
production.

Photograph by Blackdown
Horticultural Consultants

Planting the Augustenborg
Botanical Green Roof,
Malmo, Sweden, with pot
and plug plants.

Laying vegetation mats

Vegetation mats are pregrown sheets of vegetation. They are produced
on a geotextile base (a woven synthetic fabric) over which is laid a thin
layer of growing medium or substrate, into which plants are grown,
either from direct-sown seed or cuttings. The soil substrate is often
reinforced with thin plastic netting to prevent fragmentation. The mats
are usually started under cover in a galls house or polythene tunnel and
then grown outside. For large-scale plantings the mats can be rolled up
and then unrolled on site like a carpet. For smaller scale uses squares or
sections of mat can be fitted together like carpet tiles.

Vegetation mats or blankets have the advantage of instant effect.
They are usually planted with a mix of sedum species and have 90–100

Vegetation mats dominated by sedum species.

Photograph by Blackdown Horticultural Consultants

A turf roof gives a simple clean appearance, but irrigation is essential for the grass to remain lush and green.

© ZinCo

per cent vegetation cover at the outset. They are laid directly onto the substrate layer of the roof. Mats need to be laid as quickly as possible after receipt. They should be placed so that no gaps are left between mats, and then weighted down at the corners and at intervals along the sides, to avoid them being blown off, until they are securely rooted, usually after four to five weeks.

Turf can be laid onto a roof much as it is when laying a lawn, but particular attention must be paid to the edges; they should be cut as precisely as possible to avoid any areas of loose substrate being exposed, and thus liable to erosion.

Spontaneous colonization

The unaided vegetating of bare substrates is the most ecological of the planting methods described here in that only those plants that are locally available and totally suited to the roof environment will survive. Further information on spontaneous green roofs is given in the biodiversity section of chapter 2. Clearly, using spontaneous colonization involves the least expensive planting method, but it is likely to be visually unacceptable in many locations because it is virtually unavoidable to get what many people would judge to be a weedy vegetation with patches of bare ground. For tall, invisible, and inaccessible roofs this is not a problem, and the use of spontaneous greening confers many financial and ecological benefits.

The various methods discussed above vary considerably in cost. Direct sowing is the least expensive of the conventional methods, followed by strewing of cuttings, plug planting, and pot planting. The most expensive method is the use of vegetation mats. However, the increasing cost of the different methods is also associated with increasing rapidity of results and assurance of predictable outcomes. Although pregrown vegetation mats are the most expensive method, they also give an instant effect and total cover. So, which is the best method?

A spontaneously colonized green roof on a hospital in Basel, Switzerland.

Photograph by Pia Zanetti

A recent study in Sweden looked at three establishment methods: premade vegetation mats, plug plants, and *Sedum* shoots over a 4-cm (1.6-in) growing substrate. A survey after the first growing season showed that the establishment had been successful on most of the plots and across most treatments. There was an obvious initial advantage in using vegetation mats but no difference between the other two establishment methods in terms of success. The researchers concluded that the cheaper alternatives were perfectly acceptable compared to the use of mats (Emilsson 2003). There are situations in which mats may be the best choice—where rapid effect is needed and also on sloping or inaccessible situations where physical planting may be difficult. Mats also have the great advantage to non-horticulturists or non-ecologists that, because they are pregrown, no decisions need to be made about plant choices.

DESIGNING WITH PLANTS ON GREEN ROOFS

Three broad categories of plant combination for roofs can be recognized: monocultures, simple plant combinations and mixtures, and plant communities. These categories represent a gradient of complexity, with monocultures being very simple plant systems and plant communities having the potential for great complexity and diversity.

Monocultures

In this instance, one plant species or cultivar is used en masse, perhaps on its own, or alongside other single-species blocks as part of a design. This approach is essentially similar to the use of block-planted shrubs and perennials by many landscape architects or garden designers. Monocultural plantings are often visually rather uninteresting and can be susceptible to total die-back if drought or disease severely affect the plant in question. Monocultural drifts or blocks can be very effective if used in interlocking patterns.

Simple plant combinations and mixtures

Here a limited number of species or cultivars are grown together. Simple mixtures may contain plants of similar growth rate and form. A grass lawn would be a familiar example, comprising perhaps four to six varieties. The sedum mixtures used on many shallow-substrate roofs are the most important example in roof greening. More complex mixtures may contain a variety of forms (that is, low growing, mound forming, upright) to enhance the visual and structural diversity of the planting.

Mixtures are generally more preferable to monocultures because of the susceptibility of low-diversity plantings to being wiped out by disease or stress. Diverse mixtures of species are more likely to contain plants that are able to overcome or withstand such environmental hazards and therefore provide long-term integrity to the vegetation. Low-growing, drought-tolerant species may form the bulk of a mixture, with evergreen and deciduous components. Longer-lived species may be mixed with annuals or species with short life-cycles to give a dynamic aspect, and grasses or upright forbs can give visual contrast and diversity to an otherwise two-dimensional vegetation. Mixtures can compensate for stressful periods of the year for the different species—for example, with mixtures of grasses and drought-tolerant perennials in

Left: Monocultural planting can be made more interesting by using blocks and patterns of different species and by emphasizing paths as part of the design.

© ZinCo.

A small-scale creative use of simple, low-diversity roof planting.

Photograph by VegTech

The turf roof on this rammed-earth hut makes a link between the sculptured landscape and the building.

Photograph by Jane Sebire

dry climates the grasses grow during the wetter periods and the perennials will flourish and flower during hot, dry periods. Species with attractive foliage or seasonal flowering highlights can complement more sombre evergreens. A combination of low- and high-density species allows a unique ecological mixture to develop, where runners fill in the spaces between cushions.

Plant communities

Plant communities on green roofs are usually based on natural habitats: the plants are chosen and combined in proportions that approximate to their occurrence in the wild. In most cases this mixture will be based on a matrix of grasses with a minority of forbs, and in some cases dwarf shrubs as well. Plant community-based plantings tend to be self-sustaining, requiring low maintenance inputs for their upkeep. They will also, by their very nature, have an informal, naturalistic appearance.

The advantage of using a plant community such as a grass-based meadow is that it is ideal for extensive maintenance and has a visual appearance that makes it suitable for all situations, apart from where a neat and tidy visual appearance is of utmost importance. A large, purely functional site can be planted with a meadow mix that used only grass, which is always the cheapest option, whereas those in more visually important sites can have colourful flowering forbs included, too—and the more important the aesthetics, the greater variety that can be included.

While natural plant communities, comprising regionally native plants, are currently the most important model for roofs with substrates between 6 and 15 cm (2.4 and 6 in) there are good reasons for expecting the assembling of artificial plant communities using both native and non-native species to become increasingly important. In most cases these will consist of a matrix of dominant plants that provide good substrate coverage, usually native grasses or sedges, along with a variety of more decorative non-native plant varieties.

The use of regionally native plants has become a very important part of landscaping and garden design in recent years. Advocates of native

plant use (for example, Stein 1993) would prioritize the use of such plants for roof greening for the following reasons:

Non-native plant species with invasive tendencies are a major problem in some regions. The use of non-natives avoids the danger of introducing potential 'problem plants'.

Native plants support local wildlife. In some cases insect larvae will only eat a particular species and no other.

The use of regionally native vegetation replaces lost habitat.

However, not all ecologists and horticulturalists agree that the use of natives is vital, arguing that there are often circumstances where the selection of non-native species may not be as harmful as some in the ecological lobby suggest (for example, Kendle and Rose 2000), and that there may be positive advantages in doing so. These can be summarized:

Roofs are very demanding environments. There may not be many locally native species that will prove successful. Also, in many regions

Well-chosen mixtures provide diversity of form and colour but also offer a long flowering season as one set of plants takes over from another. This naturalistic plant community mix of native and exotic drought-tolerant perennials and grasses on a roof in Sheffield, England, flowers from spring through to fall: (left to right) May, June, August. Planting design by Nigel Dunnett.

there may not be local plant communities that exist in conditions that in any way resemble rooftop environments.

Where visual appearance is important, the inclusion of plants with attractive flowers or foliage over the whole growing season is vital. Locally native species may not be particularly striking or may only be so for a limited time.

There may be circumstances where non-natives have considerable wildlife value, which make them even more important in urban areas than the inclusion of natives with little wildlife value. Examples might include *Verbena bonariensis*, a plant that is a valuable nectar source for butterflies over a very long season.

A 30- to 40-year life is possible for a green roof with proper waterproof membranes and made using professional installation methods. Research is insufficient to show how long each species will live and how each species will interact with others over a long time. Therefore, each green roof is a unique long-term ecological experiment (White and Snodgrass 2003).

PLANTS FOR GREEN ROOFS

The best planting solution for large areas is undoubtedly one that relies on a natural plant community, for the simple reason that this will be tried and tested and, by using seed mixtures, cheap to install. However, for smaller situations, ones with high visibility, or where there is no viable natural community to call upon, individual plant species will have to be selected and combined. Plants can be installed as nursery-grown specimens in various sizes or a seed mixture of appropriate species made up and sown. Whereas a sown plant community requires little thought about its individual species composition, a planting combination, design, or artificial plant community requires that attention is given to the characteristics of each variety chosen.

In the early days of roof greening in central Europe the species used were generally the more showy or resilient components of dry meadow communities or species chosen from the extensive flora popular as rock-garden plants, mostly from the Alps, Pyrenees, and the mountain ranges of eastern Europe and the Balkans. Some hardier species from the Mediterranean area and eastern Asia have also been used.

Trialling of species for their suitability for roof greening was a major part of the early research work into roof greening. German researchers set up trials, with plants being evaluated by a panel, which assessed them for appearance of growth and ground coverage. Sedums consistently rated high, along with low-growing grasses such as many *Festuca* and *Koeleria* species, and alliums. Sedums have since become the bedrock of shallow-substrate roof-greening systems for their drought tolerance, year-round good looks, ease of propagation, and suitability for shallow substrates. *Dianthus* taxa, for example, *D. petraeus*, *D. carthusianorum*, and cultivars of *D. gratianopolitanus* also appeared high on evaluation lists (Kolb and Trunk 1993). But the trials also revealed surprises. For example, some species that would otherwise be suitable for reasons of drought-tolerance were found to be unsuitable because of their sensitivity to competition with grasses; *Salvia pratensis*, a major and highly decorative component of central European limestone meadow floras failed for this reason. Others were excluded for the opposite reason—invasiveness (for instance, *Anthyllis vulneraria*; Kolb 1988).

The task of selecting suitable plant species for roof greening has arguably hardly begun, and it offers potentially enormous rewards. While central and northern European flora has been well trialled, the drought-tolerant floras of the rest of the world have not, although in many cases suitable species are familiar as garden plants. Practitioners of roof greening have much exciting work ahead of them evaluating potentially suitable plant species. In this section we look at some of the commonly used and dependable plants and plant groups, before proceeding to consider fruitful areas of discovery for new green-roof plants.

The following sections give a flavour of the range of suitable plant material. We have restricted our comments here to plants that will grow on extensive roofs with different substrate depths and minimal irrigation. More comprehensive lists are found in the Roof-Greening Plant Directory appendix.

Mosses and ferns

Undisturbed tile or slate roofs colonize spontaneously in time with mosses and lichens. This process can be aided on such roofs to obtain a semblance of vegetation cover without introducing growing substrates by coating the surface with a nutrient-rich material to encourage germination and establishment of moss spores. Traditionally, stone and rock structures can be given the impression of premature ageing in this way by painting with a liquid containing milk, yoghurt, manure, and other similar products. Mosses also colonize bare patches of substrate on very thin extensive green roofs where, because of the harsh growing conditions, complete vegetation cover is rarely achieved.

Ferns are not obvious roof candidates, and indeed most are too bulky too survive and will not tolerate dry, hot sun. Many are nevertheless stress-tolerant plants adapted to hostile conditions in dry shade. The common polypody fern, *Polypodium vulgare*, can be found colonized on old tile roofs in shady situations where its creeping network of rhizomes are able to exploit gaps between the tiles, and the maidenhair spleenwort, *Asplenium trichomanes*, is commonly encountered in cracks in old walls.

Bulbs

Short-growing bulbs from arid continental climates potentially make ideal green-roof subjects. Such bulbs, which include a diverse range of species tulips, narcissi, and irises are adapted to such conditions by growing and flowering early in the year and then dying back underground to survive baking summer temperatures as the protected subterranean bulb. Indeed many need this dry, hot period for effective ripening. Where substrate reaches depths of between 10 and 20 cm (4 and 8 in) a wide range of bulbs can be grown on roofs. Species used successfully in German trials include *Crocus tommasinianus*, *Muscari neglectum*, and *Tulipa tarda* (Kolb and Schwarz 1999). However, few, if any, trials into suitable bulbs for green roofs have been carried out with results published in the English language, and the longevity of many bulb species on green roofs is not known.

The most commonly encountered bulbous genus on extensive green roofs is the onions, *Allium*. Small growing alliums, for example, *A. pulchellum*, *A. schoenoprasum* (chives), and *A. flavum*, are particularly valuable. They often flower later than the sedums and are very different in height. While slow to establish from seed, they then self-sow well, but without displacing other plants. Alliums also maintain their foliage in good condition for some time, unlike many other bulbous species. Successful iris species include *Iris germanica*, *I. graminea*, and *I. pumila*.

Chives, *Allium schoenoprasum*, survive well on green roofs under both wet and dry conditions and make dramatic mass plantings.

Photograph by Manfred Köhler

Annuals

Some annuals are suited to green-roof cultivation. These are generally desert annuals that are adapted to surviving in stressful dry, hot conditions, avoiding the most harsh time of the year as dormant seed and germinating, growing, and flowering during more benign periods. Although they do not contribute a great amount in terms of vegetation cover, they can make a big impact through their intense flower colours.

The most successful annuals for green roofs are those that will self-seed from year to year once established. There is a careful balance to be achieved here between achieving a reasonable number of annuals from year to year and preventing the species from becoming a weed. Also bear mind that if the annuals that you desire are able to survive from year to year, then so probably are undesirable annuals or weeds. Other desirable traits include a slender habit that does not crowd out or swamp other lower growing species and a compact habit that is not vulnerable to wind rock.

In small-scale trials the German researcher Wolfram Kircher found that of ten annuals trialled on an extensive green roof, only one was able to survive from year to year. This was the slender white-flowered annual *Gypsophila muralis*. Similar species that would behave similarly include fairy toadflax, *Linaria maroccana*, and red flax, *Linum grandiflorum* var. *rubrum*. In our experience, successful species on 10 cm (4 in) of substrate include Californian poppy, *Eschscholzia californica*, and scentless mayweed, *Tripleurospermum maritimum*. The deeper the soil, the greater the potential success of annuals. Under green-roof conditions it is most likely that self-seeded annuals will germinate in autumn, overwinter, and flower in spring. These annuals can be introduced simply by scattering seed in autumn or spring.

Herbaceous perennial species

The majority of extensive green-roof species are herbaceous perennials and grasses of dry habitats. Here we give a summary of some of the tried-and-tested species on European roofs. It is sensible to divide these perennial species into those that will succeed at different minimum depths of substrate. We start with those plants that survive in the thinner substrates (4–6 cm, 1.6–2.4 in). The observations are gained from the authors' own experiences and from standard German works such as Kolb and Schwarz (1999).

Perennials for shallow substrates—Only the most stress-tolerant species survive on the thinner substrates (4–6 cm, 1.6–2.4 in). By definition these tend to be highly specialized plants, many of them succulents. Many of these species will survive on deeper substrates, but as discussed above, they will tend to be eliminated through competition with more vigorous species under more productive conditions. We will look first at some of the succulent species before considering others. Succulent species have found favour for green-roof use because of their extreme drought-tolerance through storage of water in their tissues. Two main genera of succulents are widely used: *Sedum* and *Sempervivum*.

Sedums are ubiquitous on extensive green roofs because they are supremely adapted to the roof environment: the majority of sedums

Sedum album makes a dramatic display in full flower.

© ZinCo.

Close-up of mixed sedums on a green roof.

Photograph by Blackdown Horticultural Consultants

come from arid or well-drained areas where other vegetation is limited (Hewitt 2003). Indeed, species such as *Sedum acre* and *S. rupestre* (syn. *S. reflexum*), commonly find their way onto old roofs unaided in northern Europe, growing in very little or no soil and rooting into cracks or joins between tiles. The majority of sedums will survive if receiving no water for a month (Stephenson 1994), although growth is likely to be very sparse. Drought-stressed sedum roofs turn from a lush green to a dull purple. The majority of species used in European green-roof systems hail from habitats with near perfect drainage and/or high summer temperatures and low summer rainfall: few sedums originate from areas with high rainfall, and if they do they will be growing in very free-draining situations. They will not succeed if transferred to tropical and subtropical climates with high summer rainfall coupled with high summer temperatures (Stephenson 1994). While surviving well under high temperatures and drought, *Sedum* species may not be effective in thin extensive green roofs in climates with extreme cold in winter. In a Canadian study on six different herbaceous plant species grown in a range of substrate depths, the Sedum species included suffered greater frost damage at the thinner depth than the other species (Boivin et al. 2001).

Green-roof sedums are evergreen foliage plants in the main, flowering in May and June. Some species are spectacular in flower, particularly if used in large numbers. However, monocultural plantings of sedums can be rather dull visually for much of the year. Some of the more widely used sedum species are discussed below.

Sedum acre makes splashes of yellow through this green-roof planting. Planting design by Nigel Dunnett.

Sedum floriferum 'Weinstephaner Gold'

Sedum rupestre

Sedum acre (biting stonecrop) is a very widespread species in the wild, found in virtually every European country (although it is naturalized in more northern countries rather than truly native). It is one of the most effective in flower, its low mounded forms being covered completely in early summer with acid yellow flowers beloved of bumble bees. This is a variable species that has given rise to a number of horticultural forms, including very small forms, taller forms, and forms with variegated foliage. *Sedum acre* 'Aureum' has yellow foliage.

Sedum album (white stonecrop), along with *S. acre*, is one of the more attractive species for roof plantings, where the stressful conditions can limit its more exuberant nature. The airy white flowers appear in June. *Sedum album* is responsible for the purple-brown colouration of many sedum-based green roofs in dry periods—the species transforms from lush green to purple-bronze. Again, a number of cultivars are available, of which the red-leaved forms such as 'Coral Carpet' make striking contrasts when grown with green-leaved forms.

Sedum floriferum 'Weihenstephener Gold' is widely used for its flowering effect, with golden yellow flowers over a dense mat of foliage that reddens in the winter.

Sedum hispanicum is a commonly grown creeping species, similar to *S. acre*, with glaucous tufts of foliage and pink or white flowers. The shoot tips turn attractive purple or pink shades in cooler weather.

Sedum kamtschaticum is a distinctive and attractive Asian species with bold yellow flowers. The foliage rosettes tend to turn to orange or red in the summer and autumn. It is less drought tolerant than other species mentioned here (Stephenson 1994).

Sedum rupestre (syn. *S. reflexum*; reflexed stonecrop) is a useful upright species that sends vertical flowering shoots with yellow flowers up to a height of 30 cm (12 in), above rambling whorls of grey-green foliage. The cultivar 'Fosteranum' has silvery foliage resembling that of a blue spruce.

Sedum sexangulare is a distinctive species from southern Europe with an appearance of globular heads of succulent grey leaves on thin wiry shoots. It is an effective rambling species that weaves its way among others.

Sedum spathulifolium is probably the most common North American species in cultivation (Stephenson 1994), and a very attractive one, with rosettes of flattish, rounded grey-purple leaves.

Sedum spurium is another widely cultivated species, with whorls of large flat succulent leaves and pink flower heads. Cultivars are available with different leaf shapes and flower and leaf colours.

Sedum spathulifolium

Nearly all these species are European natives. They represent a small fraction of the total pool of suitable *Sedum* species, many of which have not been trialled effectively for green roof cultivation. Some native North American species that show promise are *Sedum oreganum* and the evergreen *S. divergens* (Hauth and Liptan 2003).

Sempervivum, the houseleeks, are not rapidly spreading or creeping plants like many sedums but instead tend to form clumps of rosettes that spread slowly outwards. As such, they are not prime candidates for creating complete vegetation cover but are best considered as ornamental species for close viewing. Their common name indicates that they are well adapted to very dry conditions and shallow soils and traditionally have been grown on slate and tile roofs and walls. Commonly grown species include *Sempervivum tectorum*, which has the largest rosettes, up to 8 cm (3.2 in) in diameter; *S. montanum*, a relatively rapid spreader and *S. arachnoideum*, the so-called cobweb houseleek because of the dense covering of hairs that can sometimes be found on the leaves.

Sempervivum hybrid

The succulent ice plants (*Delosperma*) have large colourful daisy flowers over mats of oval pointed leaves. They will be familiar to visitors to Mediterranean coasts, where they form extensive monocultural carpets of vegetation, and they have naturalized in milder coastal areas of the United Kingdom. Although not widely used, ice plants offer spectacular colour and are highly drought-tolerant, but do have questionable hardiness. *Delosperma cooperi* is likely to survive light frost (Hewitt 2003). It is also possible to grow cactus on a roof. The low-growing prickly pear *Opuntia humifusa* from the eastern United States possesses a degree of winter hardiness. The colourful hybrids of *Lewisia cotyledon* need free-draining soil to avoid root rotting and are relatively hardy.

One of the most successful and attractive non-succulent green-roof species is *Petrorhagia saxifraga* (syn. *Tunica saxifraga*) which has small

Delosperma cooperi

Photograph by Tom Liptan

This attractive and diverse green roof is dominated by *Petrorhagia saxifraga*.

© ZinCo

Below left: *Dianthus*, *Sedum*, and *Festuca* grasses make up much of the vegetation on this flowering green roof.

© ZinCo

pink flowers in airy panicles up to 20 cm (8 in) in height. This is an easily propagated species, rooting well from small fragments, that tends to find its own spaces among more solid cushion or spreading plants. The true saxifrages, *Saxifraga crustata* and *S. tridactylites*, carry pink or white flowers above rosettes of jagged foliage. The cypress sedge, *Euphorbia cyparissias*, is rampant if grown under fertile conditions but is less vigorous on a roof with thin substrate. It produces attractive feathery foliage, lime green flowers, and the whole plant turns a vibrant yellow in the autumn.

Herbaceous perennials for 6–10 cm (2.4–4 in) substrate depth—All the plants suitable for more shallow depths will succeed here, but at depths of up to 10 cm (4 in) a much wider range of plants is possible. Mostly these are low-growing cushion forming or spreading plants, which will mingle to form beautiful tapestries of varying colours and textures, including various species of *Dianthus*, *Thymus*, *Alyssum*, *Campanula*, and *Potentilla*. *Gypsophila repens*, for example, weaves between and beneath taller clump-forming species, and its greyish green leaves are covered with pink or white flowers for several weeks depending on the form of the plant. Some species can be used to give vertical accents among the lower plants; suitable plants include *Iris* species, *Sisyrinchium*, *Verbascum phoeniceum*, and *V. chaixii*.

This dramatic meadow is composed of the short-lived but freely seeding *Dianthus carthusianorum*.

Photograph by APP Dachgarten GmbH.

Dianthus deltoides and *Sedum acre* make a striking planting combination, flowering in June.

The sea thrifts (*Armeria*) make excellent green-roof plants with attractive foliage, colourful flowers, and good seed heads.

A sumptuous red hybrid pasque flower (*Pulsatilla vulgaris*) with lewisia, alpine phlox, and a carpet of *Sedum spurium* on the roof garden of Toronto City Hall.

Nepeta 'Walker's Low' with *Dianthus deltoides* and *Armeria maritima* 'Alba'.

Kniphofia 'Border Ballet' is an excellent, long-flowering green-roof plant in 10–20 cm (4–8 in) substrate depth. Planting design by Nigel Dunnett.

Herbaceous perennials for 10–15 cm (4–6 in) substrate depth—It is at this depth that the use of the full range of dry meadow species and many other drought-tolerant plants becomes a distinct possibility, including lower-growing *Achillea*, *Anthemis*, some late-flowering *Aster*, *Solidago*, *Centaurea*, *Leucanthemum*, and *Origanum*. The beautiful *Pulsatilla vulgaris* grows well in calcareous (chalk or limestone) substrates. We have found that the dwarf red-hot poker mixture *Kniphofia* 'Border Ballet' has survived for three years in a substrate depth of 15 cm (2 in), flowering well all summer in a sheltered location. *Nepeta* ×*faassenii* and *Calamintha nepeta* similarly flower for months on end.

Grasses and sedges

Grasses serve three main purposes on low-input green roofs: they may be used to form a matrix within which meadow flowers are embedded—in this case native grass species will usually be chosen; they may be used as ornamental plants in their own right, either in naturalistic meadow-like plantings or more formally as accent plants; or they may be the dominant or only component as in the traditional turf or grass roof.

Melica ciliata is one of the most attractive grasses for green-roof use.

Stipa tenuissima reflects the slightest breeze on this green roof.

Grasses in mixed plantings—Most grasses do not grow well in the thinnest types of extensive green roofs—this is a positive factor because it limits the need for weed control. Apart from a couple of small *Festuca* species, only a restricted range of short sedges are used on these types of roof. For example, *Carex caryophyllea* is a low grey-leaved sedge of dry calcareous grasslands that grows well on these types of roofs.

On substrates with depths of 6–10 cm (2.4–4 in), the potential range of species widens to include Festuca species such as sheep's fescue (*F. ovina*) and *F. cinerea*. One of the most attractive of the shorter ornamental grasses, *Melica ciliata*, can also be grown. This grass has narrow white inflorescences that fountain out from the foliage clump and catch low sunlight beautifully. A scattering of this grass among low-growing flowering plants creates a wonderful naturalistic effect. *Melica ciliata* grows naturally in central Europe on free-draining calcareous soils.

At substrate depths of 10–20 cm (4–8 in), the choice widens still further to include a number of extremely attractive grasses. Most of these will not attain the same height and spread on a roof as they will in cultivated conditions in a garden border. The annual quaking grass, *Briza media*, will seed itself effectively from year to year. Several *Stipa* species, the steppe grasses *S. capillata* and *S. pennata*, can be grown. These supremely graceful grasses have arching inflorescences with very long awns and respond to the slightest wind movement. The Mexican species *S. tenuissima* will only reach half its normal height in this depth of substrate but makes a fine mass planting for a visible roof—again it is a very agile grass that glows in low sun. As its name suggests, *Festuca amythystina* has purple-tinged inflorescences. *Helictotrichon sempervirens* is a larger, more robust version of the grey-leaved but rather short-lived *Festuca glauca*, and it is one of the most attractive grasses in full flower.

Grass roofs—Traditionally, grass roofs would be created from meadow turfs cut from the vicinity of the building or even from the building footprint itself. Traditional Norwegian grass roofs are heavy and use thick turfs. However, for contemporary extensive green roofs, such a weight load is not appropriate. Creating grass roofs on thin layers of substrate can be done using turf, but it is essential that the roof is irrigated until established. Sowing a grass seed mix is not only effective but cheaper. Grass or turf roof plantings on substrates of less than 15 cm (6 in) deep can only support the more stress-tolerant grasses, rather than more vigorous agricultural grasses. Fine-leaved grasses such as *Agrostis capillaris*, *Cynosurus cristatus*, *Festuca rubra* ssp. *commutata*, *Poa pratensis*, and *Trisetum flavescens* are among the grasses commonly used in wild-flower seed mixtures, and they are suitable for these situations with or without the wildflower component. Most wildflower seed companies supply a range of mixes to suit different soil types. For extensive roofs a calcareous meadow mixture is suitable and can be sown in spring or autumn.

To date, roof greening has used European turf grasses. Where the surface is going to be used for recreational purposes, the tough self-regenerating sod formed by these grasses is appropriate. In other regions, however, in situations where there will be no recreational use, it may be more appropriate to trial the use of native species, especially if these are reliably drought tolerant. Such species will almost inevitably be bunch grasses, with a different aesthetic than European turf-forming species; whereas turf grasses form an unattractive brown mat when dry, bunch grasses will have more visual structure and sometimes better colouring.

In more shaded situations, it may be more appropriate to rely on *Carex* species instead of true grasses. There is a huge diversity of sedges in the world's cooler climates, and horticulture is arguably only just beginning to realize their true value. Many are evergreen, tolerate deeper shade than grasses, and thrive on low-nutrient, often acidic soils. For this last reason, a *Carex*-dominated roof in shade would do well to have an acidic rather than calcareous substrate.

Interesting effects can be obtained by cutting different sections of a grass roof to different heights.

Deciduous woody plants

A limited number of shrubs can be used with substrates of 15–25 cm (6–10 in). As with the perennials and grasses, these tend to be drought-adapted species with small tough leaves or grey-leaved aromatic sub-shrubs. To enable them to ripen wood for winter hardiness and to prevent rotting of roots in cold saturated winter substrate, good drainage is the key to successful growth of these species. Many legumes are included in this category: *Cytisus*, *Genista*, *Caragana*, and *Ononis*.

Deeper substrates enable drought-tolerant subshrubs such as lavender to survive on green roofs.

© ZinCo.

Right: Saplings of birch (*Betula*) and larch (*Larix*) form a spontaneous woodland on this garden shelter roof at the Centre for Alternative Technology in the moist climate of North Wales.

Low creeping and suckering species include roses of sandy habitats, *Rosa pimpinellifolia* and *R. gallica*; the shrubby cherry, *Prunus tenella*; and a range of willows including *Salix lanata*, *S. repens*, and *S. retusa*. Trees are really out of the question unless grown in containers or deeper mounds of growing medium.

Conifers

On deeper substrates (a minimum of 15 cm, 6 in), conifers can make a considerable visual impact, combining particularly well with other plants that are ecologically and psychologically linked with mountain or extreme-climate habitats, such as alpines and dwarf grasses. Slow-growing taxa, of which there are an enormous number available commercially, are particularly useful. Small or prostrate junipers are particularly suitable: *Juniperus communis* ssp. *nana*, *J. horizontalis*, and *J. procumbens*, for example. Some low-growing pines are also valuable, such as *Pinus aristata* and *P. mugo* var. *pumilio*.

Conifers, however, are very sensitive to drying out, which results in leaf loss. Whereas deciduous woody plants can recover the next growing season, conifer leaf loss is more or less permanent, with a considerable reduction in visual quality. Drying out can be avoided if situations are chosen that are out of full sun or where irrigation can be easily used. With time even slow-growing conifers may become too large, necessitating some pruning. This can be turned to aesthetic advantage and bonsai-like specimens may be developed over the years.

The Chicago City Hall green roof features a combination of roof planting approaches. It was constructed and planted in 2000 as a retrofit to cover the roof of the landmark classical revival City Hall building, designed in 1911. Structural considerations meant that much of the roof is of the extensive type, with plants growing on around 10 cm (4 in) of growing medium. However, there were some points where a greater depth of soil could be supported. Over the frames of existing skylights it was possible to support semi-extensive plantings, while in localized areas over the support columns for the building it was possible to install intensive plantings with trees and shrubs. An undulating topography was created to bridge these different substrate depths using layers of extruded polystyrene laid over the drainage layer to form small hills and hollows, over which the growing medium was spread. One hundred fifty different plant species were used, mostly native species from the Chicago region. Round concrete pavers were used to give access among the plantings.

NATURAL PLANT COMMUNITIES AS
MODELS FOR ROOF-GREENING VEGETATION

While the use of drought-tolerant sedums has dominated the planting of shallow-substrate roofs, it is very much the natural vegetation of dry places that has so far been the model for extensive roof greening for substrates between 6 and 15 cm (2.4 and 6 in). Pioneer roof-greening researchers have tended to turn to their nearest dry habitats for inspiration and as sources of plant species.

In central and northern Europe the most diverse and visually attractive flora is found on shallow alkaline soils. This may be seen partly as an accident of geological and botanical history, but it also reflects the fact that low resource and stressful environments limit the growth of strong-growing competitive plants, leaving space for slower-growing species. The very nature of these habitats thus allows for more species to flourish in a given unit area than on a more fertile and moister soil.

Soils over limestone are characteristically shallow, thus drying out and heating up during the summer. Characteristic European limestone flora consists of a low turf dominated by dense tussock grasses, such as species of *Festuca*, along with a wide assemblage of colourful wildflowers, such as *Campanula rotundifolia*, *Thymus vulgaris*, and *Euphorbia cyparissias*. The short stature, visual appeal, and drought tolerance of this vegetation is thus a perfect model for roof greening. In Germany and Austria, the short wildflower-spattered turf is known as *Trockenrasen* and has traditionally been used for pasturing sheep. Centuries of grazing, along with occasional spring burning as a management practice, has tended to encourage the development of a rich flora through the suppression of the more vigorous grasses. For roof greening, there may well be lessons here for maintenance.

In Sweden, on the Baltic island of Öland, extensive areas of limestone were overgrazed by Bronze Age farmers, resulting in soil erosion and the development of a very distinctive vegetation overlaying a very thin soil, ranging between 1 and 20 cm (0.4 and 8 in) deep. The areas with the thinnest soil are dominated by succulent species of sedum.

Known as the alvar, this vegetation is one of the best natural models for roof-greening vegetation (Schillander and Hultengren 1998).

It is worth pointing out, however, that because roof greening originated in central and northern Europe, the limestone meadow flora of this region has tended to dominate the plant-selection aspects of roof greening, partly because of its eminent suitability and partly because a variety of seed mixes are readily available. Yet, outside this region this limestone meadow flora may be regarded as inappropriate or potentially unsuccessful, particularly in areas with longer and hotter summers, making it important that local mixtures (for example, shortgrass prairie) are investigated for their suitability instead.

The plant communities that develop on siliceous, acidic soils are much less diverse than those that develop on shallow calcareous ones. But they have a very distinct visual character, dominated by grasses such as *Nardus stricta* and species of *Carex*. Such a vegetation is well suited to environments where this kind of habitat is locally well developed, partly where high rainfall causes thorough leaching of nutrients both from soils and roofs. Naturally, such plant communities are also suitable for acidic substrates, but also for partly shaded roofs, which are not always suitable for a sun-loving, dry-meadow flora.

One of the most complex and visually rich of temperate zone wildflower communities, the prairie of the American Midwest, has been extensively used as a landscape element, primarily in the Midwest but also on the eastern seaboard of the United States. For roof-greening projects in these regions it is an obvious starting point. Prairie can be roughly divided into tallgrass and shortgrass, the former being typical of the moister climate between approximately 96 and 100°E, the latter of the drier areas between the Rockies and 100°E, where rainfall is on average 300–375 mm (12–15 in) per year (Cushman 1988). Shortgrass prairie is a potential model for roof greening, although some projects in the tallgrass prairie states have used this plant community with irrigation. Such a vegetation is based on the grass species that form the matrix of the shortgrass prairie plant community: predominately blue grama (*Bouteloua gracilis*) and buffalo grass (*Buchloë dactyloides*), along with little bluestem (*Andropogon scoparius*), side-oats grama (*Bouteloua curtipendula*), dropseed (*Sporobolus heterolepis*), and *Elymus canadensis* and the sedges *Carex bicknellii* and *C. annectans* (Miller 2002). Neil

Diboll, an authority on prairie restoration, thinks that some short prairie grasses are fully capable of growing in very shallow substrates under conditions of high temperatures and full sunlight. Such species enter dormancy under drought conditions and then revive rapidly following significant rainfall. The genus *Bouteloua* is particularly adept at growing in shallow soils. In more arid climates buffalo grass would be an excellent choice. Another prairie community worth further investigation is the dry gravel prairie found on very free-draining glacial moraines in the Midwest—although many component species have deep taproots to reach water at depth, others may be adapted to withstand predictable summer drought in this habitat.

The green roof on the Peggy Notebaert Nature Museum, Chicago, is based upon native prairie species, with a selection of tried-and-tested European species. The same mix of plants is grown on a range of substrate depths, from extensive (12 cm, 4.8 in substrate depth) through to intensive (30 cm, 12 in), with the aim of discovering those native species which are suitable for green-roof use in the area. The roof is irrigated. Native species selected particularly for use in extensive roofs include: *Aquilegia canadensis, Allium cernuum, Aster laevis, A. azureus, A. ptarmicoides, Baptisia leucophaea, Coreopsis palmata, Dodecatheon meadia, Geum triflorum, Helianthus mollis, Heuchera richardsonii, Liatris aspera,* and *Solidago speciosa,* together with the grasses *Andropogon scoparius, Buchloë dactyloides,* and *Sporobolus heterolepis.*

Other grassland communities may be suitable models as well, such as the California grassland and the Palouse prairie of Idaho and surrounding states. Both of these are likely to be subjected to severe drought stresses, and both have been massively damaged through the introduction of European grasses (Barbour and Billings 1988). It is possible that the clump grasses characteristic of both of these threatened habitats, could have a future on roofs, in an environment where they will be able to outcompete the non-native invaders.

In many cases plant communities can be readily established from seed mixtures sold by companies engaged in ecological restoration or the marketing of wildflowers. Dry-meadow mixtures for central and northern Europe and dry-prairie mixtures for the American Midwest and the eastern seaboard are all readily available. The great advantage of using a sown plant community such as a meadow or prairie is that no thought has to be given to the selection and combining of individual species. This makes installation ideal for people with little or no plant knowledge.

Seed mixtures have generally aimed at establishing at least twenty species. Good levels of diversity make for adaptability to a variety of environmental conditions as well as visual attractiveness. Trials have also shown that in light shade a somewhat larger number of species survives over a period of several years—presumably as a result of reduced water stress—suggesting that where floristic diversity is regarded as important, occasional watering in dry spells would be desirable (Kolb 1995).

THE NATURAL HABITATS OF POTENTIAL ROOF-GREENING PLANTS

Plants suitable for roof greening will be found in those habitats where plants are subjected to climatic extremes, especially drought and wind exposure. It therefore makes sense to concentrate the search for new roof-greening plants from among the world's floras where plants have adapted to these extremes. The following habitats stand out as having much potential.

Mountain environments—There is a considerable overlap between the species listed in the plant directory and many commonly grown rockery or alpine plants. However, there are many public misconceptions about the kind of habitat inhabited by these plants, often connected with the terminology used by nurseries to market them. True alpine plants may originate from any of the following habitats: meadows above the tree line, often with shallow soils; scree slopes of greater or lesser stability;

and rock faces, where plants root into fissures. Species from all of these are potentially useful for roof greening, although many from the third category are very slow growing and easily swamped. Note should also be made of aspect, as mountain sides that face the sun will become very much hotter than those that face away from it. The more xerophytic flora of the former will be of much greater importance, although the more shade-loving species of the latter can be of great use on shaded roofs.

High-latitude environments—There is a considerable overlap in conditions and species with mountain environments, and the three habitats above can be recognized here too. Summer temperatures will be very much lower, however, and drought will be induced by wind rather than the sun. Species from these environments are often completely unsuitable for lower latitudes.

Coasts—Maritime environments are extremely taxing for plants, and while dedicated coastal plants are relatively few, the conditions they have to survive are similar in many ways to those on roofs, for two main reasons. First, plants must have drought tolerance or avoidance strategies to survive in very free-draining sandy soils. Second, the salt-laden air and soils also promote anti-desiccation mechanisms.

Limestone vegetation—The shallow soils overlaying limestone have frequently been damaged by centuries of misuse by agriculturalists, resulting in the very specialized low vegetation of the Swedish alvar and the Mediterranean garrigue. Despite being the result of abuse and damage, these floras are often very rich, with many very attractive and stress-tolerant species.

Sclerophyllous woody vegetation—A feature of many exposed habitats is a low, dense vegetation composed of drought-tolerant shrubs or sub-shrubs, with dense twiggy growth and usually evergreen foliage showing adaptations to reduce water loss such as grey leaves or greatly reduced leaf size—technically known as *sclerophyllous* vegetation. At higher latitudes and altitudes throughout the world, such habitats are often dominated by members of the Ericaceae and in New Zealand by species of *Hebe*. In regions with a Mediterranean climate, species with grey, often aromatic, foliage from a great many families is typical. The garrigue and taller maquis of the Mediterranean region has provided a great many plants of horticultural value, while the fynbos of South Africa is one of the world's richest floras.

While these floras include many species of horticultural value, many, particularly from the Mediterranean zones, are too large for roof-greening applications, although dwarf or spreading cultivars may be useful, for example, *Ceanothus thyrsiflorus* 'Repens'. The higher latitude heath type vegetation is very wind proof but not necessarily suitable for surviving prolonged drought, with many Ericaceae, for example, being totally intolerant of drying out. However, where this is not a problem, there may be considerable potential in these floras. Similar are habitats such as south-western North American chaparral, where the flora is more varied, verging on savannah, with a mixture of trees, scrubby shrubs, and open grassland. Zones where thin soils or an exposed aspect limit tree or large shrub growth will be particularly rich in species suitable for roof greening.

Semi-desert—Such areas occupy large areas of the globe, with considerable variation in temperature range. Those regions which experience low winter temperatures as well as drought should be rich sources of potential roof-greening plants. Regions where changes in terrain and geology over relatively short distances create a complex of different habitats have particularly high potential, especially if these different habitats have a large proportion of endemic species. In some cases, large areas of these habitats are dominated by one species, for example, *Perovskia atriplicifolia* in the drier regions of Russia and Ukraine or the sagebrush *Seriphidium tridentatum* in the United States. However, other smaller and more useful species may often be found with them. In some areas the opposite effect may be seen, with very high levels of biodiversity, parts of the Ukrainian steppe having a flora of up to 80 species per square metre (7.4 per square foot), an indication of the potential of roof greening.

The plant-hunting that has given the modern garden and suburban landscape such a high level of diversity, or at least potential diversity, if the stock lists of innumerable specialist nurseries were to be used more adventurously by garden designers, has to date concentrated largely on species suitable for conventional garden conditions. The more xerophytic and stress-tolerant floras have tended to remain the preserve either of botanists with no interest in the practical or aesthetic applications of plants or of specialist plant collectors, concerned often with alpines or bulbs. With roof greening becoming an important part of the new built environment, it is increasingly important that more attention is paid to sourcing new plant material from habitats in the wild where conditions approximate those on rooftops and other problem urban situations. Regions with potential for the temperate zone rooftop horticulturalist include:

the Mediterranean basin and Turkey, with more cold-tolerant species in the dry mountainous areas of Iran across to Tibet and into the semi-desert of central Asia,
the coast of the Cape Province of South Africa and high-altitude regions in South Africa,
the coast and semi-desert regions of the southern cone of South America,
semi-desert and dry regions of the western United States and Mexico, and
Australia.

PLANT SELECTION AND INVASIVENESS

As long as people have been moving plant species around the globe, certain species have spread aggressively, ousting native flora, occasionally forcing some into extinction, and sometimes taking over and threatening entire ecosystems. As globalization continues apace, the threats posed by invasive non-native species is greater than ever. People involved in roof greening and other aspects of bioengineering have a responsibility to ensure that introduced species do not spread into and damage local ecosystems, especially since the areas where the plants are being grown are potentially large. At times, this may mean having to forego using some extremely valuable plants. An example is English ivy,

Hedera helix, which has escaped in the Pacific Northwest of North America and poses a major threat to local woodland ground flora. Yet, this is potentially a very useful plant for a variety of landscape applications including roof greening.

There are two ways of eliminating invasiveness as a problem. One is to use locally native species, which often are of more benefit to wildlife in any case, and the other is to restrict the use of introduced species to those that have been in cultivation locally for a long time without causing any problems. These options may not always be possible or even desirable, however, as the combination of having to find species that will grow in testing conditions and that may need to be ornamental or at least fulfil demanding functional and aesthetic criteria may require looking beyond locally native or tried-and-tested commercial species.

There are as yet no horticultural industry protocols on the risk assessment of introduced species. However, the following points cover the main issues:

Given that roof greening is physically so separate from other places where plants may grow, species that present a problem through invasive rooting systems present a low risk. However, the disposal of unwanted material or roof plantings that are no longer needed must be considered.

All species new to cultivation in a particular region should be trialled for a number of years before being sold commercially or used on a large scale. Although it sounds like common sense not to sell new plants on a large scale until they have proved their worth in the local climate, the pressure in the horticultural industry for novelty means that this does sometimes happen.

Plant species that self-sow readily in the nursery should be regarded as suspicious. In actual practice, however, only those that will self-sow and grow to adult size among already established vegetation need be a concern.

Plants with berries are often much more of a problem, as they can be scattered far and wide by birds.

Climate and existing native vegetation plays the most important role in whether or not non-natives are likely to become invasive. The level of risk can therefore be expressed reasonably confidently on a regional basis. North-western Europe has an extremely aggressive grass flora and a maritime climate that favours a limited number of semi-ever-green herbaceous species, and thus risks are low. Other cool temperate areas are generally medium risk, with large-growing short-lived species setting large quantities of seed being the most easily identified problem, along with berry-bearing climbers and scramblers. Areas with seasonally dry climates seem to be high risk, possibly because of the large number of areas of bare ground open to seeding that develop between plants where water resources are limited.

PLANT SELECTION FOR THE TROPICS

Finally, it may be worth briefly considering the unrealized potential of roof greening in the humid tropics, where runoff from heavy downpours in urban areas is a major problem and where the buffering effect of green-roof vegetation could be of major benefit. While the epiphytic flora of the tropics is vast, much of it is dependent upon partial shade, rendering it unsuitable for rooftop use. However, there is also a lithophytic flora—species that grow on rocks—which in places can be extremely diverse and is often better adapted for exposure to sun and prolonged drought. The value of this flora has been little realized, although the garden designer and artist Roberto Burle Marx collaborated with botanists on several expeditions in the southern states of Brazil where there is a particularly rich lithophyte flora (much of it orchids or bromeliads), introducing several species to cultivation and making great use of a number of species in his design work, notably the bromeliad *Vriesea imperialis*.

The Bromeliaceae is a family of major importance for ornamental planting in the tropics, generally for areas of medium to high visual importance. The plants are able to thrive with little or no attention, although many have the habit of not letting go of their old leaves, which can build up to look very untidy unless periodically removed. Nearly all bromeliads have a central urn which stores water, making them potentially very useful plants for water management. The Araceae also contains many species with roof-greening potential, with genera such as

Philodendron, *Monstera*, *Rhaphidophora*, and *Scindapsus* typically grow-ing as epiphytes on tree trunks, clinging to their host with aerial roots. These all have an obvious potential as roof-greening plants where extensive ground coverage is needed and where the substrate is shallow.

MAINTENANCE

The completely maintenance-free green roof is probably an unreach-able goal. However, for extensive and semi-extensive type roofs, main-tenance can be limited to a set of simple annual tasks.

Feeding—Roof greening works with stress-tolerant plants; nevertheless some attention to feeding after plants have become established does often enhance growth and hence the appearance of the planting. In particular, grass roofs, which constantly lose nutrients when the clip-pings from mowing are collected, need feeding. Two years after plant-ing is often a good time to feed, as plants will be well established and much of the nutrient content that was in the substrate initially will have been exhausted. Slow-release feeds are usually the best option, at 15–20 g per square metre (0.05–0.07 oz per square foot) for extensive roofs, or 40 g per square metre (0.14 oz per square foot) for intensive roofs. Organic alternatives based on animal products such as bone meal can also be used. On grass roofs that are not mowed, an equilibrium is reached where a cycle returns nutrients from dead stems and leaves to the substrate, and thus to new growth—analogous to the way nutrient recycling works in natural habitats.

Plant protection—Pest and disease problems are few with green roofs, partly because the species used are not generally badly affected with particular pest problems. When diverse plant communities are used, if one species becomes adversely affected, there are always plenty of oth-ers in perfect health around, so that any problems do not become conspicuous. One problem that can sometimes occur is patches of fun-gal diseases in wet autumns, often triggered by accumulating tree leaves. Keeping leaves from building up will generally prevent this.

Drainage—Effective drainage is key to the success of green roofs. Inadequate drainage or drainage systems that become blocked can lead to pooling of water, which may result in damage to the roof surface and consequent leakage, together with damage to plant root systems, followed by fungal damage and decay. Points where drainage systems may become blocked need to be identified and their regular inspection specified into schemes of maintenance.

Weeding—There are several tricks to minimize weeding requirements. Achieving continuous vegetation cover reduces the space available for unwanted plants to establish. Maintaining a coarse, very dry surface to the green roof will make germination of weed seeds less likely. Nevertheless, there is a high likelihood that wind-blown seeds will find their way onto the roof and establish. Tree and shrub seedlings such as birches and willows are a particular problem because of the danger of their roots damaging the underlying roof membrane. Other problem species are wind-dispersed annuals that can gain a toehold, grow and set seed rapidly, and contaminate the rest of the vegetation. As a result, where roofs are accessible, it is recommended to check for weed seedlings and saplings on a regular basis and to undertake light hand-weeding once or twice a year at the opportune moments before weeds go to seed and start the cycle again.

CHAPTER 5
Façade Greening

Façade greening is essentially a living—and therefore self-regenerating—cladding system for buildings. Climbers, or in some cases trained shrubs, are used to cover the surface of a building. This is a practice that is long established in parts of Europe, and it is quite common to see houses in France and Germany covered in Virginia creeper (*Parthenocissus tricuspidata*) or vines in those regions with a more Mediterranean-influenced climate. Traditionally, self-clinging climbers have been used, as they require no supporting network of wires or trellis. Modern façade greening, however, favours the use of climbers supported by steel cables or trellis. Whereas traditional self-clinging façade greening involved allowing climbers to attach themselves directly to the building surface, with obvious implications for any building works that needed to be carried out, modern practice is more likely to involve holding the plants away from the surface itself.

Climbers have conventionally been used for largely, but not entirely, ornamental purposes. Large climbers are frequently seen on the sides of houses, although their use tends to be somewhat localized, occurring in certain geographical regions with certain plants but not in others, and the supporting structure for large climbers is often completely inadequate. Species and cultivars of wisteria, particularly *Wisteria sinensis*, are among the most popular really large climbers, and there are few sights more magnificent than a huge plant, which may be more than a century old, smothered in its smoky blue-violet flowers in early summer. Yet, supporting frameworks for large climbers like this are rarely seen that make the best use of the plant; usually they are simply too small and there are a lot of stray new shoots visible flailing wildly at thin air, trying to find somewhere to latch onto. All too often these shoots return to wind themselves around the parent plant, resulting in large tangled masses of growth, unattractive and increasingly structurally unsound with age.

Façade greening at the time of writing is still a relatively new discipline that builds on previous knowledge and experience. Much of the technical and research literature is concerned with the problems that arise from inappropriate planning or implementation, and how they may be avoided. New support materials and their increasing availability through an international network of manufacturers and suppliers are making façade greening a much more practicable and realistic option for those professionally involved with buildings. Owing to occasional incidents of damage, some look unfavourably on having climbers on buildings. With new technologies and with many contemporary buildings offering extensive surfaces suitable for coverage, and fewer sites for damage to occur, the combination of climbers and architecture needs re-evaluating.

This section of the book is not intended to repeat the extensive horticultural literature on climbing plants, but rather to look at the potential for a more dramatic and sophisticated use of climbers. While it is aimed largely at those concerned with the use of climbers on a large scale, domestic gardeners with large expanses of wall will hopefully find it useful, too. Although the horticultural literature on climbers is extensive, it is often frustratingly inadequate regarding technical details—how climbers actually hang on and the physical characteristics of the supports they need. Information given here should supply some of this information.

Vines (*Vitis* species) in particular have often been used on the sides of buildings for summer cooling in some warm-summer climate zones or growing over extensive pergola type constructions designed to give shade below. Climbers have also long been used for screening on the sides of utilitarian domestic buildings such as sheds and garages. Despite their potential for screening extensive areas of blank wall on commercial or industrial premises, climbers have been used little for this purpose. Given that so little structural work is needed to make it possible to grow climbers up to several storeys high, this use does seem to have enormous potential.

The early years of the twentieth century saw extensive use of climbers, particularly *Parthenocissus tricuspidata*, in German-speaking

A good example of well-managed ivy (*Hedera helix*) on a four-storey building in Zürich, Switzerland.

countries. This was part of a movement towards integration of house and garden that, broadly speaking, grew out the *Jugendstil* (Art Nouveau) movement in art and architecture. An analogous movement towards surrounding houses and residential areas with greenery occurred at the same time in Britain, as is illustrated by the garden city movement and the first development of suburbia in the United States, often with a link to the arts-and-crafts movement. Pergolas and other structures that linked architectural features and climbing plants were increasingly common features in gardens and parks throughout western Europe, but it was only in German-speaking countries, and to some extent in France, that climbers were so extensively used on houses and other buildings. The use of façade greening declined from the 1930s onwards, and arguably today's use of climbers is a revival rather than a new field. Modern façade greening is still very much in its infancy.

A survey conducted in 1982 in Berlin gave an overview of the status of façade greening prior to the recent growth in interest and development of a more technological approach to the subject. Forty per cent of the use of climbers was on south-facing walls, with other aspects covered more or less in equal proportions. *Parthenocissus tricuspidata* was the most widely used, in 60 per cent of the examples and 80 per cent of the total area covered. *Hedera helix* came second, *Parthenocissus quinquefolia* third, and *Fallopia baldschuanica* fourth. The two most popular are self-clinging, arguably requiring more effort to restrict their growth once established than to encourage them. *Parthenocissus quinquefolia* is more or less self-clinging. The fallopia, while requiring support, is extremely vigorous (Köhler 1993).

Greening the walls of a building has potentially more effect on the building environment than roof greening, as the surface area of the walls of buildings is always greater than the area of the roof. With high-rise buildings this can be as much as twenty times the roof area. Low buildings may have large climbers trained over the roof, further extending the shading and insulating benefits. Traditionally, some climbers were allowed or encouraged to do this, but the results were often less than satisfactory. Russian vine, *Fallopia baldschuanica*, for example, will readily scramble over low-gradient or flat roofs but often looks untidy and eventually forms an uneven mass of very tangled woody material, which can be difficult to remove. The modern approach would be to use the same kind of cable or trellis system on the roof as on the walls.

THE ADVANTAGES OF FAÇADE GREENING

Effects of climbers on building temperature

Climbers can dramatically reduce the maximum temperatures of a building by shading walls from the sun, the daily temperature fluctuation being reduced by as much as 50 per cent, a fact of great importance in warm-summer climate zones. The effectiveness of this cooling is related primarily to the total area shaded rather than the thickness of the climber (Köhler 1993). Together with the insulation effect, temperature fluctuations at the wall surface can be reduced from between 10°C (14°F) and 60°C (140°F) to between 5°C (41°F) and 30°C (86°F; Peck et al. 1999).

Buildings are most effectively insulated against high summer temperatures by shading rather than by building insulation into the structure, for the simple reason that shading stops the heat entering in the first place—climbers are one of the most effective ways of achieving this. It has been calculated that a 5.5°C (10°F) reduction in the temperature immediately outside of a building can reduce the amount of energy needed for air-conditioning by 50–70 per cent (Peck et al. 1999). The use of climbers to reduce solar heating is most effective if they are used on the wall that faces the sun, together with the west wall, which experiences afternoon heating. Windows may also be shaded by climbers on a seasonal basis, which has a particularly dramatic effect on reducing summer heating because their foliage will stop solar energy entering the building. Solar energy heating the side of a building will generate more powerful convection currents than it will on a horizontal surface, which climbers through their cooling effect and the creation of complex air flows can minimize. There is thus a contribution to the reduction of the heat island effect (see chapter 2, "Green roofs and the urban heat island effect") and dust generation. In climates with cold winters, it makes sense to have deciduous climbers on walls which receive sunlight, as this enables them to absorb more solar radiation. The use of evergreen climbers on walls which do not receive sunlight, on the other hand, helps reduce heat loss in winter.

Evergreen climbers provide winter insulation, not only by maintaining a pillow of air between the plant and the wall but by reducing wind chill on the wall surface. One-third of a home's demand for winter heating is generated by wind chill, either through draughts or the cooling of the walls, at least in climates where cold-season winds are a regular feature. Reducing wind chill by 75 per cent reduces heating demand by 25 per cent (Peck et al. 1999). Reduction of wind chill is also reduced to some extent by the interwoven stems of deciduous climbers during winter. The effectiveness of winter insulation is related to the thickness of growth, which is generally related to the age of the plant. In some cases, however, growth patterns change as the plant ages, for example, there may be a reduction in the dense twiggy growth that forms the most effective insulation. *Fallopia baldschuanica*, for instance, becomes less effective after ten years. German research results show *Hedera helix* with a thickness of 20–40 cm (8–16 in) is the most effective insulator.

A mixture of climbers and wall shrubs is used at the Danish Museum of Modern Art: cultivars of ivy (*Hedera helix*), the twiner *Actinidia kolomikta*, and a *Cotoneaster* species. Annual maintenance keeps growth away from the gutters and eaves. The cotoneaster is a shrub rather than a climber and is kept cut back.

Right: Russian vine, *Fallopia baldschuanica*, is very effective for covering large expanses of wall, given strong supports. Its bulky growth provides excellent cover for bird roosting and nesting.

Photograph by Fritz Wassmann

Other benefits of façade greening

Climbers and urban trees are highly effective at trapping dust and concentrating certain dust-derived pollutants in their tissues, particularly in those tissues that are then discarded. In a study of *Parthenocissus tricuspidata*, lead and cadmium concentrations were shown to be highest in dead leaves and dead wood. These heavy metals are thus taken out of the atmosphere and rain and concentrated in a form that then falls to the ground (Köhler 1993). The removal of dead leaves and branches and their disposal in sites where the concentrated heavy metals can do minimal environmental damage is thus a key factor in reducing the dangers presented by these elements. Trapping of dust is proportional to the amount of leaf surface to wall area, which can be expressed by a leaf area index, the higher the index, the more effective the plant. Indices for three commonly used species are: *Parthenocissus quinquefolia*, 1.6–4.0; *P. tricuspidata*, 2.0–8.0; and *Hedera helix*, 2.6–7.7 (Köhler 1993). Figures from German research show that 4 g per square metre (0.012 oz per square foot) can be captured by *P. tricuspidata* in the course of a growing season, and 6 g per square metre (0.018 oz per square foot) by *Hedera helix* (Köhler 1993).

Climbers on buildings can help protect the surface of the building from damage from very heavy rainfall and hail, and may play some role in intercepting and temporarily holding water during rainstorms, in the way that green roofs do. They also help to shield the surface from ultraviolet light, which might be an important consideration for both certain traditional as well as modern cladding materials.

Façade greening and wildlife

The presence of climbers on walls is of considerable benefit to wildlife, and it can do much to improve the biodiversity of urban areas. Detailed research has shown the presence of a wide variety of invertebrate species, which can form the basis for a rich web of life. The invertebrates are a food source for birds, particularly summer migrant species, as well as bats. In addition, established climbers may provide good roosting and nesting sites for birds, especially for songbirds such as thrushes, and small insectivorous species. Some climbers may contribute to biodiversity directly as food sources for insects, either in the form of nectar, with the late-flowering *Hedera helix* particularly valuable in this respect, or as primarily the case with some native species, the leaves could be eaten by larvae. In the latter case, this may not be desirable, if heavy infestation reduces the functional and amenity aspects of the climbers. Climbers can also be a valuable hibernation site for insects, such as lacewings (Chrysopidae species), butterflies, and moths. *Hedera helix* is a good example of specialized hibernation niche as the outline of its leaves is similar to that of the outline of the European brimstone butterfly (*Gonepteryx rhamni*), which makes the plant a safe hiding place. Evergreens such as *Hedera* species might also play a significant role in providing sheltered winter roosting for small birds, many of which can be very vulnerable to winter cold.

THE POTENTIAL FOR FAÇADE GREENING

The opportunities for using large-scale climbers are dependent on the nature of the buildings to be found in a given area. However, in many urban areas, where there is little in the way of plant life or space to develop green areas of any extent, there may be a strongly felt need for greenery. Those working with climbing plants will need to address a variety of issues in order to shoehorn plants into environments that were never designed for them.

Examples might be old industrial areas, where warehouses built in the late nineteenth century and early twentieth have been converted into studios, fashionable lofts, or other living spaces, but where the environment is still desperately short of life. Many countries, particularly in central and eastern Europe, have large amounts of court housing, where multiple-storey buildings purpose built for multiple residency are built around a large central yard. By modern standards the exterior of the building and the central area may be bleak or even Dickensian. Large climbers have great potential to bring nature into these courtyards, where there is often virtually no open ground for planting, creating a valuable green oases. In former Communist countries in eastern Europe there may large urban areas with this kind of housing stock, where regeneration projects seek to improve the environment in relatively poor economies—façade greening has huge potential for maximum improvement at minimal cost. Brutalist architecture of the 1960s, featuring extensive areas of raw concrete, can also benefit. High apartment blocks and other buildings with very high façades present a challenge to the engineering skills of those involved in installation, but the visual improvement that can be made is enormous. Climbers are capable of reaching tall forest trees, so a maximum height of 25–30 m (82–98 ft) can be regarded as practicable. The expression "urban jungle" can now take on a new and more positive meaning.

Industrial and commercial buildings dominate many urban or peri-urban areas, often presenting dull, featureless façades to the world. In many cases façade greening could be used to create a living surface, one that changes with the seasons and actively contributes to the local environment. Multiple-storey car parks are another example of a highly functional and often unattractive façade which can be greatly improved by the addition of training wires and large climbers.

In situations where there is multiple occupancy, that is blocks of flats, apartments, or maisonettes, the approval and support of residents is vital for façade greening. Those planning greening must listen to any concerns residents may have. Regular maintenance will be an issue in keeping the support as the plants grow, so that windows are not obscured and wayward stems will not create an untidy appearance.

For those living in estates or in areas of extensive nineteenth-century terracing, large numbers of identical houses, and identical streets, façade greening is an opportunity to create some sense of identity, to bring a distinctive touch to one's property. Climbers can be used for screening and to create privacy as well, if free-standing supports are used. For those who live in flats or apartments, but who have balconies or terraces, climbers can be grown in containers, either for growing up walls or as privacy-creating screens. Large climbers may even be grown hydroponically in such a situation, although this system of growing plants is only suitable for climates where there is no prolonged winter freezing. Very tall buildings can be greened by having a second set of plants growing in planter boxes at several stories height, for example, on a balcony. Lightweight planting media can be used in conjunction with an automated watering system and a regular application of slow-release feed.

Finally, with a greater realization of the contribution that vegetation can make to city life, modern buildings are being realized that actively involve plants in their design. When this happens, ideal locations for particular plants species can be created, and designs of great ecological integrity can result. The finest example at the time of writing is the MFO Park in Zürich, Switzerland. See pages 136–137.

Walls, windowless structures, and noise barriers

Façade greening is a very useful technique for covering a variety of walls such as noise barriers or to screen unattractive large windowless structures such as garages. An added advantage for noise barriers is that the plant growth will absorb some sound and dust, adding to the effectiveness of the barrier. On wooden walls and other structures, species with very heavy growth or a thick branching habit should be avoided, as the structure may not be able to support the weight. *Fallopia baldschuanica* has commonly been used for these purposes owing to its large size and fast growth rate, but it is not always suitable. If the support is lower than its eventual maximum height (18 m, 59.4 ft), it tends to form a more tangled woody mass at the top of the structure than most other climbers, potentially reducing the stability of the structure and adding to wind loading. However, where there is a flat top or roof where there is space for the plant to spread horizontally, this is less likely to be a problem.

THE MFO PARK

Zürich's MFO Park (for Maschinenfabrik Oerlikon, the name of the business that formerly occupied the site) is part of the redevelopment of a former industrial area for new uses, combining the commercial, residential, and recreational. The central feature of a series of interlinked green spaces is a futuristic pergola, intended as a new kind of public open space, a contemporary version of the traditional European square, a place for meeting and play but also for organized events such as theatre, concerts, and film.

The MFO Park is a double-walled, three-sided construction which evokes the structures that have been used in European gardens since at least the Renaissance, known in French as "treillage" and "carpenter's work" in English. Forerunners of the pergola, they were temporary structures employed in aristocratic gardens, sometimes supporting climbing plants. Within seven to twelve years, luxuriant climbers will scramble up the steel cables of the parkhouse, with more covering the roof, rooted in high-level troughs of lightweight growing medium. A series of stairs and gangways allow for public access to the upper levels, where a sundeck gives extensive views over the surroundings.

The park measures 100 m long × 35 m wide × 17 m high (328 × 114 × 49 ft) and is built of steel, with tensioned cables supporting the climbers. Paving at ground level is broken up by hedges of yew and beech to make for a distinctly contemporary environment where architecture and horticulture are integrated in a way that is all too rarely seen. Zürich city authorities chose the design after a competition, the concept and planning was undertaken by Burckhardt & Partner, landscape architects Raderschall and many other specialists, with Fritz Wassmann as planting consultant. It was formally opened in May 2002.

An artist's impression of the completed MFO Park.

A detail of the structure in the first year after completion.

The interior of the structure, two years after completion.

Photographs © Grün Stadt Zürich

Client: Grün Stadt Zürich (Former Parks services)
Projektteam: Burckhardt Partner and Raderschall Landschaftsarchitekten AG.

Metal structures such as street furniture and outside stairs

Climbers can be used on such structures, if there is no risk of their function being impaired by the plants' growth and the structure can take the additional wind loading. Outside stairways such as fire exits may seem an attractive option for roof greening, especially if they are of the very functional but visually obtrusive metal kind, but the reality is that regular maintenance is vitally important to keep the plants from attaching themselves to the handrails or growing across the stairs themselves, where they could present a considerable hazard.

USING CLIMBERS

Before questions of design and plant selection are considered, it is important to understand the basic means by which climbers are supported and the various ways climbing plants use to climb. Climbers may be self-clinging or they may need supports. Broadly speaking there are three means of supporting those species that need it: trellis or a framework made up of vertical and horizontal elements, horizontal supports, or vertical supports. Conventional support systems have made great use of the first two and very little of the third. However, some of the most exciting modern façade greening has made use of vertical supports.

How climbers hold on

For our purposes, climbers can be classified into the following categories:

Self-supporting woody plants trained as wall shrubs
Climbers and plants that need support
 lax shrubs, often termed *ramblers* or *scramblers*
  ramblers with thorns
  ramblers without thorns

True climbers with methods of attachment to supports
  self-clinging climbers
    climbers with aerial roots
    climbers with suckers
  twining climbers
  climbers with specialized leaves for attachment, such as tendrils.

Self-clinging climbers—These climbers are the easiest to use as they require no supports. While *Parthenocissus* species offer the most attractive results among self-clinging species, the evergreen ivies offer a remarkably cheap and easy way to provide walls with an additional layer of protection against the elements. *Parthenocissus* are useful for their very shallow profile, which *Hedera* species have as well, until they either begin to age or to reach the limits of where they can climb, when they can become arborescent, producing much thicker growth. Other self-clinging climbers tend to have a more shrubby habit, such as *Euonymus fortunei*, although *Hydrangea petiolaris* and related plants such as *Schizophragma hydrangeioides* are very useful for shaded walls.

Self-clinging climbers are capable of making very considerable amounts of growth. *Hedera helix*, for example, can reach 30 m (98 ft) and cover 600 square metres (6500 square feet). There are an enormous number of ivy cultivars, with varying rates of growth, but there is relatively little to choose from among other self-clinging genera. New introductions are increasingly available from specialist nurseries, however. Specialist ivy nurseries will be able to advise on a selection of varieties for either restricted or extensive areas of wall. Ivy's ability to cover large areas independently is very useful for dealing with extensive windowless walls, for example, the sides of the final house in a row of terraced houses.

Most ivies, and certain other species, notably climbing members of the Hydrangeaceae, use small roots that emerge from the stem to penetrate the interstices of rough surfaces, tree bark, or rock. These aerial roots must have enough roughness on a surface for their microscopic root hairs to grab onto, for example, stone, brick, render, or cement. Smooth or shiny metal or plastic surfaces are in theory not suitable. Neither are walls where soft traditional mortar between stone or brick might allow deep penetration of roots, nor tiled walls, where there is

Aerial roots on
*Schizophragma
hydrangeoides.*

Right: Suckers on
Parthenocissus tricuspidata.

scope for roots to grow behind tiles. Timber-frame and infill, as in traditional European black-and-white houses, is unsuitable, too, as there are always cracks between wood and render. Buildings coated in traditional limewash (that is, whitewash) have a powdery surface, which also makes them unsuitable. Very brightly painted surfaces (those that are very reflective) can also discourage the attachment of self-clinging climbers.

Other self-clingers, particularly the Virginia creeper genus *Parthenocissus*, use a gluelike substance which allows specialized tendrils, resembling small octopus suckers, to attach themselves to somewhat shinier surfaces, such as painted stone. However, their ability to cling onto surfaces such as metal or plastic cladding or polished stone is not so secure, and in some circumstances the weight of a large plant may pull it away from the wall. Species which use this climbing mechanism are much less likely than those which use aerial roots to penetrate cracks, and they are thus much less likely to cause damage. *Parthenocissus tricuspidata* is exceptionally good at self-clinging, whereas others of the genus are less so. With increasing numbers of different cultivars and stock derived from different geographical provenances commercially available, the assessment of self-clinging ability is an important consideration.

Most self-clinging climbers have a strong tendency to grow upwards towards the light (phototropism). Whereas some climbers can be forced to go in a particular direction by attaching their stems to supports, self-clingers will often fail to attach themselves to surfaces if their growing tips are led away from the light. This has implications for their planting

Left: *Parthenocissus* species have weak phototropism and in good light can actually grow downwards, ensuring very thorough coverage of walls. In contrast, *Hedera* species will only grow upwards.

Well-maintained ivy or other self-clinging climbers can form a visually pleasing green skin on buildings.

positions, as plants have to be planted at the darkest end of where it is they are wanted. The degree of phototropism varies between species, side shoots of *Parthenocissus tricuspidata*, for example, may frequently be seen growing downwards on a sunny wall, and this species has a much greater ability to spread sideways for long distances than do *Hedera* species, which tend to form an inverted triangle shape on walls. Aerial roots and suckers display negative phototropism (that is, they move away from the light) as they seek to attach themselves to something.

In their early stages, self-clinging climbers may be encouraged to root onto the substrate by means of a small-mesh trellis or wire-netting type material that presses them against the substrate. Alternatively lightweight vertical training wires about 5 cm (2 in) from the wall can be used.

Twining climbers—These vary enormously in eventual size, with some species of wisteria potentially reaching 30 m (98 ft). Because they have a very strong natural tendency to go vertically, it is difficult to train them along long horizontal stretches of support—or indeed any support at an angle less than 45 degrees, which is why the traditional practice of training them to horizontal supports requires regular tying in and pruning. Larger twiners can become woody with age, with almost treelike trunks and branches. Not surprisingly the weight of these can be considerable.

In theory twiners only need vertical supports. For large and heavy climbers, however, supports need to be of a material whose surface roughness will eliminate the possibility of the plant's weight causing it to slip; steel cable and fibreglass both offer enough surface friction. The cable or other support needs to be round in cross-section with a diameter of 4–30 mm (0.2–1.2 in). Large climbers can also grab hold of and twist the support, resulting in its fixings being pulled out of the wall. This can be overcome by using a special slippage attachment at the base or by retensioning the cable annually. In some cases vertical cables are actually designed to break once the tension gets too high; the plants are held at the top and firmly rooted at the base, so this does not matter.

Despite the labour involved in training twining climbers onto horizontal structures, this practice is frequently seen, and for walls where the horizontal run is longer than the vertical, this is the best means of training. It could be argued that twining climbers are not the best species to be used in such situations, but many are happy to make an exception for wisterias.

Tendril and leaf-twining climbers—Tendril climbers, such as the true vines (*Vitis* species), attach themselves by means of tendrils on the younger stems. The tendrils can last for several years but eventually die. In nature the tendrils serve to pull the plant onwards and upwards, leaving its older and heavier stems to be supported by the trees on which they are growing. In façade-greening situations this opportunity is not possible, so the weight must be taken by the supports. Leaf-twining climbers, primarily clematis, depend upon leaf stems, nearly always deciduous, to hold on. During the winter the dead leaf stems continue to hold onto the support, although they are now much more brittle. Much of the weight is taken by the plant's stems being intertwined around the supports.

Trellis-type supports, with vertical and horizontal members, offer the variety of handholds needed by these climbers and the opportunity for weight to be put onto horizontal supports. Vertical and horizontal members need to intersect at 10- to 20-cm (4- to 8-in) intervals for less vigorous climbers such as *Clematis* hybrids, but 25- to 50-cm (10- to 20-

in) intervals are often enough for large-growing species such as *Wisteria* and *Vitis*. Trellis to support tendril and leaf-twining climbers is traditionally made of either equidistantly spaced horizontal and vertical elements or diagonally arranged elements. Both are suitable for all species, but the growth habits of certain species lead to their growing best on one or the other. There is some evidence that the shape of the cross-section of the supporting material can make a difference to how well these plants hold on, too, with many possibly preferring an angled cross-section rather than round, perhaps because there is less likelihood of slippage.

Ramblers and scramblers—Ramblers and scramblers are in a way not true climbers, as they do not have the sophisticated means of attachment that others have. Many plants of this type use thorns as a means of hanging onto the woody growth or stems of other plants in order to climb. Their means of growing is often rather haphazard, as even those with thorns, such as roses, often do not make a good job of climbing up artificial supports, ending up forming large thickets of impenetrable growth at ground level, in contrast to the vigour and enthusiasm with which they run up trees. Those without thorns, such as *Plumbago capensis*, can only lean on their supports, and once at the top sprawl out across the tops of shrubs or trees.

Ramblers are inherently somewhat ill-disciplined, and do not lend themselves to making their own way politely up supports, but need constant monitoring and tying in to supports. This is especially important when they have thorns and there is public access nearby. Trellis with sharp angles, for example, made up of rhomboid shapes made from material with a thin cross-section, is particularly effective for climbers with thorns, as it allows for plenty of potential handhold. Dimensions of mesh of 25–50 cm (10–20 in) are recommended. Ramblers can be particularly effective and most easily handled if trained in a largely horizontal rather than an entirely vertical direction. Indeed, they can be extremely difficult to train up without very frequent tying in. This quality renders them very useful for long horizontal stretches with little vertical range. In such cases the optimum vertical distance between supports is 40 cm (16 in).

Many climbers can be grown as trailers from planters at high level or from the soil at the top of retaining walls. Ivies and *Parthenocissus* are frequently grown this way and are highly effective, as are some clematis, in particular *C. montana*. Large-leaved plants such as *Actinidia* or *Vitis* species may be particularly dramatic. Little systematic research has been done on trailers, but it can be speculated than only twining species are completely unsuitable as they would twist round each other and form a knot of Gordian proportions.

Hanging plants are particularly useful for covering large areas of blank wall where there is little opportunity to plant at ground level, where passing traffic or vandalism make damage likely, or where the ground level is too dark for good growth. The maximum length that climbers will hang for (at least in temperate zones) is around 5 m (17 ft). Some scandent shrubs such as *Jasminium officianale* are effective as hanging plants, along with ground-hugging species such as *Cotoneaster dammeri*.

OTHER PLANTS FOR FAÇADE GREENING

Large perennial climbing species are generally used in façade greening. However, there is also a role for annuals and non-climbing plants. These are discussed in many books on climbers and so only their role and potential in more extensive situations will be mentioned here.

Annuals

Annual climbers which can grow to considerable sizes in one year or herbaceous perennials grown as annuals (such as *Cobaea scandens*) may be used to provide temporary cover while permanent climbers establish themselves, although care should be taken that their growth is not so exuberant that the growth of the perennials is overwhelmed. There may also be a role for the use of annuals in situations where there is little or no requirement for foliage in the winter, for example, terraces or seating areas which are only used in the summer or which require shading then but not in the winter. Annual climbers never become as large as many perennial climbers and thus do not present the same technical problems. In warm climate zones, however, annual climbers can make considerable growth, giving them great potential for shading purposes.

There are a limited number of herbaceous climbers that can be used for façade-greening purposes, shading especially. The hop (*Humulus lupulus*) is one suitable for cool temperate climates. Kudzu vine, *Pueraria lobata*, is sometimes used for this purpose in Mediterranean climates, although, given how rampant it can be, this is perhaps only advisable in places where winter frosts ensure it is only herbaceous (see "The future of plant selection" below, on the plant's invasive potential).

Wall shrubs and fruit trees

Wall shrubs are woody species that are grown against walls and then trained and sometimes clipped to ensure that they stay close to the wall. Certain species are traditional in some regions, for example, *Magnolia grandiflora* seems almost de rigueur against Georgian era (that is, eighteenth century) houses in England. In this case, and with most wall shrubs, a large part of the *raison d'être* is to enable somewhat tender species to be grown. However, large wall shrubs can fulfil many of the same functional and aesthetic roles as climbers, although there are few suitable for growing higher than two stories. Less of a support system will be needed and in some cases none at all. Nevertheless design and practical considerations often require a very shallow profile for the shrubs. To maintain this at least an annual pruning will be needed as well as regular tying in of branches to the wall, usually by means of horizontal training cables (neater looking than traditional wires) attached to the wall.

Wall shrubs can add considerably to the appeal of a building, especially if they are regularly maintained to keep a straight outline and a flat surface-hugging aspect. They can also serve to hide an unattractive surface, and thick growth may have a considerable ability to protect the building from extremes of weather. In central Europe, for example, columnar conifers such as cypress or *Picea omorika* are occasionally planted close to houses to provide a sheltering windbreak. (*Picea omorika* is very tolerant of shallow soils and to some extent of air pollution.)

An unusual use of fruit trees trained as self-supporting espaliers used to create screening for a veranda.

Photograph by Fritz Wassmann

Nevertheless the high maintenance requirement needs to be borne in mind, especially where heights of more than two stories create difficulties of access.

Fruit trees trained as espaliers are sometimes seen used as a façade-greening option in mainland Europe. The results can be very elegant, especially in winter with the branches highlighted against a wall. However, for traditional varieties, regular and expert pruning will be needed, and so installation of such an option is recommended only if this is assured. Modern miniature varieties, such as 'Ballerina', need only very low maintenance.

DESIGNING FAÇADE GREENING

The design of façade greening can be seen as potentially fulfilling two broad criteria: one being to hide ugly or boring surfaces and the other to enhance existing features. With the former, the requirement for most situations is to simply encourage the plants to cover as much of the surface as possible, whereas with the latter much greater care needs to be taken.

It is often possible to enhance existing features using climbers; for example, horizontal or vertical supports can emphasize the lines of the architecture. Columns can be created using narrow bands of vertical supports; twining climbers such as *Aristolochia* or *Wisteria* are often the most successful to use for these. On a wide or long façade, such columns repeated at regular intervals can create a striking effect. Corner plantings can be particularly effective. Horizontal runs of growth can also be used, between rows of windows, for example, but given that climbers all want to go up rather than along, more attention needs to be given to training. Climbers that use tendrils, such as *Vitis* species, are more suitable than twiners. Ramblers, which initially at least need to have their main shoots tied to supports, are particularly effective for long runs of horizontal planting, but they are liable to produce many side shoots which arch out and downwards for considerable distances. Climbers can often be lead around windows and doors to cover large areas of wall or be lead up tall vertical supports to then run free on a larger expanse above the top of the support. If there is a complex pattern of supports on a building, however, it is essential that there are clear routes for the plants to run from one to another.

Traditionally, trellis has often been used to offer support, with the design of the trellis itself playing an important part in the overall design. Complementary colours can be an effective way of achieving this, for example, a blue trellis against a yellow wall. With an increasing range of support systems available, however, it is now more feasible to build a less visible network of supports.

When designing façade greening, one must bear in mind that during the winter the structure of the supports and the bare branches are all that will be seen. In many climates it is traditional to use evergreens on the side facing away from the sun and deciduous climbers on the sunny side, so that the latter will shade the wall and windows in the summer but allow solar heating to warm the wall and the sun to enter the windows in the winter.

Young wisteria plants on a large trellis, where heavy-duty members support a network of finer wires, to which the plants attach themselves.

STRUCTURES TO SUPPORT
LARGE CLIMBERS

Key to the success and safety of façade greening is the selection of appropriate support systems for the plants and their correct installation. In cases where the plants are to exceed two storeys in height, professional advice should be sought. It is easy to get carried away with the visual and ecological possibilities of façade greening, leaving out a proper consideration of the technical issues concerned, with potentially serious long-term problems. It is crucial that knowledge of plant sizes and habits of growth are related to the capacities of the support system.

The maximum height that can be realistically greened is 24 m (78 ft), or around eight storeys. Although some climbers may reach up to 30 m (98 ft), it is unwise to rely on them reaching this height. Planting on balconies can extend the height at which they are used, although only large containers that are well supplied with nutrients or hydroponic systems can support extensive growth. It is common sense to design façade greening that avoids plants obscuring windows or other light-transmitting surfaces or decorative façades. There may well be issues over the greening of historic buildings, both from physical and heritage perspectives. Self-clinging climbers can do particular damage to heritage buildings as it is extremely difficult to remove marks left by pulled-off suckers or aerial roots.

Materials

Modern façade greening relies on high tensile steel cables, trellis, spacers, and ancillary equipment. Nevertheless smaller scale or domestic projects, up to two or three storeys, may be carried out with traditional materials.

Wooden trellis—When suitably treated, wood may last for twenty-five years as a trellis material. Traditionally, wooden trellis was a support for climbers on houses in France and Germany, and its strong outlines were a decorative feature in their own right. Wooden trellis may be painted with weatherproof paint or a tinted preservative, but in time the material will peel or fade. Once covered in climbers repainting is

Two versions of traditional wooden trellis: (left) discrete areas of wall are covered to give support to *Vitis vinifera*, here shown after pruning in winter, and (right) where trellis is constructed in situ to cover a whole wall, providing support for both twining climbers and for wall shrubs, which can be tied to it.

not generally a viable option. If renovation or renewal of a wooden trellis is ever needed, ramblers and tendril and leaf-twining climbers can, if necessary, be removed from the old woodwork and reattached to the new. With twiners, however, this is not possible.

Under very dense growth, wooden trellis is liable to decay more rapidly than when exposed, especially in high-rainfall climates. Positioning it well away from the wall can help increase airflow and hence reduce decay. The type of timber used and the way it is prepared can have a major impact on how long it lasts. Timbers such as larch, oak, *Robinia pseudacacia*, or elm will last the longest. Wood that is cleaved, rather than cut, will throw water off and help prevent decay.

Metal trellis—Corrosion-proof metal trellis is a long-lasting alternative to wood, and if designed well it can be a visual feature in its own right. Stainless steel is an obvious material to rely on. Galvanized steel products may be used but quality can vary enormously. The minimum thickness recommended is 55 mm and a coating of zinc at 380 g per square metre (1.14 oz per square foot), which will last for ten to twenty years in city conditions, considerably longer in the country, but only five to ten years in polluted industrial or coastal situations (Köhler 1993). Products painted with corrosion-protective paint or cold galvanized are not durable enough to be recommended. Note, however, that in acidic polluted environments, corroded zinc will add to heavy metal pollution.

In areas where air pollution or sea spray create a particularly corrosive environment, stainless steel or aluminium are the best materials. Plastic-coated products, designed for long-term exterior use, may also be used. Where pollution- or salt-induced corrosion are not problems, rebar (steel reinforcing bars) may be used to build trellis structures, with a life span of twenty years plus to be expected. The material is very heavy to put into place but immensely strong, and in the right setting rebar can be attractive. With the support of strong personnel and welding and cutting equipment, it is possible to construct imaginative pergola-type structures that join onto façade greening, enabling climbers to cover both parts. The material lends itself to contemporary, postmodern environments. Steel-reinforcing mesh can also be used, but is not generally thick enough to support large climbers or to be durable long term.

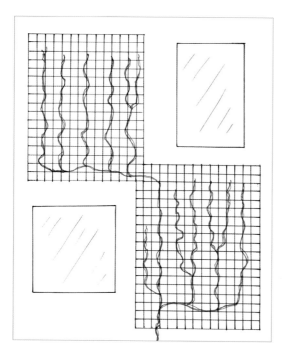

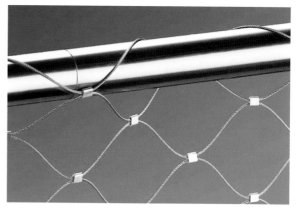

Steel cables can be used to make extremely strong flexible nets which can be stretched between rigid supports, a contemporary method with potentially many applications.

© Jakob AG

Tailor-made trellis is often an effective way of guiding climbers up large areas of blank wall, around windows, or other areas that need to be kept free of growth.

Metal supporting materials can become extremely hot in the sun, leading to shoot damage and stunted growth. Dark and large-diameter supports will absorb more heat, so the use of narrow profile or pale or reflective material is recommended where exposure to sun is an issue. Heat damage is exacerbated by close proximity to the wall. Twining climbers, whose delicate young shoot tips do not touch the support and whose new growth then shades it, are less at risk than tendril and leaf-stem climbers.

Cable and wire—Traditional wire and fixings, known as "vine-eyes," will support climbers to two storeys but become increasingly unsatisfactory above this, especially with large heavy climbers. Wire is usually stretched horizontally between the vine-eyes, usually at around 2-m (6-ft) intervals, with each wire at a spacing of around 30–50 cm (12–20 in). Used either horizontally or vertically, it is very difficult to supply enough tension to get the wire straight, resulting in an amateurish appearance, unless a tightening attachment is used at the end of each run of wire. Large-scale projects need to rely on purpose-designed products.

The advantage of cables (or wire for smaller-scale projects) is that, compared to rigid constructions like trellis or frameworks, they are easy to transport to the site, enable the construction of support over a wide area, and offer great flexibility in design. Rigid frameworks either have to be pre-assembled or constructed on site, which usually involves greater expense in transport and the use of scaffolding and lifting equipment during their erection. High-tensile stainless steel cables offer long-term strength that many wire products cannot offer.

The new generation of steel rope products that are used for vertical supports have been adapted to provide new approaches to trellis construction. Vertical and horizontal ropes stretched across a wall can be connected by cross clamps at the points where they intersect, or two sets of cables may be laid across a wall to intersect diagonally. In either case, the result is a nonrigid trellis. Steel rope can also be used to create a net-type construction which can be stretched between tensioned vertical and horizontal supporting ropes. In some regions, hybrid cables may be available: steel coated with hemp or other natural fibres. Hybrid cables have the advantage of looking attractive when exposed but when the outer coating decays the durable steel core will be hidden in growth.

Plastics and glass fibre—Currently available plastic products rarely have the strength and durability necessary to support plants on sun-baked walls. Glass fibre products, however, have considerable potential as the material has good tensile strength, does not corrode, and is lightweight. Dyes can be added in the manufacturing process to produce different colours, enhancing its design appeal. Specifications recommended for glass fibre cables are a diameter of at least 7.75 mm (0.31 in) and a glass content of 80 per cent with an uneven surface texture or coating to give plants something to grasp (Köhler 1993). The material is expensive, however, and is best limited to situations where its unique combination of strength, flexibility, and weight make it the only suitable option.

Rope—Made of hemp, manila, or other natural materials, ropes offer good adhesion for climbers but simply do not have the durability needed for long-term plantings. For short-term projects or for annuals, rope is a cheap, easy to use, and visually attractive material.

In contrast to traditional horizontal training, a more contemporary training of wisteria uses vertical supports; although suitable only for heights of several storeys, much less work is needed for maintenance.

Photograph by Fritz Wassmann

Constructing supports

For heights greater than two storeys, choosing supports and their installation for climbers moves into engineering rather than horticultural territory. The following material is intended only to outline the main technical issues and provide guidance so that professionals from the construction and engineering trades may make informed decisions. The advice of such professionals is strongly recommended before large projects are undertaken.

Selection of the appropriate method of support depends upon the following factors: climbing mechanism of the plant; plant vigour and eventual size; the degree of exposure to various climatic variables, especially wind and snow; and design factors.

Climbing mechanism of the plant—As discussed earlier, different types of plant climbing mechanisms require different kinds of support. The most essential distinction is between those which can make do with only vertical supports, often the easiest and most elegant solution, and those which need the support of both vertical and horizontal elements in the form of a trellis.

Plant vigour and eventual size—As a general rule the more vigorous the climber the more space it needs between supports. Climbers of average or below average vigour need a denser network of supports to effectively clothe the surface against which they are planted: vertical supports of 20–40 cm (8–16 in) apart or lattices of around 15 × 25 cm (6 × 10 in). Vigorous plants need supports approximately 40–80 cm (16–32 in) apart for vertical cables or lattices of approximately 30 × 40 cm (12 × 16 in). The distance from the wall that the support needs to be varies depending upon the thickness of the plant stems. As a general principle, this is at least 2 cm (0.78 in) wider than the thickest stem characteristic of the species. The following are guidelines:

10 cm (4 in) for those with thin stems, for example, *Akebia*, medium-sized *Clematis*, and *Lonicera*;

15 cm (6 in) for those with thicker stems, for example, *Actinidia* and *Vitis*; and

20 cm (8 in) for large woody climbers, such as *Celastrus* and *Wisteria*.

Degree of exposure to various climatic variables—In calculating what materials are necessary for a safe support system, the following factors need to be considered: plant weight; weight of support system; additional weight of water after rain or dew; additional weight of snow, where this is a likelihood; and the wind load on the plants and structure. Plant weight can vary enormously, between 1 and 50 kg per square metre (0.09 and 4.5 lb per square foot) of plant area. To this must be added the weight of rain and snow loading: for deciduous plants this is plant weight × 2 and for evergreens plant weight × 3.

Wind load results from direct pressure, turbulence, and suction. Wind resistance is least on those climbers with a shallow profile. Plants that build up a considerable pillow of leaves and branching can catch the wind particularly easily, subjecting supports to enormous stresses. In situations where wind may be a problem, it is an important maintenance task to remove such growth.

As a rough guideline, the following values for the various forces exerted on supports should be taken into account: approximately 0.5 kN per square metre for heights up to 8 m (26.4 ft) above ground, 0.8 kN per square metre between 8 and 20 m (26.4 and 66 ft) above ground, and 1.1 kN per square metre above this height. If the entire weight is to be taken only by supports at the top and bottom, then the upper supports must be able to take the entire load plus half the wind load, while lower supports need take only half the wind load (Jakob 2002).

Some climbers which become very large and support themselves by twining (for instance, wisterias) end up by twisting any flexible materials (such as cables) they are attached to, which can pull spacers out of the wall. This can be overcome by the use of an overload clamp at the bottom with an extra length of cable. The clamp is designed so that an extra length of cable can be pulled through the clamp when gripped tightly by the growing climber.

In some public situations there may be a problem with people attempting to climb supports. Where this is a possibility, the supports need to start at a distance above ground which makes it impossible to reach the supports, and the plants need to be led up to the support through a temporary lightweight support.

Modern materials combined
with vigorously growing
climbers can make
extremely durable screening
for industrial installations.

Photographs © Jakob AG

Stainless steel fixings are
used to support extensive
networks of both horizontal
and vertical steel cables in
many modern façade-
greening systems.

Design factors—The aesthetics of the structure may be of importance
and will have consequences for the design. Vertical supports, tensioned
ones especially, are the most minimal, and in many situations, especially on very contemporary buildings, this will mean favouring the use of
twining plants.

Fixings and load bearing

This is a crucially important area. Failure to attach fixings that can take
the weight of the climbers will result in either the failure of the fixing
and possible collapse of the climber and its supports or the wrenching
of the fixing out of the wall, possibly doing considerable structural
damage as it does so. Structural engineers should be consulted regarding fixings if there is any doubt about the ability of a building to support them. Manufacturers of steel cable and other support systems
often can supply technical advice as well, and their catalogues can be an
important source of information in themselves.

The weight of façade greening compared to the weight of a building
is minimal; however, not all walls are designed to be load bearing.

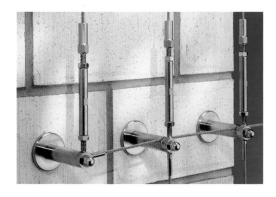

The choice of fixing for cables is of crucial importance. Fortunately, a wide range of tailor made products is now available.

Networks of cable can be constructed by the use of appropriate load-bearing attachments, allowing imaginative structures for the support of climbers to be created.

Traditional stone or brick walls can have load-bearing fixings attached straight into them, although the supports need to be in good condition. Buildings which are clad in any way present greater difficulties, as cladding is not designed to take any loading, although the very widely distributed loading of shallow-profile self-clingers does not present a problem. It is often possible to drill through the cladding to attach supports to a load-bearing surface beneath. Certain kinds of modern construction involve walls that are not load bearing, for example, steel-framed buildings. Timber-framed buildings also include walls that are not load bearing, but fixings may be attached through the outer skin to the framework, although the precise location of the framework must be known. In all these cases where it is not possible for the exterior surface to support any weight, climbers may be supported instead from the ground up on a rigid support or from the top of the building. These methods are discussed in the section below.

Varieties of vertical support system—Loading can be transferred to the structure either through the wall or to particularly secure parts of the building or the ground. Direct wall fixing is a common system of support for vertical elements (see [1] on page 156). It involves using a relatively

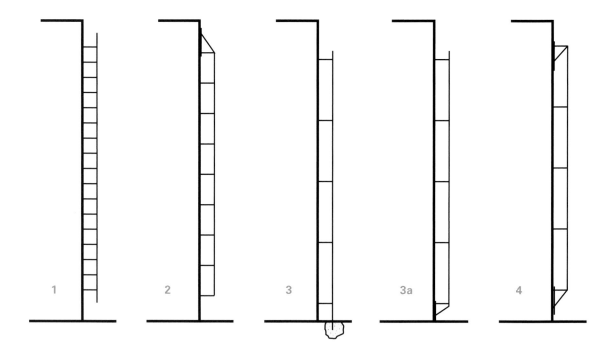

Vertical support systems

rigid bar (of metal or glass fibre) attached by regular rigid fixing points to the side of the building. The weight is carried proportionately by each fixing so that, for example, weight can be carried either by a few very strong fixings or many less strong ones. This system is ideal for surfaces such as stone or concrete, which can take considerable loading.

A hanging system (2) is hung from one very strong fixing at the top of the building using subsidiary lower fixings—not to carry vertical loading but to prevent sideways movement, such as that caused by wind. This system allows the climber to be held further away from a building than direct wall fixings as well as thermal expansion of the vertical element and stretching. It is ideal for situations where the wall itself can take little loading.

Standing a rigid rod upright (3) allows the weight to be taken by the ground, through a suitable foundation (for example, concrete), with fixings to the building taking only horizontal wind loading. Like the hanging system, it is ideal for situations where the wall itself can take little loading. A variation is to use a supporting bracket at the base of the building sufficient to take all vertical loading (3a).

Various tensioning methods can be used to hold rigid a relatively flexible support, such as steel cable or glass fibre (4). Tensioned systems are the most sophisticated option as they minimize the need to have supports up the building, creating a less cluttered look. They are ideal for structures where there is little opportunity for fixings to be inserted into the wall. Using steel cable/rope, this system is finding most favour with contemporary practitioners and is enabling façade greening to make dramatic progress.

HORTICULTURAL ASPECTS OF FAÇADE GREENING

Soils

Climbers tend to not be fussy about soil content and chemistry, generally not preferring acid or alkaline, sands or clays, just so long as it is fertile. Vigorous shoots depend upon healthy roots. Strong growth is demanded of climbers for façade greening, and so deep fertile soils are best, with a constant supply of moisture but never experiencing waterlogging. A high organic matter content helps to hold moisture and nutrients. Consequently, adequate soil preparation is of great importance, especially if the soil is thin or of poor quality. In many cases the foundations of buildings limit root penetration. In itself, this is not a problem because roots can and will find their way to sources of water and better soil. But moisture at least does have to be there, and there must be a pocket of good soil to start the plants off in.

There may be circumstances where there is little good soil at the surface, and plants may be grown in bottomless planters or relatively small areas of quality soil. Their roots may penetrate to considerable depths to extract moisture, but the small size of the soil pocket may restrict growth through a lack of nutrients. Regular feeding will be needed—often best carried out with one of the widely available resin-coated pelleted feeds. These last a whole growing season, releasing nutrients at a rate dependent upon temperature. Regular application of a mulch of well-rotted manure or composted greenwaste helps to keep organic content up.

Buildings often cast a rain shadow, exacerbating the drying effects of foundations. Before committing to planting it is wise to ensure that plants will get adequate moisture, at least until they get to a size when their roots penetrate into deeper soil layers. Irrigation may be necessary. Mulches will also limit dry-season water loss and can even be ornamental, as with the use of stones or pebbles.

Aspect

Conventional garden wisdom describes the ideal position for clematis as having its feet in the cool and its head in the sun. This could be extended to the majority of climbing species, with the exception of those few which are definite shade lovers. It is difficult to generalize about aspect across wide geographical regions, however, and the following are points that should be considered.

With increasing altitude and latitude, temperatures will drop, so a shade plant in one location may grow well in the sun higher up or in more northerly regions. Guidance on aspect should be sought from plant suppliers and horticultural texts written for the locality. For shading purposes, façade greening is often most desirable on the sunny side of a building. However, species chosen must be able to take the full heat of the sun and have adequate, indeed generous, irrigation.

Cold winds either in winter or in spring, when young growth is tender, can do enormous damage, especially to evergreens and species originating from warmer climates than that of the planting site.

There is little doubt that providing a cool root run is very beneficial to all climbers, they are, after all, plants used to having their roots in shaded forest-floor conditions. The best way to do this is to design planting beds so that they are protected from the most direct solar heating. Where this has not happened, mulching with stones is one of the most effective methods.

Combining climbers

Climbers may be combined to scramble together, creating a wild and romantic effect. They need to be carefully matched in vigour, however, otherwise the stronger will overcome the weaker. Aesthetic considerations will play a part in choosing species to put together, too: complementary flowering times to provide a succession of colour or autumn foliage colour alongside spring- or summer-flowering species. Maintenance of mixed climbers is often higher than of separately planted ones, as inevitably one will prove slightly more vigorous and therefore need harder pruning to keep a balance. Of course, it is impossible to exactly predict how a combination will work out.

Planting

As with trees and shrubs, attention to detail at planting time will reap its rewards. No special planting techniques are required for climbers with the exception of self-clinging species, both aerial root and sucker species. Self-clinging species benefit enormously from being encouraged to develop a more extensive root system by letting their stems run along the ground for a year or two before encouraging them to climb, allowing them to develop an extensive root system. They will then climb much more quickly. It is possible that the failure to do this accounts for the widespread reputation of some climbers, particularly species of the Hydrangeaceae, to be so slow growing. Because only young stems produce suckers or roots that can cling, cutting young plants back to the base will also encourage the production of new stems with a strong urge to attach to a vertical surface.

It is debatable whether purchasing extra-large specimens really gives much of an advantage. In many cases younger plants will adapt to new circumstances more quickly, negating the effect of buying a large plant. Self-clinging climbers will never reattach themselves from the aerial roots or suckers on existing stems, and the best thing to do with them on planting is to cut them down to ground level and so encourage production of several vigorous new stems. Plants generally take a year or two to settle down, after which they will start to grow at their normal

A fig (*Ficus carica*) grown as a wall shrub alongside Virginia creeper (*Parthenocissus tricuspidata*) and ivy. Combined climbers can create considerable visual interest.

Photograph by Fritz Wassmann

rate. In the case of larger vigorous species, growth may be as much as 3–4 m (9.9–13.2 ft) per year, resulting in their maximum height, but not thickness of canopy, in as little as five years.

SELECTING CLIMBERS

Plant selection for the garden involves consideration of the suitability of various plants for the site environment as well as aesthetic factors. Façade greening also involves the consideration of various practical factors. As with selecting plants for roof greening, functional concerns clearly outweigh aesthetic ones.

Climate and aspect

Climbers on the side of buildings are subject to climatic extremes, with wind damage a particular potential problem, both through physical buffeting and the wind chill factor. This is liable to increase greatly with height, as exposure may be very much greater at the fourth storey than at the second. Thus, species selection needs to relate to conditions at the height at which the plants will receive the most extreme conditions. Many tall buildings also create turbulence or powerful downdrafts which can exacerbate exposure problems. Above all, one must recognize that wind direction at height may be completely different to that at ground level, either because of turbulence or because adjacent buildings, trees, or the lie of the land protect the observer at ground level from the site's prevailing winds.

The number of climber species increases enormously from cool to warm climate zones, and to a great extent so does the visual appeal. It is therefore a temptation to choose plant species that are not reliably hardy. A frost-damaged climber several storeys high is not a pretty sight, and removal can be expensive. A run of warm winters can be a siren call that lulls the unwary into thinking that they can get away with it. With façade greening it is safest to assume the worst and plan with the hardest winter of the last twenty years in mind.

Size

There is no reason why a climber that can grow eight storeys cannot be put on a two-storey house—after all, the vast majority of wisteria are on buildings of this size—but there has to be provision for at least occasional maintenance. Where it is not possible to guarantee this, the maximum size of the climber must be carefully matched to the size of the building. As a general rule, it is better that supports are larger than the maximum size of the plant, which will reduce the problems of tangled growth and self-strangulation that can occur when supports are too small. Climbers vary considerably in speed of growth, from *Hydrangea petiolaris*, eventually large but only after a long time, to *Fallopia baldschuanica*, one of several species known as mile-a-minute vine. There may be circumstances where speed of coverage is regarded as the most important factor.

The profile of a climber refers to how thick it is, that is, how much it projects from the surface to which it is attached. A narrow profile is essential where space is at a premium, for example, adjacent to pavements. Design considerations also sometimes require a shallow profile because shallow-profile species have a much neater appearance than others.

Support mechanisms

The primary plant choice is between self-clingers and those that need supports. Where either is a practical choice, factors that favour supported climbers include the importance of the support in the overall appearance of the buildings, the need to limit the growth of the climber (the growth of self-clingers is more difficult to constrain), and the visual appearance of the climber. There may be instances where design considerations dictate the use of particular forms of support, maybe even because the support itself is regarded as a design feature. Where only vertical supports are desired, only twiners can be used.

Visual aspects of plant selection

Evergreen climbers are unfortunately few and far between in cool temperate climates. Whereas many climbers have traditionally been grown for their flowers, the foliage is generally more important with façade greening. Fortunately, most available species have good-quality foliage, and the range is getting better all the time, both through new introductions and the selection of improved or distinct cultivars from established species. Many hardy climbers have large and dramatic leaves, for example, species of *Aristolochia*, *Vitis*, and *Actinidia*. Many, too, have autumn foliage that is as good as that of the very finest oaks and maples and, unlike oaks and certain other autumn-colour species, they colour reliably whatever the soil type.

Fruit may be an added visual bonus, or it may have its down side: slippery rotting fruit on the pavement below or a carpet of bird excrement. In the case of some fruiting species, for example, *Actinidia*, plants are single sex, so males may be selected if fruit is not wanted.

Ecological aspects of plant selection

There is a strong presumption that native species are better for wildlife. However, unless a particular species is known to be a food source for particular insect larvae, there is little real ecological advantage to using only native species. There may be a strong ecological disincentive to using non-native species, however, if they could possibly spread and become invasive. Generally, the ecological value of climbers is dependent upon the following factors:

Roosting and nesting space for birds and hibernation opportunities for insects: As a general rule, the thicker the climber and the more twiggy its growth, the more opportunity there is for a variety of wildlife to find a home. Narrow-profile climbers are therefore much less valuable. Thick evergreen climbers are especially valuable as they offer winter protection.

Nectar sources for insects: Flowers are potentially a valuable nectar source, and those which flower very early, such as *Clematis armandii*, or very late, such as *Hedera helix*, are especially valuable.

Fruit for birds and insects: Fruit-bearing vines are a valuable resource for birds during winter months. Fruit can also be a food source for insects, which provides a benefit to insect-eating birds and bats.

PROBLEMS WITH FAÇADE GREENING

Self-clinging climbers and surface damage

Disputes over possible damage to building surfaces caused by climbers has been discussed for over a century, with many in the conventional construction industry expressing the view that self-clinging species are likely to weaken the surface of the building, particular where it consists of a render. The popular wisdom of gardeners, however, is inclined to the opposite view, that self-clinging climbers can actually help preserve surfaces, as they "hold the mortar together."

The survey in Berlin discussed above also involved an inspection of the condition of the render: where self-clinging species were used, 83 per cent of walls were undamaged, 16 per cent showed some damage, and 1 per cent had severe damage (Köhler 1993). Those that showed damage were generally very old or had poor-quality render. Most extensive greening in the past has involved self-clinging species of *Parthenocissus* and *Hedera*, whereas contemporary greening is more focused on the use of cables to support plants at a distance from the surface, so there is no question of plants attaching themselves to the building surface. In addition, most modern cladding materials are not suitable for self-clinging plants to attach themselves, and if the plants are able to, the materials are less likely to be damaged than traditional renders.

Damage caused by self-clinging climbers is most likely to occur when they are pulled off, either because they are dead and unsightly or as part of pruning or trimming operations. The aerial roots or suckers are then liable to either pull off pieces of render or leave behind hairline cracks. Those self-clinging climbers with aerial roots are the only ones that are at all likely to cause damage while still living, owing to the fact that on poor-quality or already decaying render their roots can penetrate cracks and widen them.

Walls that are clad with tiles, shingles, or similar materials are generally regarded as unsuitable for aerial root climbers, because of the danger of the plants rooting behind such materials. Where tiles are loose other types of climbers, such as twiners, may send stray shoots into gaps behind the tile, resulting in contorted growth behind the tile levering it away from the wall. The same can happen to large sheets of cladding if there is any possibility of shoots getting behind or between them.

Although self-clinging climbers may not do the damage many think they are capable of, they can undeniably create a variety of inconveniences. Because they are unconstrained by any kind of framework, self-clinging climbers are free to go where they will, which can mean into gutters, eaves, or over windows, necessitating annual pruning, which may create problems of access. Where there is any well-founded concern over possible damage or inconvenience, it would be advisable to grow climbers that use supports.

More general problems

Potential damage to buildings or climber support systems has been extensively studied in Germany, with different species evaluated for different risks (Brandwein and Köhler 1993). Damage occurs for a variety of reasons:

supports are installed that are too small for the species used;

supports are installed of insufficient strength;

supports are not adequately fixed to the building;

allowances are not made for growth, particularly the development of thick stems;

climbers and supports are properly installed but cause damage to failing building surfaces;

maintenance is insufficient for the size of the supports, leading to:

self-strangulation and unattractive growth;

tangled growth, leading to masses of projecting stems causing over loading and additional wind loading; and

shoots going where they are not intended to, such as over windows and into gutters.

Increasing stem girth is the cause of some of the more intractable problems. Large climbers often build up stems and branches of considerable thickness—up to 45 cm (18 in) in diameter in the case of *Wisteria* species. If supports are not far enough away from the wall, large climbers can lever the supports or fixings away. The thickest trunk development will occur at the base, and the design of supports, particularly rigid ones like trellises, needs to allow for possible removal, repositioning, or detachment when plants reach maturity.

Climbers can also penetrate failing expansion joints and any other cracks and crevices that open up in aging or poorly built façades. While a thin shoot will do little damage, as it grows it will exert considerable forces sideways, which can tear apart whatever is on either side. Shoots, particularly those of aerial root climbers and strong twiners, can continue to grow in the dark for some distance, especially if there is light at the other end—up to 7 m (23.1 ft) under roof panels.

Ivy and ruins go together in the imagination like strawberries and cream. But what of allowing large ivy plants to grow on buildings that are still in use? The conventional wisdom, outlined in this book, is that ivies will cause no damage on surfaces where their aerial roots cannot penetrate. However, they may cause damage if the roots can enter cracks in, for example, crumbling mortar, the small aerial roots then growing into true roots, with the result that the ivy becomes a semi-lithophyte, actually rooted into the fabric of the house. More unconventional builders have suggested that in fact where this has happened, it may be better to leave the ivy in situ and manage it to prevent further growth rather than remove it. A living ivy plant will hold together the structure its roots have penetrated very effectively, whereas removal would have to be followed by complete rebuilding of the area affected. Ivy foliage throws rainwater off the building and roots serve to remove all moisture from the fabric of the building. There is, then, a possibly good case to argue that where ivy has taken a hold it is doing a very good job in keeping the building secure and dry (Randall 2003).

Plants encouraging a damp atmosphere on the walls to which they are attached is another worry that is occasionally voiced. However, the evidence suggests climbers, at least while they are in leaf, actually throw rainwater off the wall, thus reducing humidity at the wall surface (Köhler 1993). As just noted, ivy, being evergreen, is particularly useful for this (Rose 1996).

Much like young children, very vigorous climbers may grab hold of things they are not meant to: window fittings, drainpipes, exposed cables. One of the functions of regular maintenance is to prevent this happening. As a general rule, very large strong-growing climbers cause more problems than less vigorous ones but only because they are planted in situations where there is opportunity to cause damage. Yet, to restrict them to situations where there is no possibility of anything going wrong is to unduly limit exciting visual opportunities. No one would ever have planted a wisteria on a house, and we would all be very much poorer. The answer is regular maintenance and an assessment at the planning stage of how frequent and skilled maintenance will need to be. The more restricted the site and the more the opportunities for problems, the more frequently maintenance will be required.

Another concern, closely related to concerns over trees—often fuelled by overanxious insurance companies—is that of damage to foundations or drainage systems. Certain trees, willows and poplars particularly, are noted for causing subsidence to buildings through drying out soil, but no climbing species is noted for extracting comparable quantities of water from the atmosphere. Root damage to foundation or cellar walls is not unknown but is extremely rare, while cases of damage to pipes is limited to old and already failing systems (Köhler 1993). Root entry into drainage pipes around buildings is a potential problem, however.

MAINTENANCE

A programme of regular inspection and maintenance of façade greening is essential. With good planning and implementation, however, an annual inspection is often all that is needed and can be included in the annual inspection generally carried out by anyone responsible for the fabric of a building. In the case of domestic houses and smaller buildings, responsible owners and tenants always keep an eye out for problems in any case. Issues such as creepers entering gutters, getting too close to eaves, and vines grabbing hold of window fittings are all easily noticeable in the normal course of life.

Young climbers or those on new buildings should be inspected every two years. Large ones, or those that are close to installations which could be damaged, should be inspected annually. Supports and fixings need to be checked at least every five years (Arbeitskreis 'Fassadenbegrünung' 2000). Essential maintenance tasks comprise:

training plants and tying onto supports, if necessary;
pruning shoots going in the wrong direction or which might grab hold of gutters or cables, or thinning out overly thick or tangled growth; unattractive loops of growth that stick outwards should be removed as well, as they may eventually put considerable leverage stress on the support;
clearing shoots and debris out of gutters; and
cutting back shoots that are near sites where they could penetrate between materials in the building, for example, under tiles, cladding, or roofs.

Façade greening does not present an appreciable fire risk, although it is possible that if large quantities of dead material (leaves, twigs, branches) were to accumulate, then a localized risk is possible.

THE FUTURE OF PLANT SELECTION

To date façade greening has been developed in central Europe, mostly using plant species native to North America and eastern Asia. The same species proven successful can therefore be expected to be successful in all cool temperate climate zones. As the nursery trade actively seeks out new species and selects cultivars and breeds (deliberately or otherwise), the façade-greening industry will no doubt benefit. Arguably, there is a need for more adventurous plant selection. Those involved with plant selection need to pay attention to selecting new taxa on the basis of several characteristics: the visual qualities of the foliage, the colour, texture, and leaf shape. In many cases the garden centre and nursery trade can be relied upon to come up with an endless range of improvements in this respect. Plant size and vigour must also be considered. It would be very convenient for specifiers if there was a greater range of plant sizes within a particular species or species group. Where several cultivars of a species are grown, for example, *Clematis montana*, it is well known that they vary enormously in eventual size. Whereas most conventional selection concentrates on flowering and purely aesthetic qualities, façade greening needs a greater concentration on selecting on the basis of growth habit and functionality.

It is something of a mystery—a result no doubt of geological history and the ebb and flow of the glaciers during the ice ages—that the geographical distribution of cool temperate climbers is so varied. The number of large climbers native to Europe can practically be counted on one hand, whereas North America has many more, and eastern Asia is a veritable treasure trove. There is little doubt that façade greening will benefit enormously from the introduction of new species and new forms of species already in cultivation from this region. Much valuable work is being done in this respect by Bleddyn and Sue Wynne-Jones, who run a nursery in Wales and have established important links with botanists and others in eastern Asia, bringing many new taxa into the nursery trade (*Crûg Farm Nursery Catalogue* 2003).

New species offer exciting and dramatic possibilities for the visual enhancement of buildings, while the introduction of new forms and the selection of new cultivars and hybrids will allow greater precision in specifying plants. In many species in cultivation, only one geographical variant is commercially available, and in some cases all the plants in horticulture are clonal. The importance of collecting a range of geographical races from the wild and making them commercially available can be appreciated from the following list of characteristics relevant to façade greening:

Variations in hardiness may be considerable within the species' natural range of latitude and altitude. Continentality may also be a factor. Provenance is thus of great importance in plant selection.

Size, vigour, and growth habit may vary across a species' range. In some cases, climbing mechanisms themselves may vary within a species, for example, with geographical races having a greater or lesser number of adhesive tendrils in the case of *Parthenocissus* species.

Visual factors, such as leaf shape and flower colour, often vary considerably.

The use of non-native species can sometimes lead to problems. One of the worst examples of a runaway species concerns a climber, a salutary and appropriate reminder for those involved in façade greening. In the early twentieth century the kudzu vine, *Pueraria lobata*, was introduced from Japan into the south-eastern United States to control erosion. Having naturalized, this extremely aggressive climber has smothered whole tracts of woodland, even houses, and proved very difficult to eradicate. Other problem climbers include *Lonicera japonica* and *Celastrus orbiculata*. Both these species have spread via birds eating their fruit. Before widespread planting of new species, an assessment needs to be made of the likelihood for it to spread through the transportation of seed.

FAÇADE GREENING IN
WARM CLIMATE ZONES

The opportunities for façade greening in warm climate zones are enough to make practitioners in cool temperate climbers weak at the knees. The range of species is vastly greater, with a mind-boggling selection of every imaginable flower and leaf colour and shape. In addition many, if not most, warm-climate climbers grow very large.

The need for shade and the cooling of buildings is of course vastly greater in warm climates. Undoubtedly, there is enormous potential for considerably improving the quality of life of those who live in warm climate zones through the extensive use of pergolas to shade walkways and recreation areas and of climbers on buildings to facilitate cooling, shading, and a reduction in air-conditioner use.

However, there are also problems that have to be overcome. One concerns irrigation, at least in those climates which experience seasonal drought. Many large climbers are used to having their roots in the cool shade of the forest, and the high temperatures and reduction in soil moisture at the foot of buildings is a problem that will need to be addressed. Another concern is the danger posed by venomous snakes and spiders having better access to buildings, and the problems of public acceptability posed by the mere thought of these creatures lurking in undergrowth right next to open office windows. In many cases this is a question of design, and in regions where dangerous animals are an issue, the clear separation of climbing plants and people may be required. Nevertheless, if these problems can be overcome, there is the possibility that warm-climate façade greening may become one of the most exciting and dynamic areas of horticulture and landscape design in the twenty-first century.

Indoor greening

Many warm-climate species can be used indoors if there is enough light. They can play a major role in improving office environments, as the plants absorb and break down potentially toxic volatile organic compounds and help to cool the air. Fundamentally important, however, is plants' role in raising humidity levels to the 45–65 per cent necessary for comfort and respiratory health at comfortable working temperatures of 20–22°C (68–72°F). Plants are good for the psyche as well, and it has been found that absenteeism is reduced in green offices.

Vigorous foliage plants (for instance, *Rhoicissus rhomboidea*, *Tetrastigma voinierianum* and *Cissus* species) have been found to be most effective and easy to care for in office environments where light levels are 1000–1500 lux. *Ficus pumila* is highly effective as a self-clinger, and on rough concrete *Philodendron* species can be used as well. Flowering plants such as *Thunbergia grandiflora*, *Mandevilla suaveolens*, and *Tecomaria capensis* need higher light levels, 2000 lux and above (Wassmann 2003).

Indoor greening is a new area of enormous potential, especially as increasing numbers of people spend more and more of their lives inside. Given the scale of many modern buildings, climbers and façade-greening techniques will have a major role to play.

CHAPTER 6

Living Walls, Structures, and Surfaces

In chapter 5 we looked at covering walls or other vertical structures with climbers that were rooted in soil or some sort of growing medium at the base of the wall, whether natural or in containers, and which covered the wall through a self-clinging mechanism or with the aid of physical supports. In this chapter we look at covering walls and other structures with vegetation that is either rooted within those structures or is able to survive independently on the structure without the need to root in surrounding soil. Specifically, we shall consider various types of living walls, the use of vegetation mats, vegetated retaining structures, and other types of what is often called "ecotechnology." Many of the things we shall discuss are routinely used in engineering applications such as slope stabilization, highway boundaries, and the containment of stream and riverbanks. Because they involve the use of vegetation to solve problems usually tackled with concrete and heavy machinery, these techniques have come to be known as "bioengineering." Both ecotechnology and bioengineering techniques are usually employed in a functional manner, achieving a specific job in the most efficient way. Although fairly widely used in their particular contexts, they have rarely made the jump into designed urban landscapes where visual appeal assumes more importance. The techniques do, however, offer much creative potential, especially where space is limited or flat space is at a premium.

Richly planted dry stone retaining wall, Sleightholmdale Lodge, Yorkshire, England.

WALL PLANTING

Over the last century, we have lost our taste for planted walls, perhaps preferring the pristine clean lines of modern constructed structures instead of what might be seen as the more chaotic and fuzzy outlines of walls covered in vegetation. The situation was rather different in Britain at the turn of the twentieth century when the Arts and Crafts movement, fuelled by romantic visions of the traditional cottage garden, encouraged garden walls to become obscured by billowing cushions of trailing and mounded plants. Indeed one of the towering horticultural figures of the time, William Robinson, devoted a separate section of his classic book, *The English Flower Garden*, which guided a whole generation of gardeners, to wall planting. In fact, he considered walls in some ways to be a better setting for alpines than the artfully constructed rock garden because the limited soil and harsh conditions of the wall environment meant that there was little danger of the alpine plants becoming overrun by weeds. A further testimony to the popularity of wall planting was the publication in 1901 of *Wall and Water Gardens* by the other dominant horticultural figure of the period, Gertrude Jekyll, who created often elaborate sunken and terraced gardens through the extensive use of planted dry stone walls. Her famous collaboration with the architect Edwin Lutyens overturned many of the ground rules of the Victorian age by deliberately perforating retaining walls and leaving spaces in the joints of paving and steps for Jekyll's planting (Bisgrove 1992). This legacy has again largely been forgotten, swept away by the purity of the modernists, and we are now left with the suburban rockery as the rather dismal memory of former times.

In this chapter we consider three main types of wall or vertical planting: retaining walls where plants can root into material behind the wall façade, retaining walls where the rooting medium for the plants is contained within the wall structure, and vegetation layers that are independent of the main wall structure. Of course, walls can be two dimensional, having only one visible surface, as is the case with standard retaining walls or building façades, or they can be three dimensional, as in the case of free standing screens or dividing structures, where in effect the wall has an exposed front and back.

Dry stone walls

These are part of the traditional or vernacular landscape of many parts of the world and, because they are generally made from stone from the immediate vicinity, help convey a sense of local distinctiveness to that landscape. For that reason it is often desirable to use local stone, where appropriate, for new dry stone wall construction. Dry or battered walls are particularly appropriate for planting because the joints between the stones are not mortared. Thus, there is plenty of opportunity for plants to root back into the wall itself. While free-standing dry stone walls may colonize with plants in time, any vegetation growth is likely to be rather sparse because, unless pockets of soil or substrate can be incorporated into the structure of the wall, there is very little rooting material available for plant growth. There is much greater scope for vegetation establishment where the wall is retaining soil behind it and plant roots can reach back into this. Unmortared vertical retaining walls are only safe up to a certain height (usually 1 m, 3 ft) before there is a danger of collapse. To achieve greater stability, dry stone retaining walls should be constructed at an angle (approximately 5 cm [2 in] for every 12 cm [4.8 in] in height) for optimal plant growth. This not only gives greater strength to the wall but also enables rainwater to percolate down to the roots of any plants growing in the wall (Bisgrove 1992).

Stacked constructions and modular walls

Dry stone walls stay upright because of careful placement of interlocking stones, jigsaw fashion. If free standing, they will only be able to reach a certain height before becoming unstable, even if on a slope. This is because these unmortared constructions are basically held together by gravity and become top heavy when too tall. By stacking wider flat material such as stone flags or paving slabs at an angle, however, it is possible to build much larger structures. The supreme example of this is the work of the Dutch architect Louis G. LeRoy, who from the 1960s onwards has had a profound influence on ecological design in The Netherlands. He has been a powerful advocate of community participation in neighbourhood design and developed a

trademark approach in open spaces of creating piles and structures of bricks, rubble, and tipped material that, as well as being fostering grounds for imaginative children's play, were allowed to colonize and vegetate spontaneously, as a metaphor for the relentless power and movement of nature. Today, there remains a tradition in The Netherlands among ecologically inclined gardeners (of which there are many) of using waste brick and tile structures to support free-growing vegetation. Ironically, while these can be chaotic affairs, LeRoy's crowning glory and life work, the EcoCathedral, situated in a field at Mildam in the north of Holland, is a strictly ordered and geometric creation. The EcoCathedral has taken thirty years to build to date and is planned to be continued by future generations until the year 3000. It is constructed entirely of demolition materials—bricks and pavers from a nearby town—the material is tipped on site at regular intervals. Once built, the structures are left to colonize naturally by vegetation, together with some judicious planting. Spaces within raised three-dimensional structures built with this approach are filled with crushed smaller material such as bricks or tiles, and these again make a suitable basis for specialized plant growth.

The principle of stacking is also utilized in modular wall systems, or stacked retaining walls. These systems consist of interlocking, dry-stacked precast concrete blocks of varying dimensions with holes inside them that can be filled with gravel and compacted soil. The modules often feature small precast holes through which steel rods can be inserted for added reinforcement. Such modular walls are being used increasingly to retain slopes and embankments along highways or as noise control barriers. But they can also be used to raise land against a slope to enable construction to occur there. There is no need for a slope to be present—the interlocking systems can be used to create free-standing structures of varying shapes.

Because each module can be filled with soil they can be planted, often with hardy shrubs and vines, or seeded with grass mixes. Because the walls are usually specified by engineers, however, the range of planting options has yet to be fully utilized. These modular systems have the same advantages of dry stone retaining walls in that, because they are not totally sealed surfaces, there is no build up of hydrostatic pressure behind them. Conventional sealed retaining walls (such as vertical

Top left: Detail of Louis G. Leroy's EcoCathedral.

Top right: Stacked wall of bricks, tiles and clay pipes, with sedums growing along the top. Oase Garden, Holland.

Bottom left: Stacked walls of reclaimed paving slabs create a sunken garden.

Bottom right: Dry stacked retaining walls optimize opportunities for growing alpines. Design by Wolfram Kircher.

concrete walls) require massive reinforcement as a counter to this pressure, as well as extensive drainage systems to remove water. Because the faces of modular walls are totally plantable, the wall itself can be quickly hidden by vegetation and there is a further advantage that the wall becomes graffiti-proof.

Gabions

The examples above rely on gravity to maintain their structure. Rocks can be held in place in vertical structures without the help of gravity by placing them in wire baskets which themselves then become walling units. These rock-filled wire baskets are called gabions and are similar to structures used by the ancient Egyptians to stabilize riverbanks, only in this instance baskets were filled with reeds. Gabions are commonly used in slope stabilization or for retaining embankments, but they are also used as an alternative to bricks and blocks in some situations where walls are required. Gabions are usually left unvegetated, or in less formal situations such as riverbanks left to colonize spontaneously with vegetation—often this means that vigorous vegetation adjacent to the gabions encroaches on them and hides them.

Gabions are not ideal planting structures because there are usually large gaps and air spaces between the rocks. In time they will revegetate as the structure collects soil and the airborne or waterborne seeds of local vegetation, thereby creating a locally appropriate planting. Planting can be fostered by filling the visible face of the gabion basket with rocks and then backfilling with soil or using a mix of rock sizes when filling the gabions. Alternatively, the top of gabion structures can be planted by filling the top 10–15 cm (4–6 in) with a suitable growing medium.

Vegetation can be established more rapidly by the use of gabion mattresses. These are shallow gabion structures lined with geotextile and filled with a mix of stones, rocks, and growing substrate. A filter mat is placed on top before the lid of the gabion is attached. The entire structure can then be seeded with grass or a meadow seed mix, or the gabion can be planted with seedlings or plug plants inserted through the fibre mat.

Top left: This stacked modular wall blends seamlessly into the surrounding desert landscape.

Top right: Stacked modular walls enable planting to be established on near vertical surfaces.

Centre left: English ivy and Virginia creeper root freely into this modular, soil filled wall.

Centre right: Modular walls enable awkward spaces and slopes to be stabilized and vegetated.

Photographs by Soil Retention Systems, Inc., California

These gabions, containing regularly sized blocks, make an attractive wall in themselves and are enhanced by wall plants placed in planning pockets within the wall.

Mortared walls

The difference between a mortared wall and a dry stone wall is that the components of the wall, whether they be natural stone or man-made material such as brick, are held together by mortar and therefore present a sealed surface and barrier to plant establishment and growth. Mortared walls do, however, enable greater height to be achieved (provided adequate foundations have been installed). Planted mortared walls are a rarity, particularly in contemporary constructions. An exception is the remarkable 300-m (990-ft) length retaining wall in the Grift Park in Utrecht, The Netherlands. This wall (2 m, 6.6 ft) in height, has been constructed in brick with regular unmortared gaps between bricks into which plug plants have been inserted. The plants used are a mix of dry meadow native species (such as lady's bedstraw, *Galium verum*), alpines and succulents (sedums and sempervivums), and typical wall-growing species (for instance, *Antirrhinum* and *Centranthus ruber*).

While all the structures discussed above, both mortared and unmortared, exist as free-standing entities or as retaining walls, they also have many applications against buildings, as a means of creating a vegetated façade in front of an existing wall. As with a green roof, the important factor here is to ensure that the original building wall is protected against moisture and damage from plant roots, through the use of a protective waterproof membrane or liner. The retaining wall structure is then built up in front of the original wall and backfilled with growing medium. As with green-roof media, the material should be lightweight and free draining. If the facing structure is to be taller than 1 m (3.3 ft) then foundations must be installed and some form of reinforcement at the front, such as a metal grid or batons, will be necessary to prevent collapse. Irrigation may be needed where thin substrate layers are being used. This can be introduced at the top of the structure, possibly as rainfall from overlying roofs and the water allowed to percolate down.

Top left: The richly planted wall in Grift Park, Utrecht, The Netherlands, is 300 m (990 ft) long.

Top right: Many plants in the wall are familiar alpines or wall plants: rockroses, harebells, wall flowers, sedums, houseleeks.

Lower left: *Sempervivum*, *Sedum*, and *Campanula* planted into mortar-free gaps in the wall.

LIVING WALLS

So far we have looked at vertical structures that to the eye are clearly part composed of hard construction materials and part composed of vegetation. But it is also possible to create vegetated walls that are composed completely of vegetation. These so-called living walls employ plants that are rooted into some sort of growing medium on the outward face of the wall, rather than behind the façade of the wall as in the previous examples. Like green roofs, such vertical gardens exploit previously underutilized upright structures. And in some ways their construction and mode of operation is similar to green-roof technology. In this section we will look at three related approaches: hydroponic systems, vegetation mats, and living fences.

Hydroponic systems

The concept of hydroponic systems to create living walls was pioneered by the French researcher and designer Patrick Blanc, who was an internationally celebrated tropical botanist long before developing his living plant walls. Blanc's research led him to discover the many ways that plants exploit vertical surfaces in humid environments, whether it be a tropical forest or the rock face behind a waterfall, and how they are able to survive in the absence of soil. Blanc sought to reproduce this effect for buildings and boundary walls. The method he uses is based upon the horticultural practice of hydroponics, or growing plants without soil using balanced nutrient solutions to provide all the plant's food and water requirements. His systems involve the use of an outer layer of propagation felt or capillary matting that is fixed over a waterproof PVC sheet that isolates the wall structure from the vegetation supporting felt. The entire system is very thin: around 13 mm (0.5 in; Hill 2001). Small young plants are placed into pockets cut into the felt blanket. The plants root into the felt and help reinforce its structure. The system is kept constantly moist through a drip irrigation system that provides all the requirements for successful growth of the plants. Such systems can be put on the front of existing building walls or created on free-standing structures. Two well-known examples by Blanc in Paris include a large installation in the Parc de Bercy and a façade at the Foundation Cartier.

Blanc uses large-leaved plants, many of them evergreen, to produce a lush, tropical effect (the opposite of the drought-resistant flora of the dry stone wall). Typical plants include *Ficus* and *Salix*, with sun-seeking species such as *Buddleja globosa* near the top of the wall and more shade-tolerant ferns, saxifrages, mosses, and lichens at the base. Once established, maintenance is limited to annual clipping and removal of dead foliage. These walls are clearly intensive in their resource requirements and water dependence, but produce a spectacular effect.

Vegetation mats

We have already discussed the idea of vegetation mats as a means of introducing the plant layer onto a green roof. Although the technology

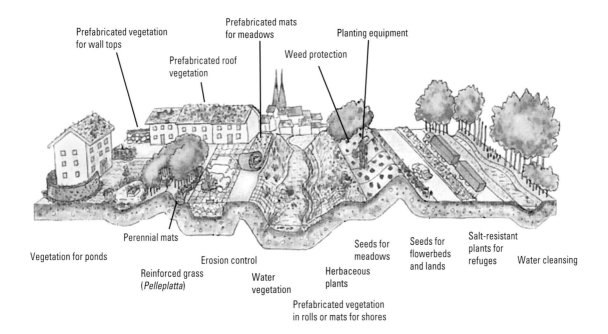

Prefabricated vegetation for wall tops

Prefabricated mats for meadows

Planting equipment

Prefabricated roof vegetation

Weed protection

Vegetation for ponds

Perennial mats

Erosion control

Reinforced grass (*Pelleplatta*)

Water vegetation

Herbaceous plants

Prefabricated vegetation in rolls or mats for shores

Seeds for meadows

Seeds for flowerbeds and lands

Salt-resistant plants for refuges

Water cleansing

has largely been developed for this application, it is suitable for any application where vegetation might be required where there is no direct link between plants and underlying soil. In fact, lateral thinking opens up a very wide range of potential uses for these vegetation mats.

Because of their development for green-roof technology, most vegetation mats consist of drought-resistant sedums. These require sun for best performance, but are not, as many people assume, completely drought resistant. The wall environment is in some ways even more harsh than a rooftop, being potentially completely free draining and often in the rain shadow of a building and therefore not receiving a great deal of direct rainfall. Add to that the buffeting effect of wind, and plant growth on a thin layer of substrate becomes difficult. In addition there is the effect of shade on the lower portions of the wall, again causing problems for sun-requiring species. Vertical sedum walls are being seen on demonstration and show gardens and appear very lush and pristine, but their success in the long term is not guaranteed, unless permanent irrigation is available to help the vegetation through dry periods. As well as the pinning of the mats to the supporting structure behind, netting stretched tight along the front of the wall will help prevent bulging and hold the vegetation in place.

The applications of ecotechnology and the creative use of vegetation in built developments offers boundless possibilities, as this diagram from the Swedish green-roof company VegTech indicates.

Drawing by VegTech

The use of sedum vegetation mats for ground cover between tram lines is relatively common-place in some European cities.

Right: Sea thrift, *Armeria maritima*, a good green-roof plant, is used here in a similar exposed, harsh environment.

Photographs by VegTech

Angling the support structure for the vegetation mat will help overcome shading and water-capture problems. There is more chance of success for vegetation mats at ground level—they are seen relatively commonly in some European cities along pavements or sidewalks as a low maintenance ground cover beneath light trees or as infill between tramlines for example. There is no reason why vegetation mats should be restricted to sedum or green-roof communities—research is currently being conducted in Germany into the use of mats as a means of establishing presown and germinated meadow mixtures of both native and exotic plants. There is really little difference in considering these options for establishing flowering herbaceous vegetation and establishing lawn grass through turf or sod.

Living fences

Most of the vegetated structures discussed above are one-dimensional in that they present a single face to the viewer, whether it be the façade of a building or the edge of a bank or slope. All can be converted into three-dimensional structures for screening or dividing spaces as a living alternative to fences or trellis. That is, of course, what a hedge does. But in some circumstances a different structure may be more appropriate. For example, it may not be possible to establish woody plants in the ground—where the screen is over a hard surface or off the ground, such as on a balcony or roof. A screen or structure that is not rooted to the ground can be moved around. There may be less maintenance involved

Left: Stone hedge with a topping of spontaneously colonized meadow.

Stone hedge with a turf top.

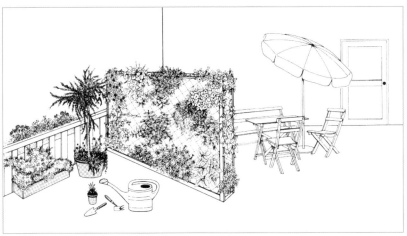

Self-contained living walls can be constructed using lightweight growing media held back by geotextiles within a metal or wood grid or framework.

© Eugen Ulmer GmbH & Co, Stuttgart.

than with a hedge—the living fence will stay the same size and it can also give instant impact. There is also the possibility of changing the planting in an artificial structure.

Living fences consist of a supporting framework which keeps the whole structure upright, vegetation layers, and internal growing medium.

This sloping, double-sided triangular stacked structure makes an impressive living fence, colonized with red valerian (*Centranthus ruber*) at the Centre for Alternative Technology, Wales.

The tops of walls also provide opportunities for growing plants as well as the sides.

They are in effect a sandwich of substrate between vegetation layers. As such they are a designed version of traditional hedges of the west country in the British Isles, where dry stone walls enclose a central core of soil, and which, because of their free-draining, infertile nature, become rich vegetated habitats.

There are innumerable ways in which living fences, or "fedges," may be constructed. Timber frameworks can hold wire grid sections which contain the substrate on each side. A geotextile mat must be used to stop the substrate spilling through the holes in the grid. Slits cut into the geotextile allow plants to be inserted into the walls. Again, irrigation during very dry periods is essential to maintain vegetation cover. On a large scale, noise protection barriers along highways and railway lines are constructed along similar principles, with galvanized metal grid elements linked together to form upright screens filled with subsoil and covered with vegetation.

PLANTS FOR WALLS AND
VERTICAL STRUCTURES

Most of the plants that are suitable for green roof planting will be successful as wall plants, particularly the lower growing and creeping plants: mountain pinks (*Dianthus*), harebells (*Campanula*), alpine wall flowers (*Cheiranthus*), toadflax, wall ferns, alpine phloxes, stonecrops, houseleeks, thymes, *Corydalis*, sea thrift (*Armeria*), and cranesbills and storksbills (*Geranium* and *Erodium*). Walls are also very suitable for species with a more trailing habit, such as *Alyssum*, *Arabis*, *Aubretia*, some *Campanula* species, *Cerastium*, and rockroses (*Helianthemum*).

One of the best methods for deciding what to grow on walls in different regions and countries is to look at the spontaneous flora of old walls. This will vary considerably according to climate but also to the pH and other characteristics of local rock types. For example, even in a relatively small country such as the United Kingdom, the spontaneous flora of walls varies considerably. In the maritime west, walls become clothed in swaths of ferns, grasses, and meadow plants, depending on position and aspect, whereas in the dry south-east, walls are much more sparsely clothed and lush growth is restricted to shade conditions.

Walls offer an additional advantage of varying conditions through their height profile: in the lower portions there is likely to be greater moisture and shade, thereby enabling ferns and other more-moisture-demanding species to be grown. In the United Kingdom, for instance, species such as Hart's tongue fern (*Asplenium scolopendrium*) thrive at the base of shady walls. As with roof greening, there is great scope for experimentation.

Because of the very free-draining nature of walls, plants that are not normally considered hardy can be grown, because they are able to ripen more effectively under the warmer conditions of a sunny wall, and because they have less tendency to succumb to root rot in cold wet winter soils.

Plants can be introduced during construction of dry stone walls. In *The English Flower Garden*, William Robinson described how plants

Prefabricated wetland vegetation, established through preplanted rolls of coir, rapidly achieves an established effect.

Photographs by VegTech

are lined out during dry stone wall construction—placing the roots into crevices and gaps as the stones are put into position, covering the roots with grit or sand, and then filling the space behind with gritty earth.

BIOENGINEERING

The field of bioengineering is concerned mainly with ecological solutions to slope stabilization, in contrast to traditional engineering solutions that tend to solve problems through large quantities of concrete. Bioengineering techniques harness the binding power of plant roots in holding a slope together, as well as the protective value of foliage cover in preventing erosion and washing away soil following heavy rain. Slope stabilization techniques include the use of woven biodegradable Hessian geotextiles to prevent slope erosion following the sowing of grass and wildflower seed mixtures. Trees and shrubs can also be planted through these mats. Willows are used extensively because of their propensity to root from inserted dormant shoots. And there is increasing use of vegetation technology—the use of pregrown or seeded ready-made vegetation or plant communities that can be put into place for instant effect. We have already mentioned the examples of the use of vegetation mats. Another similar type of product is the use of rolls of coconut fibre, or coir, that are seeded and planted with wetland vegetation and placed along the edge of streams, rivers, and canals to provide instant bank stabilization. Although not yet available to smaller scale users, such pre-established wetland vegetation could be very beneficial in the planting of new ponds and lakes. Of all these techniques the one that has made the jump into the mainstream is the use of willow as a structural component. Building upon the use of direct-planted willow cuttings in slope stabilization, willow structures are now widely used to produce tunnels and screens and are particularly attractive to children.

Linking building to landscape: water is the key

This book has been concerned with the many opportunities for establishing vegetation on and around buildings. We haven't dealt with the well-known aspects of balconies, window boxes, and containers but have instead looked at how the building surfaces themselves can be the starting point for vegetation establishment. We have dealt with them as separate entities: planting on roofs, walls, and other above-ground structures. We have seen that there are many similarities between them, however, in terms of construction and not the least in that they present harsh, water-limited environments for planting. This has meant that a similar suite of plants is suitable for many of these different settings. The range of techniques and approaches discussed mostly focus on how to optimize the value of limited space for planting, and most offer creative opportunities for innovation that have yet to be exploited fully. Perhaps unintentionally, many of our examples show an intriguing mix of formality in construction and the use of hard materials softened by naturalistic and free vegetation.

Water is also the key to how these different elements come together to tie the building into its surrounding landscape. While green roofs may limit and slow down runoff from a roof, what water there is must go somewhere. Often it may go directly into a mains drainage system, but this is in many ways to waste a useful resource. A more integrated approach would be to feed excess runoff into a series of pools and wetland areas where it can provide habitat and visual amenity and also infiltrate back into the groundwater. Such rain gardens are attracting a lot of interest in the United States. Taking things still further, water from the roof can be used to irrigate the sort of wall plantings that have been discussed here and in chapter 5.

Roof-Greening Plant Directory

This plant directory lists in detail those species that have been tried, tested, and proved reliable in central Europe. Other genera are included which should also prove successful. We do not pretend that these are exhaustive listings. Given that roof greening is still a young subject, there is much trialling of species that remains to be done, and so the inclusion of genera with less detailed information is intended very much as an indication of their potential. We are only listing species that are suitable for extensive and semi-extensive roofs, that is, those that will survive on shallow and relatively shallow substrates and are tolerant of some moisture stress, unless specifically noted otherwise.

In the following lists we have indicated species that are suitable for various depths of substrate: extensive roof plants categorized as those which will be successful in depths of 4–6 cm (1.6–2.4 in) and 6–10 cm (2.4–4 in), and semi-extensive roof plants that will be successful in depths of 10–15 cm (4–6 in) and 15–20 cm (6–8 in). Note that these are depths of growing medium, not total green roof depth, including drainage layer. It should also be noted that these are suggested minimum depths for successful growth—most of the species listed will also grow successfully at greater depths than those in which they are listed—in fact growth is likely to be more vigorous. The listings also assume low levels of irrigation and substrate humus content. Many of the species listed will grow in the next shallow depth category to that in which they are listed if regular irrigation is provided or humus content is increased.

The use of a grass-based vegetation for roof greening involves the combination of appropriate grasses, with visually striking forbs. These forbs may be successful in conjunction with grasses but not necessarily

Allium schoenoprasum

without them, because the competition with grasses keeps them relatively compact. Without this competition they tend to grow taller than is usually regarded as visually appropriate for roof greening. Examples include *Centaurea* species and *Cichorium intybus*.

We organize the listings by genera and provide the family name to give some idea of the character of the plant. We then give brief general descriptions of the characteristics of that genus. Growth form definitions fall into five categories, with the first two having indefinite spread: (1) carpet-forming plants have stems which spread over the substrate surface, rooting as they go (that is, stoloniferous); (2) the stems of mat-forming plants spread over the surface and eventually root, but they are not stoloniferous; (3) clump-forming plants form moderately tight or loose clumps, not carpets; (4) cushion-forming plants form tight cushions of growth; and (5) rhizomatous plants spread through horizontal roots. Finally, we suggest species within that genus that have proven successful. Our intention, however, is to encourage experimentation with other species and cultivars within the genus.

For each genus we give general information regarding height, drought tolerance, and aspect—these do not necessarily apply to all species within the genus. The same genus may appear in different depth categories. The drought tolerance categories indicate low, moderate, and high drought tolerance. Low-tolerance species require moist or shady conditions and humus-rich substrate. Moderate-tolerance species—the majority—come from dry habitats but will not withstand prolonged summer drought or long periods of intense heat and respond well to some humus content in the substrate. High-tolerance species are from arid or alpine habitats and can succumb to winter decay in moist substrates. These grow best in mineral substrates with low humus content.

PERENNIALS

Extensive: 4–6 cm (1.6–2.4 in) substrate depth

Acaena (Rosaceae)
Creeping, open clump-forming perennials. Dense foliage in a variety of colours and a dense habit make these some of the most valuable plants for decorative, slightly shaded roofs. Evergreen pinnate bronzed leaves, red-brown burrlike seed-heads, summer. Height 10–15 cm (4–6 in), drought tolerance moderate, aspect partial shade.
Species: *A. microphylla* is widely available. *A. buchananii*, 10 cm (4 in), blue-grey foliage. *A. caesiglauca*, 10 cm (4 in), grey-green foliage. *A. inermis* 'Purpurea', 10 cm (4 in), purple-toned foliage.

Acinos (Lamiaceae)
Creeping perennials with small diamond-shaped leaves and purple flowers in early summer. Height 15 cm (6 in), drought tolerance high, aspect sun.
Species: *A. alpinus*. Several similar suitable species exist.

Carlina (Asteraceae)
The carline thistle is a stemless thistle that produces an attractive rosette of slivery prickly leaves and a central flower. Height 5 cm (2 in), drought tolerance high, aspect sun.
Species: *C. acaulis. C. acanthifolia* is similar but makes a large rosette.

Chiastophyllum (Crassulaceae)
Spreading rhizomatous evergreen perennial with rounded fleshy evergreen leaves and drooping yellow racemes. Height 15 cm (6 in), drought tolerance moderate, aspect sun.
Species: *C. oppositifolium*

Euphorbia (Euphorbiaceae)
A useful group of perennials, predominantly with glaucous foliage and green or yellow flowers. Height 20–30 cm (8–12 in), drought tolerance high, aspect sun.
Species: *E. capitulata. E. cyparissias* has ferny foliage that colours well in autumn and yellowish green flowers in spring. Can be invasive.

Fascicularia (Bromeliaceae)
This is a small genus of colourful xerophytic terrestrial bromeliads able to tolerate light frosts that has potential value in tropical, subtropical, and frost-free climates.

Herniaria (Illecebraceae)
Carpet-forming perennial with tiny yellowish green leaves. Height 2 cm (0.8 in), drought tolerance high, aspect sun.
Species: *H. alpina*

Jovibarba (Crassulaceae)
Clump-forming perennial with evergreen succulent rosettes. Bunches of green-yellow flowers, summer. Height 20 cm (8 in), drought tolerance high, aspect sun.
Species: *J. sobolifera* is very similar to sempervivum and equally drought tolerant.

Mazus (Scrophulariaceae)
Mat-forming perennial with rooting stem making a carpet of small densely packed leaves and purple blue flowers in late spring. Height 5 cm (2 in), drought tolerance low, aspect partial shade.
Species: *M. reptans*

Petrorhagia (Caryophyllaceae)
Clump-forming perennial with small linear leaves and small pale pink flowers throughout summer. Height 20 cm (8 in), drought tolerance high, aspect sun.
Species: *P. saxifraga*, vigorous and can self-seed, potentially either very useful or invasive.

Raoulia (Asteraceae)
Prostrate mat-forming perennial with tiny silver-hairy leaves on ground-hugging stems and yellow flowers in summer. Height 1 cm (0.4 in), drought tolerance moderate, aspect partial shade.
Species: *R. australis. R. glabra* and *R. hookeri* are similar and often confused with *R. australis*, but are sensitive to winter wetness.

Rosularia (Crassulaceae)
Clump-forming perennial with evergreen succulent leaves in rosettes and yellow flowers in midsummer. Height 5 cm (2 in), drought tolerance high, aspect sun.
Species: *R. aizoon.* Several related species.

Sagina (Caryophyllaceae)
Mat-forming perennial forming cushionlike mounds. Tiny linear leaves and white flowers in early summer. Height 1 cm (0.4 in), drought

tolerance low, aspect partial shade.
Species: *S. subulata.* The yellow-foliage form 'Aurea' is the most commonly grown.

Saxifraga (Saxifragaceae)
Cushion- or mat-forming perennials with evergreen rosettes and sprays of white or pink spring flowers. Height 10–20 cm (4–8 in), drought tolerance high, aspect sun.
Species: *S. paniculata* has sprays of white flowers on tall stems in spring. *S. crustata. S. tridactylites.*

Scutellaria (Scrophulariaceae)
Mat-forming perennial with tiny silvery leaves and yellow flowers in summer. Height 15 cm (6 in), drought tolerance high, aspect sun.
Species: *S. orientalis*

Sedum (Crassulaceae)
A large genus of succulents that has been widely exploited for extensive green roofs. Carpet- or clump-forming rosettes of evergreen leaves and yellow, white, or pink flowers in summer. Height 10–20 cm (4–8 in), drought tolerance high, aspect sun.
Species: *S. acre, S. album, S. anacampseros, S. cauticolum, S. cyaneum, S. dasyphllum, S. ewersii, S. floriferum, S. fosterianum, S. hispanicum, S. hybridum, S. kamtschaticum, S. lydium, S. nevii, S. ochroleucum, S. reflexum, S. sediforme, S. sexangulare, S. spathulifolium, S. spurium.* Many hybrids and cultivars are available.

Sempervivella (Crassulaceae)
Mat-forming perennial with runners. Light

Sedum spurium

Sedum hybridum 'Immergrunchen'

green evergreen succulent leaves in rosettes and white flowers in summer. Height 5 cm (2 in), drought tolerance high, aspect sun.
Species: *S. alba*

Sempervivum (Crassulaceae)
Perennials forming tight cushions with rosettes of evergreen leaves and flowers of greenish

white, pink, or purple on upright stems. Height 20 cm (8 in), drought tolerance high, aspect sun.
Species: *S. arachnoideum, S. montanum, S. tectorum*. Many hybrids and cultivars are available.

Extensive: 6–12 cm (2.4–4.8 in) substrate depth

Alyssum (Cruciferae)
Clump-forming perennials with silvery grey foliage and yellow flower-heads. Height 10–20 cm (4–8 in), drought tolerance high, aspect sun.
Species: *A. argenteum, A. montanum, A. saxatile*

Antennaria (Asteraceae)
Mat-forming stoloniferous perennials with semi-evergreen grey-green foliage and white or pink fluffy flower-heads in late spring. Height 5 cm (2 in), drought tolerance moderate, aspect sun.
Species: *A. dioica*, several cultivars exist with pink flowers, such as 'Rosea' and 'Nyewood'. *A. alpina* is slightly taller but otherwise similar.

Anthericum (Liliaceae)
Rhizomatous perennials with linear foliage and lilylike trumpet flowers in late spring. Height 40 cm (16 in), drought tolerance moderate, aspect sun. Important components of limestone meadow flora.
Species: *A. liliago. A. ramosum* is taller (to 60 cm, 24 in), rhizomatous, and with smaller, more star-shaped flowers.

Anthyllis (Fagaceae)
Clump-forming short-lived but free-seeding perennials found naturally on sand dunes and calcareous free-draining soils. Height 30 cm (12 in), drought tolerance moderate, aspect sun.
Species: *A. vulneraria* has flower-heads of yellow, also red and pink variants, early summer, but can be very invasive to the detriment of other species. However, combining several different colour forms can create spectacular effects. *A. montana* (10–20 × 60 cm, 4–8 × 24 in) is longer-lived, cloverlike heads of pink, red, or purple.

Armeria (Plumbaginaceae)
Supremely useful group of attractive and resilient plants. Evergreen cushion-forming perennials with narrow leaves in tight rosettes. White, pink, or red flowers, drying to papery seed-heads. Drought tolerance high–moderate, aspect sun.
Species: *A. juniperifolia* is only 5–8 cm (2–3.2 in) tall, with flower-heads varying from purple to white. *A. maritima* has given rise to many hybrids. *A. pseudoarmeria*.

Asplenium (Aspleniaceae)
Clump-forming fern which prefers acidic humus-rich substrate. Height 15 cm (6 in), drought tolerance moderate, aspect partial shade.
Species: *A. ceterach*, *A. septentrionale*, *A. trichomanes*

Astragalus (Leguminosae)
Semi-shrubby habit with white-mauve flowers in midsummer. Height 20 cm (8 in), drought

Armeria maritima

tolerance moderate, aspect sun.
Species: *A. alpinus*. Many other related species but few are available commercially.

Aubrieta (Crucifereae)
Cushion or mat-forming perennials with very bright showy purple flowers in late spring. Height 5–10 cm (2–4 in), drought tolerance moderate, aspect sun to partial shade. May be suitable for shallower substrates if summer drought not severe.
Species: Very many hybrids are available. 'Red Cascade' is one of the most widely available.

Babiana (Iridaceae)
An extensive genus of South African geophytes often with highly coloured flowers in spring and early summer, becoming dormant in midsummer. Suitable for frost-free regions.

Centaurium (Gentianaceae)
Upright perennial with small pink flowers, found naturally on free-draining calcareous substrates. Height 15 cm (6 in), drought tolerance high, aspect sun.
Species: *C. erythraea*

Cerastium (Caryophyllaceae)
Creeping mat-forming perennials with silvery grey leaves and white flowers in spring and early summer. Useful to weave among other more upright plants. Height 15–20 cm (6–8 in), drought tolerance moderate, aspect sun.
Species: *C. tomentosum*, can be invasive.

Coronilla (Fabiaceae)
Perennial with long trailing stems, bearing pink and white pea-flowers early to late summer. Potentially invasive, smothering slower growing species, but useful for difficult sites or for fast coverage and erosion control. Height 25 cm (10 in), drought tolerance moderate, aspect sun.

Corydalis (Papaveraceae)
Rhizomatous perennial forming mounded growth with golden yellow, spurred flowers in spring and summer and finely divided foliage. Seeds freely. Height 30 cm (12 in), drought tolerance moderate–high, aspect shade or light shade.
Species: *C. cheilanthifolia* has yellow flowers but very distinct fern like foliage. *C. lutea*.

Cymbalaria (Scrophulariaceae)
Ivy toadflax is a carpet-forming perennial with blue and yellow flowers throughout summer.

Invasive, but this may be a useful characteristic. Height 5 cm (2 in), drought tolerance high, aspect partial shade.
Species: *C. muralis*, common natural wall plant.

Dianthus (Caryophyllaceae)
A very valuable showy genus of mainly tufted, mat-forming perennials with attractive narrow grey or green evergreen foliage and usually with colourful pink, purple, red, or white flowers in early to midsummer. Height 10–20 cm (4–8 in), drought tolerance high–moderate, aspect sun.
Species: *D. anatolicus* is a vigorous spreader with pink flowers. *D. arenarius* (height 20 cm, 8 in), fringed white flowers, early summer. *D. carthusianorum* is a slender upright perennial or biennial with small deep dark pink flowers and is decorative with grasses and best grown as a meadow plant, freely seeding. *D. deltoides* is similar with flowers in a variety of red and pink shades. *D. erinaceus* forms very low tight mats, pink flowers. *D. gratianopolitanus* is similar in size with large pink flowers. *D. plumarius* bears usually bearded pink or white flowers in summer.

Draba (Cruciferae)
Carpet-forming alpines with bristly rosettes of leaves and small yellow, white, or violet flowers. Height 10 cm (4 in), drought tolerance moderate–high, aspect sun.
Species: *D. aizoides, D. dubia, D. lasiocarpa*

Duchesnia (Rosaceae)
Mat-forming perennial, spreading by runners with trifoliate strawberry like leaves and small

yellow flowers in spring, strawberry like fruit in summer. Height 5–10 cm (2–4 in), drought tolerance moderate–low, aspect partial shade.
Species: *D. indica*

Echeveria (Crassulaceae)
A large and widely used genus of rosette-forming succulents with considerable potential in frost-free drought-prone climates. Height 20 cm (8 in), drought tolerance high, aspect sun.

Erinus (Scrophulariaceae)
Tufted alpines with pink spring flowers. Height 10 cm (4 in), drought tolerance moderate, aspect sun.
Species: *E. alpinus*

Hieracium (Asteraceae)
Useful composites for meadow plantings. Clump-forming perennials with low rosettes and flower-heads in early summer. Height 20 cm (8 in), drought tolerance high, aspect sun.
Species: *H. aurantiacum* has brilliant coppery orange flowers. *H. lanatum* and *H. villosum* have silvery leaves. *H. pilosella* is invasive and sometimes self-sows aggressively, but good in grass or with other strong-growing perennials.

Hypochaeris (Asteraceae)
Similar to *Hieracium*, the cat's ears are yellow-flowered composites for meadow plantings. Height 20 cm (8 in), drought tolerance moderate–high, aspect sun.
Species: *H. glabra. H. maculatum*, the spotted or leopard cat's ear, has leaves attractively blotched with chocolate spots. *H. radicata.* All self-seed freely.

Iris (Iridaceae)
Rhizomatous perennials with sword-shaped leaves and flowers usually in shades of blue in early summer. Height varies with species, drought tolerance high, aspect sun.
Species: *I. flavescens. I. pumila. I. tectorum* has lilac flowers with darker markings and pale crest; like sempervivums, the roof iris has been traditionally grown on roofs with minimal substrate. *I. variegata* has pale yellow flowers with brown and violet veins borne in early summer and is one of several so-called bearded irises, which have contributed to a vast number of hybrids, the shorter ones of which are all suitable for roof greening.

Leontodon (Asteraceae)
Useful late-summer- and autumn-flowering yellow rosette-forming perennials for naturalistic and meadow plantings. Height 20 cm (8 in), drought tolerance moderate–high, aspect sun.
Species: *L. taraxacoides. L. autumnalis* will flower sporadically from August to November.

Leptinella (Asteraceae)
Carpet-forming evergreen with finely divided, aromatic foliage and reddish flowers in summer. Height 4 cm (1.6 in), drought tolerance low, aspect partial shade.
Species: *L. squalida* is one of many species, most with yellow buttonlike flowers, which make very good surface covering, but only with constant moisture.

Lysimachia (Primulaceae)
Spreading perennial rooting from prostrate

stems. Rounded leaves held tight to the ground and yellow flowers borne in summer. Height 5 cm (2 in), drought tolerance low, aspect partial shade.
Species: *L. nummularia* is an effective and sometimes rampant ground cover. 'Aurea' is a yellow-leaved form.

Minuartia (Caryophyllaceae)
Mat-forming perennial with tiny narrow leaves and white flowers. Height 10 cm (4 in), drought tolerance moderate, aspect sun.
Species: *M. laricifolia, M. verna*

Oxalis (Oxalidaceae)
Mat-forming rhizomatous perennial with divided, cloverlike and nodding white flowers in spring. Height 5 cm (2 in), drought tolerance low, aspect partial shade.
Species: *O. acetosella*. Given the reputation of many *Oxalis* species for invasiveness, it might be worth assessing locally native species for roof greening.

Paronychia (Caryophyllaceae)
Mat-forming perennial with silvery white bracts in spring. Height 1 cm (0.4 in), drought tolerance high, aspect sun.
Species: *P. argentea, P. kapela*

Polypodium (Polypodiaceae)
Spreading rhizomatous fern. Height 20 cm (8 in), drought tolerance moderate, aspect partial shade.
Species: *P. vulgare*, numerous cultivars

Potentilla (Rosaceae)
Useful group of clump-forming or trailing perennials with colourful yellow, red, or white flowers. Drought tolerance moderate–high, aspect sun.
Species: *P. argentea*, silverweed (15 cm, 6 in), is a stoloniferous species with ferny silver-backed leaves and yellow flowers; makes good ground cover but can be invasive. *P. argyrophylla. P. aurea* is a carpeting species with a long succession of yellow flowers. *P. cinerea. P. erecta. P. neumanniana* has large yellow flowers over a long summer period. *P. reptans.*

Primula (Primulaceae)
Clump-forming perennials with rosettes of oval leaves and heads of yellow flowers in spring. Height 10–20 cm (4–8 in), drought tolerance moderate–high, aspect sun to partial shade.
Species: *P. veris*, cowslips, have many applications, whether as a spring element among other perennials or as a component of grassy meadows. Can self-sow and form a dramatic spectacle. *P. vulgaris* requires moisture-retentive substrate in partial shade.

Prunella (Lamiaceae)
Spreading mat-forming perennial with deep purple flower-heads, early summer. Height 15 cm (6 in), drought tolerance moderate–low, aspect sun to partial shade.
Species: *P. grandiflora* is vigorous but resents drying out. *P. vulgaris* is a smaller version.

Saponaria (Caryophyllaceae)
Spreading mat-forming perennial with small

oval bright green leaves and masses of 1-cm (0.4-in) pink flowers in early summer. Height 20 cm (8 in), drought tolerance moderate–high, aspect sun.
Species: *S. ocymoides* is easy and vigorous but can swamp slower growing plants. *S. pumilio* reaches 8 cm (3.2 in) in height.

Serratula (Asteraceae)
Clump-forming perennial with finely divided leaves on branching stems and pinkish purple thistlelike heads in late summer and autumn. Height 20 cm (8 in), drought tolerance moderate, aspect sun.
Species: *S. seoanei* is an extremely useful species because of a late flowering season.

Sisyrinchium (Iridaceae)
A useful genus with grassy foliage and star-shaped flowers in spring and summer. Height 15–20 cm (6–8 in), drought tolerance high, aspect sun.
Species: *S. angustifolium, S. graminifolium.*

Teucrium (Lamiaceae)
Aromatic subshrubs and perennials with blue, pink, and purple flowers. Drought tolerance moderate–high, aspect sun.
Species: *T. chamaedrys* (10 cm, 4 in), *T. montanum* (10 cm, 4 in), *T. pyrenaicum* (5 cm, 2 in).

Thymus (Lamiaceae)
Aromatic carpet- or clump-forming subshrubs with pink or purple flowers. Self-seeding. Height 10–30 cm (4–12 in), drought tolerance high, aspect sun.

Species: *T. doerfleri, T. praecox, T. pulegioides, T. serpyllum, T. vulgaris*

Vancouveria (Berberidaceae)
Creeping rhizomatous perennial with bright green leaves somewhat variable in shape and small white flowers in spring. Height 20 cm (8 in), drought tolerance low, aspect partial shade.
Species: *V. hexanda. V. chrysantha* has more leathery evergreen leaves.

Verbascum (Scrophulariceae)
Rosette-forming perennials or biennials often with woolly or hairy foliage and upright spikes of usually yellow flowers. Very freely self-seeding. Height 60–100 cm (24–40 in), drought tolerance high, aspect sun.
Species: *V. chaixii, V. phoeniceum*

Extensive/semi-extensive: 10–15 cm (4–6 in) substrate depth

Achillea (Asteraceae)
Carpet-forming perennials with attractive silvery feathery foliage and generally white or yellow flat flower-heads. Height 20–25+ cm (8–10+ in), drought tolerance moderate, aspect sun.
Species: *A. ageratifolia, A. chrysocoma, A. clavennae, A. millefolium.* Many other potentially suitable species.

Aethionema (Cruciferae)
Subshrubs with pink flowers in late spring. Height 10–15 cm (4–6 in), drought tolerance high, aspect sun.

Species: A. grandiflorum has light pink flowers. *A. speciosum* is 10 cm (4 in) and pink and *A. stylosum* is 8 cm (3.2 in) and pink; neither as long-lived as *A. grandiflorum*.

Ajuga (Lamiaceae)

Low, stoloniferous perennials with glossy, purple-tinged foliage and blue flower spikes in spring. Height 15 cm (6 in), drought tolerance low, aspect partial shade.
Species: *A. pyramidalis* is clump forming with dark leaves and blue-violet flower spikes up to 15 cm (6 in) high. *A. reptans*, various cultivars available, largely distinct through having variegated or deeper toned foliage. 'Catlin's Giant' is a particularly good form with large leaves.

Alchemilla (Rosaceae)

Attractive mat-forming perennials with lobed leaves and pale yellowish green flower-heads in summer. Height 20–40 cm (8–16 in), drought tolerance moderate, aspect partial shade.
Species: *A. alpina. A. conjuncta* is more upright (20–30 cm, 8–12 in) with more blue-green leaves. *A. erythropoda*.

Anacyclus (Asteraceae)

Mat-forming perennial with highly divided grey-green foliage and white daisy flowers in early summer. Height 5 cm (2 in), drought tolerance high, aspect sun.
Species: *A. pyrethrum* var. *depressus*

Anaphalis (Asteraceae)

Clump-forming perennials with silvery grey narrow leaves and heads of white everlasting flowers in early summer. Height 30 cm (12 in), drought tolerance moderate, aspect sun.
Species: *A. margaritacea*, *A. nepalensis* var. *monocephala*, *A. triplinervis*

Anthemis (Asteraceae)

Clump- or mat-forming perrenials with divided foliage and yellow or white daisy flowers in summer. Height 20–50 cm (8–20 in), drought tolerance high, aspect sun.
Species: *A. nobilis*, *A. sancti-johannis*, *A. tinctoria*

Aquilegia (Ranunculaceae)

Upright perennials with divided foliage and columbine flowers. Short-lived but seeding freely. Height 40–60 cm (16–24 in), drought tolerance moderate, aspect partial shade.
Species: *A. alpina*, *A. canadensis*, *A. flabellata* (only 10 cm, 4 in high), *A. vulgaris*

Arabis (Crucifereae)

Evergreen mat-forming perennials with grey-green leaves and white spring flowers. Height 15 cm (6 in), drought tolerance high, aspect partial shade.
Species: *A. caucasica*, *A. procurrens*

Artemisia (Asteraceae)

Aromatic perrenials and subshrubs with divided silvery grey foliage. Height 10–30 cm (4–12 in), drought tolerance high, aspect sun.
Species: *A. schmidtiana*, *A. stellariana*, *A. umbelliformis*

Asarum (Aristolochiaceae)

Evergreen carpet-forming rhizomatous

perennials, with shiny heart-shaped leaves. Height 8 cm (3.2 in), drought tolerance low, aspect shade.
Species: *A. caudatum*, *A. europaeum*

Aster (Asteraceae)

Clump-forming upright perennials. Valuable late-flowering genus with potential for experimentation on green roofs. Height 30–50 cm (12–20 in), drought tolerance moderate, aspect sun.
Species: *A. amellus* has blue flowers (pinkish purple in hybrids). *A. linosyris* has yellow pincushion flower-heads in late summer and autumn.

Calamintha nepeta

Bergenia (Saxifragaceae)

Spreading perennials with large glossy evergreen leaves and clusters of pink, purple, or white flowers in early spring. Height 30 cm (12 in), drought tolerance moderate, aspect partial shade.
Species: *B. cordifolia*, *B. purpurascens*, many hybrids.

Billbergia (Bromeliaceae)

Billbergia includes some of the hardiest bromeliads and many lithophytic species. They have potential in climates with minimal winter frost.

Calamintha (Lamiaceae)

Aromatic perennials with white or pink flowers in late summer. Height 40 cm (16 in), drought tolerance high, aspect sun to partial shade.
Species: *C. grandiflora*, *C. nepeta*

Campanula (Campanulaceae)

The bell flowers are a varied group with a good number of suitable species for green roofs, mostly with clear blue summer flowers. Height 10–30 cm (4–12 in), drought tolerance moderate, aspect sun.
Species: *C. carpatica* has large mauve-blue bells, long-flowering in summer.
C. cochleariifolia is similar but smaller and more delicate looking. *C. glomerata* is an upright species of calcareous meadows with globular flower-heads of deep blue flowers.
C. portenschlagiana. *C. rotundifolia* (harebell) forms rhizomatous clumps.

Carlina (Asteraceae)

The smaller thistles offer potential in certain situations. They produce upright prickly stems and leaves and purple flower-heads. Height 30 cm (12 in), drought tolerance high, aspect sun.
Species: *C. vulgaris*

Centaurea (Asteraceae)

The perennial cornflowers offer great potential for roof greening, having attractive foliage, colourful flowers, and sculptural seed-heads. Clump-forming perennials with rosettes of foliage and upright flower stems, usually with purple or pink flowers. Drought tolerance moderate, aspect sun.

Species: *C. nigra* is a coarser species for maritime climates. *C. rupestris. C. ruthenica. C. scabiosa,* large purple flower-heads. *C. triumfettii* ssp. *stricta.* lavender flower-heads, early summer. Many other species are worth trialling

Centranthus (Valerianaceae)

Clump-forming perennial with shiny medium green leaves and pinkish red flowers in early summer, also pink and white forms. Height 30 cm (12 in), drought tolerance high, aspect sun.

Species: *C. ruber* is a commonly found on walls and cliffs.

Cheilanthes (Adiantaceae)

A group of ferns which are unusual in that they are very drought-resistant, the fronds shrivelling in dry conditions to recover after rainfall. While none are especially large or effective as ground-covers, they deserve trialling. Height 10–20 cm (4–8 in), drought tolerance moderate, aspect sun.

Daucus (Apiaceae)

Upright biennial with finely divided foliage and cream-coloured heads, turning pink. Found on calcareous substrates. Height 40 cm (16 in), drought tolerance high, aspect sun

Species: *D. carota*

Davallia (Davallliaceae)

A genus of epiphytic and lithophytic ferns with extensively creeping rhizomes and fronds which die back during the dry season. Height 10–20 cm (4–8 in), drought tolerance low, aspect partial to full shade.

Delosperma (Aizoaceae)

Creeping mat-forming succulent with evergreen leaves and bright magenta daisylike flowers borne in summer. Height 10 cm (4 in), drought tolerance high, aspect sun.

Species: *D. cooperi* is the hardiest of a large and colourful genus with considerable potential in mild winter climate zones.

Dryas (Rosaceae)

Mat-forming subshrubs with white or yellow flowers borne in late spring. Height 5 cm (2 in), drought tolerance moderate–high, aspect sun.

Species: *D. drummondii* has yellow flowers. *D. octopetala* has white flowers. *D. ×suendermannii* has particularly large decorative leaves.

Edraianthus (Campanulaceae)

Loose tufted perennial with bell-shaped purple flowers in early summer. Height 15 cm (6 in), drought tolerance high, aspect sun.

Species: *E. graminifolius, E. tenuifolius*

Epimedium (Berberidaceae)

Rhizomatous perennials, evergreen or deciduous usually with white or yellow spring flowers. Height 30 cm (12 in), drought tolerance moderate–low, aspect shade.

Species: The genus contains many species

suitable for covering surfaces in shaded locations. Some (for instance, *E. ×rubrum*) have evergreen foliage. *E. alpinum* has divided foliage and yellow and red flowers.

Erigeron (Asteraceae)
Clump- or mat-forming perennials with glaucous foliage and blue or pink daisy flowers. Height 10–20 cm (4–8 in), drought tolerance moderate–high, aspect sun.
Species: *E. glabellus* ssp. *pubescens, E. glaucus*

Eriophyllum (Asteraceae)
Clump-forming perennial with white woolley foliage and bright yellow daisy flowers in summer. Height 15 cm (6 in), drought tolerance high, aspect sun.
Species: *E. lanatum* is one of several suitable species in the genus. Can be vigorous enough to overwhelm smaller plants.

Erodium (Geraneaceae)
Cushion- or clump-forming perennials with pink, white, or purple flowers through summer and finely divided leaves. Height 10–30 cm (4–12 in), drought tolerance high, aspect sun.
Species: *E. cheilanthifolium. E. cicutarium. E. manescavii* is very showy and seeds freely. Many other suitable species. All have attractive divided foliage and pink, reddish, or purple flowers.

Eryngium (Apiaceae)
The lower growing species offer potential. Prickly, tough glaucous foliage and spiky blue flower-heads. Tap roots mean that shallower substrates are not suitable. Height 20–30 cm (8–12 in), drought tolerance high, aspect sun.
Species: *E. bourgatii, E. maritimum, E. planum*

Euphorbia (Euphorbiaceae)
A useful genus with many drought-tolerant species. Often with glaucous foliage and green or yellow inflorescences. Height 20–30 cm (8–12 in), drought tolerance high, aspect sun to partial shade.
Species: *E. myrsinites. E. polychroma.* Many other species may be suitable. *E. amygdaloides* and *E. amygdaloides* var. *robbiae* are tough, hardy species for partial shade.

Filipendula (Rosaceae)
A perennial herb with ferny divided foliage and creamy flower-heads. Found in limestone grasslands. Height 25 cm (10 in), drought tolerance high, aspect sun.
Species: *F. vulgaris*

Fragaria (Rosaceae)
The strawberries have potential as green-roof species in partial shade or in substrates that do not dry out completely (for example, at the base of a sloping roof). Trailing stoloniferous perennials with white flowers in early summer. Height 10 cm (4 in), drought tolerance moderate–low.
Species: *F. vesca* is the true wild strawberry. *F. viridis.* Cultivated large-fruited forms may also be suitable.

Galium (Rubiaceae)
Creeping or trailing perennial herbs with whorls of narrow leaves along their stems and small star-shaped white or yellow flowers.

Height 10–20 cm (4–8 in), drought tolerance moderate–high, aspect sun, partial shade, or shade, depending on species.

Species: *G. mollugo* and *G. saxatile* (hedge and heath bedstraws) are worth experimenting with on roofs that are not susceptible to prolonged summer drought. *G. odoratum* is successful on shady damp roofs. *G. verum*, lady's bedstraw, grows commonly in calcareous meadows or sand dunes. In dry situations it is much less vigorous and shorter than in fertile productive soils.

Gentiana (Gentianaceae)

A large genus with much potential application of species from calcareous grasslands. Height 10–20 cm (4–8 in), drought tolerance moderate, aspect sun.

Species: *G. acaulis*, *G. alpina*, *G. verna*

Geranium (Geraniaceae)

A large genus with much potential application. Clump-forming or spreading perennials with divided leaves, flowers in late spring to midsummer usually in shades of pink or blue. Height 10–30 cm (4–12 in) drought tolerance moderate–high, aspect sun to partial shade depending on species.

Species: *G. cinereum*. *G. dalmaticum*. *G. endressii* (30 cm, 12 in) has bright pink flowers in early summer and again later; the species has many cultivars. *G. macrorrhizum* has deep pink flowers and is a useful species for partial shade; several cultivars and hybrids are available. *G. sanguineum* grows naturally in limestone grasslands and sand dunes and has pink flowers. *G. sessiliflorum* 'Nigricans' will grow in shallow substrate layers.

Glechoma (Lamiaceae)

Mat-forming perennial with runners with light blue flowers. Potentially invasive but can be used to underplant larger perennials. Height 10 cm (4 in), drought tolerance low, aspect partial shade.

Species: *G. hederacea*

Globularia (Globulariaceae)

Woody cushion-forming perennial with glossy dark green leaves and deep blue rounded heads. Height 5 cm (2 in), drought tolerance high, aspect sun.

Species: *G. cordifolia*, *G. nudicaulis*, *G. punctata*

Gypsophila (Caryophyllaceae)

Clump-forming or mat-forming perennials with glaucous foliage and white or pink flowers. Height 10–20 cm (4–8 in), drought tolerance moderate–high, aspect sun.

Species: *G. paniculata* has clouds of star-shaped white flowers. *G. repens* and *G. repens* 'Rosea' are excellent creeping and weaving plants with white and pink flowers, respectively.

Hedera (Araliaceae)

Self-rooting climber or trailer with deep, dark, glossy green evergreen leaves and green flower-heads in winter. Height 20 cm (8 in) when prostrate, drought tolerance moderate, aspect shade.

Species: *H. helix*. There are a great many variegated and other cultivars. Very invasive but useful for carpeting roofs in deeply shaded situations.

Helianthemum (Cistacaceae)
Mat-forming subshrubs with small evergreen leaves and large flat flowers in early summer. Height 10 cm (4 in), drought tolerance moderate–high, aspect sun.
Species: *H. nummularium* has rich yellow flowers. Many similar species and cultivars, with white, cream, yellow, and orange flowers. Can be short-lived.

Horminum (Lamiaceae)
Clump-forming perennial with lush rosettes and deep violet flowers in spikes borne in early summer. Height 20 cm (8 in), drought tolerance moderate, aspect partial shade.
Species: *H. pyrenaicum*

Hypericum (Guttiferae)
The St John's worts are yellow-flowered perennials and shrubs with some useful green-roof species.
Species: *H. olympicum* (20 cm, 8 in) has glaucous leaves and yellow flowers in midsummer. *H. perforatum* (30 cm, 12 in) is suitable for meadow communities in sun and partial shade. *H. reptans* is a ground-hugging species. Several other alpine species are worth a trial.

Inula (Asteraceae)
Upright clump-forming perennials with yellow flowers. Drought tolerance moderate, aspect sun.
Species: *I. ensifolia* (20 cm, 8 in)

Iris (Iridaceae)
Rhizomatous perennials with sword-shaped leaves and flowers usually in shades of blue in early summer. Height varies with species, drought tolerance high, aspect sun.
Species: *I. aphylla*, *I. graminea*, *I. pallida*. Short and medium beared iris cultivars.

Jasione (Campanulaceae)
Sheep's bit scabious is a clump-forming perennial with rosettes of basal leaves and pincushion heads of light violet blue, occurring on acid substrates. Height 20 cm (8 in), drought tolerance high, aspect sun to partial shade.
Species: *J. montana*

Jasione montana

Leucanthemum (Asteraceae)
Tufted perennial with dark green toothed leaves and large white and yellow daisies borne in early summer. Height 40 cm (16 in), drought tolerance moderate, aspect sun.

Species: *L. vulgare* (oxe-eye daisy) is short-lived but readily self-sows. Only suitable for meadows or low-nutrient substrate, as otherwise it will become large and aggressive.

Limonium (Plumbaginaceae)

The sea lavenders offer much potential. Most have attractive foliage and airy flowering sprays of pink or purple. Height 40 cm (16 in), drought tolerance high, aspect sun.
Species: *L. gmelinii*, *L. latifolium*, and many other species.

Linaria (Scrophulariaceae)

Slender short-lived but readily self-sowing perennials with linear foliage and blue or pink flower spikes. Height varies with species, drought tolerance high, aspect sun.
Species: *L. alpina* (15 cm, 6 in) is a low growing trailing species with yellow-centred mauve flowers for shallower substrates. *L. purpurea* (40–50 cm, 16–20 in) has violet purple flowers (pink and white forms also). Several other species.

Linum (Linaceae)

The flaxes are slender upright perennials with open saucer-shaped, usually blue flowers. Height 30 cm (12 in), drought tolerance moderate, aspect sun.
Species: *L. flavum* has yellow flowers. *L. perenne* has blue flowers.

Liriope and Ophiopogon (Liliaceae)

Two genera widely used as a grass-substitute ornamental ground cover in humid warm temperate or humid subtropical climates. If used for roof greening, access to adequate irrigation would be vital for success. Not rapidly growing enough for use in cooler regions.
Species: *L. muscari*, *O. japonicus*

Lychnis (Caryophyllaceae)

Clump-forming perennials. Height 40 cm (16 in), drought tolerance moderate–high, aspect sun.
Species: *L. coronaria* is short-lived but freely seeding with rosettes of silvery grey leaves and magenta flowers.
L. viscaria has panicles of purple-red flowers.

Malva (Malvaceae)

The mallows have open saucer-shaped flowers usually in shades of pink. Height 40 cm (16 in), drought tolerance moderate, aspect sun.
Species: *M. moschata* has bright pink flowers and attractive divided foliage.

Nepeta (Lamiaceae)

Aromatic grey-leaved clump-forming perennials with blue flowers. Many species flower continuously for many months. Height 30–50 cm (12–20 in), drought tolerance moderate–high, aspect sun.
Species: *N. camphorata*, *N. ×faassenii*, *N. mussinii*, *N.* 'Walker's Low'

Oenothera (Onagraceae)

Clump-forming upright or trailing perennials with yellow (sometimes pink) saucer-shaped flowers. Drought tolerance high, aspect sun.
Species: *O. acaulis* (10 cm, 4 in), *O. fruticosa* ssp. glauca (40 cm, 16 in), *O. macrocarpa* (15 cm, 6 in)

Ononis (Fabiaceae)

Low shrubby perennials with pink pea flowers. Height 20 cm (8 in), drought tolerance high, aspect sun.

Species: *O. cristata, O. fruticosa, O. rotundifolia, O. spinosa*

Onosma (Boraginaceae)

Hairy alpine with yellow spring and early summer tubular yellow flowers. Height 10 cm (4 in), drought tolerance moderate–high, aspect sun.

Species: *O. alborosea, O. stellulata*

Opuntia (Cactaceae)

The prickly pears cactuses have flat spiny pads and are relatively hardy. Several low-growing or prostrate species are worth experimentation. Height 30 cm (12 in), drought tolerance high, aspect sun.

Species: *O. humifusa*

Origanum (Lamiaceae)

Rhizomatous perennials forming discrete clumps with rounded aromatic leaves and deep mauve-pink flowers in summer and autumn. Valuable perennials for late summer bloom. Height 40 cm (16 in), drought tolerance high–moderate, aspect sun.

Species: *O. laevigatum* and various cultivars. Many related species including *O. vulgare*.

Pachysandra (Buxaceae)

Evergreen ground cover for moist substrates. Height 15 cm (6 in), drought tolerance low, aspect partial shade to shade.

Species: *P. terminalis*

Penstemon (Scrophulariaceae)

Pink tubular flowers and reddish tinged foliage. Height 15 cm (6 in), drought tolerance moderate, aspect sun.

Species: *P. hirsutus* 'Pygmaeus'

Phlox (Polemoniaceae)

The alpine phloxes are cushion-forming perennials covered in star-shaped white, pink, and purple flowers in spring and early summer. Height 15 cm (6 in), drought tolerance high, aspect sun to partial shade.

Species: *P. amoena, P. douglasii, P. stolonifera, P. subulata.* Many cultivars.

Phlox douglasii

Pulsatilla (Ranunculaceae)

Clump-forming perennial with finely divided, hairy leaves and nodding flowers in early spring. Grows on calcareous substrates. Height 20 cm (8 in), drought tolerance high, aspect sun.

Species: *P. vulgaris* has deep purple flowers. Red and white forms exist, along with various cultivars and seed strains. *P. halleri* and *P. patens* are similar.

Ranunculus (Ranunculaceae)
Clump-forming perennial with palmate leaves and yellow flowers in early summer. Height 30 cm (12 in), drought tolerance moderate, aspect sun.
Species: *R. bulbosus*

Rhodiola (Crassulaceae)
Clump-forming perennial with upright stems, greyish leaves, and umbels of yellow-green flowers in early summer. Height 20 cm (8 in), drought tolerance high, aspect sun.
Species: *R. rosea* is commonly available. Many other related species.

Sanguisorba (Rosaceae)
The salad burnet makes a rosette of divided leaves and heads of greenish flowers in summer. Height 20 cm (8 in), drought tolerance high, aspect sun.
Species: *S. minor*

Saxifraga (Saxifragaceae)
A variable genus. Mossy saxifrages produce cushions of finely divided foliage and short inflorescences of white, pink, or purple flowers. The London pride saxifrages (*S. urbium* types) have leathery rosettes and panicles of pink flowers. Height 10–20 cm (4–8 in), drought tolerance moderate–low, aspect partial shade.
Species: *S. ×arendsii* hybrids, *S. cuneifolia*, *S. geranioides*, *S. ×urbium*

Scabiosa (Asteraceae)
Clump-forming perennials with pincushion blue or pink flowers. Height 20 cm (8 in), drought tolerance high–moderate, aspect sun.
Species: *S. canescens*, *S. columbaria*, *S. lucida*

Sedum (Crassulaceae)
Succulent rosettes of glaucous foliage and flat flower-heads in late summer. Height 30 cm (12 in), drought tolerance high, aspect sun.
Species: *S. spectabile*, *S. ×telephium*

Silene (Caryophyllaceae)
Clump or mat-forming perennials with glaucous foliage and open star-shaped flowers in spring and summer. Height 20 cm (8 in), drought tolerance moderate, aspect sun.
Species: *S. schafta*, *S. uniflora*

Solidago (Asteraceae)
Upright perennials useful for their late yellow flowers. Height 10–20 cm (4–8 in), drought tolerance moderate, aspect sun.
Species: *S. culteri*, *S. virgaurea* ssp. *alpestris*. Other low-growing species are worth experimentation.

Tanacetum (Asteraceae)
Mat-forming woody perennial with very finely divided, silvery, evergreen foliage and yellow daisies in late summer. Height 15 cm (6 in), drought tolerance high, aspect sun.
Species: *T. haradjanii*

Tiarella (Saxifragaceae)
Clump-forming perennials with hairy lobed leaves, often with attractive dark markings and

spikes of small fluffy white flowers in spring. Height 15 cm (6 in), drought tolerance low, aspect partial shade to shade.

Species: *T. cordifolia*. There are several related species and increasing numbers of hybrids, many of them very ornamental, making this a genus of considerable potential.

Verbascum (Scrophulariaceae)

Rosette-forming perennials and biennials with hairy leaves and upright flower spikes. Height 40–150 cm (16–60 in), drought tolerance high, aspect sun.

Species: *V. nigrum. V. thapsus*, a tall freely self-seeding species with yellow flowers.

Veronica (Scrophulariaceae)

Creeping or rhizomatous perennials with spikes of blue flowers. Height 10–30 cm (4–12 in), drought tolerance moderate, aspect sun.

Species: *V. incana. V. prostrata* is a compact ground covering species. *V. spicata. V. surculosa.*

Vinca (Apocynaceae)

Creeping perennial rooting from stems with violet blue flowers. Height 15 cm (6 in), drought tolerance moderate, aspect partial shade.

Species: *V. major. V. minor* is very similar, but lower growing. There are a many cultivars of both, with flower colours ranging from white to dark purple and wine red, and others with variegated leaves.

Viola (Violaceae)

Mat-forming creeping perennial with heart-shaped pale green leaves. Height 15 cm (6 in), drought tolerance moderate, aspect partial shade.

Species: *V. biflora* has yellow flowers in late spring. There are a great many other *Viola* species suitable for green roofs, but few have the creeping habit of *V. biflora. V. labradorica* is a creeping species that often self-sows readily; dark purple leaves and pale purple flowers.

Semi-extensive: 15–20+ cm (6–8+ in) substrate depth

Aloe (Aloeaceae)

A succulent genus of major importance for frost-free climates with a pronounced dry season. Many thrive in minimal soil or rocky sites and are very ornamental. Aloes have considerable potential. Height 30–60 cm (12–24 in), drought tolerance high, aspect sun.

Betula (Betulaceae)

Only one species has potential.

Species: *B. nana* is a low-growing, spreading, and suckering birch that forms useful thickets but is not tolerant of dry soils.

Brachyglottis (Asteraceae)

A genus of low-growing evergreen shrubs including some widely used in landscaping as ground covers. Inhabiting rocky places in New Zealand and Australia, they have potential for deeper substrate roof greening in maritime climates where prolonged summer drought is not a severe problem. Height 1 m (40 in), drought tolerance high, aspect sun.

Buddleja (Loganiaceae)
Buddlejas exploit derelict urban sites, often growing in hot exposed sites on skeletal substrates of brick rubble or crushed concrete or in cracks in walls or abandoned roofs. The shorter forms are most suitable for roof planting. Height 1–2 m, drought tolerance high–moderate, aspect sun.
Species: *B. davidii* has given rise to a number of compact cultivars, such as 'Nanho Blue'.

Buphthalmum (Asteraceae)
Clump-forming perennial with yellow daisy flowers in mid to late summer. Height 30–40 cm (12–16 in), drought tolerance moderate, aspect partial shade.
Species: *B. salicifolium*

Calluna (Ericaceae)
Subshrubs with needle-shaped foliage and pink and purple flowers in late summer. Although *C. vulgaris* and many species of *Erica*, *Gaultheria*, and *Vaccinium* thrive in exposed situations on shallow low-nutrient soils, their suitability for roof greening is limited by their sensitivity to dehydration, which leads to foliage loss. Height 30 cm (12 in), drought tolerance low, aspect sun.

Ceanothus (Rhamnaceae)
Shrubs of Mediterranean climates and poor soils which should have considerable potential, although only a few cultivars have the ground-hugging habit that would make them useful. *C. thyrsiflorus* 'Repens' is one such.

Ceratostigma (Plumbaginaceae)
A genus of low-growing and useful late-flowering subshrubs, often used for ground cover. Potential in climates where prolonged drought is unlikely. Height 60 cm (24 in), drought tolerance moderate, aspect sun.
Species: *C. plumbaginoides*, *C. willmottianum*

Cichorium (Asteraceae)
Upright perennial with a rosette of toothed basal leaves and pure blue daisylike flowers borne in early to midsummer. Grow best in calcareous substrate. Height more than 1 m (40 in), drought tolerance high, aspect sun.
Species: *C. intybus*

Cistus (Cistaceae)
Shrubby genus of major importance in the Mediterranean maquis flora and for the landscape industry, for their showy flowers, evergreen foliage, ground-covering potential, and drought tolerance. Any of the smaller species or cultivars have potential.

Cotoneaster (Rosaceae)
Low-growing shrub with small, deciduous, dark green leaves and white flowers in spring and red berries in autumn. Height 20–30 cm (8–12 in), drought tolerance moderate, aspect sun to light shade.
Species: *C. adpressus. C. dammeri* is similar but evergreen. *C. horizontalis* 'Saxatilis' is a low-growing form of the familiar species.

Cytisus (Fabaceae)
The brooms are generally too large and vigorous for green-roof planting, but the

hybrid *C.* 'Amber Elf' is the first of a new breed of low-growing dwarf forms. Height 30 cm (12 in), drought tolerance high, aspect sun.
Species: *C. procumbens* is a ground-hugging species.

Echium (Boraginaceae)
Short-lived species with bristly leaves and blue, white, pink, or red flowers. Grows best in calcareous substrates. Height 30 cm (12 in), drought tolerance high, aspect sun.
Species: *E. russicum* produces red flower spikes 40–60 cm (16–24 in) in height. *E. vulgare* is an upright biennial with bristly elongated leaves and blue flowers in early to midsummer.

Eriogonum (Polygonaceae)
Subshrub for a sheltered position with pink flowers. Height 50 cm (20 in), drought tolerance moderate, aspect sun.
Species: *E. fasciculatum*

Erysimum (Cruciferae)
The perennial wallflowers are relatively short-lived, woody, spring-flowering plants. Height 40 cm (16 in), drought tolerance moderate, aspect sun.
Species: *E.* 'Bowles' Mauve'

Genista (Fabiaceae)
Low-growing shrubs with small linear leaves on grey-green branches and masses of golden yellow flowers in early summer. Height 40 cm (16 in), drought tolerance moderate, aspect sun.
Species: *G. lydia* is covered with yellow flowers. *G. pilosa* is similar, 40 cm (16 in) high. *G. pilosa* 'Procumbens' grows to only 20 cm (8 in).

Erysimum 'Bowles' Mauve'

G. sagittalis is 20 cm (8 in) with distinctive winged green stems.

Hebe (Scrophulariceae)
Widely used shrubs in ornamental horticulture. High-altitude species from exposed moorland environments are wind-proof and frost-hardy and have potential for roof-greening, although their drought-tolerance is poor. Height 20–30 cm (8–12 in), drought tolerance high, aspect sun.

Heuchera (Saxifragaceae)
A genus of woodland perennials of growing importance in horticulture, for the wide range of leaf shapes and sometimes showy pink flower spikes. Potentially useful for more shaded roofs where prolonged drought is unlikely.

Jasminum (Oleaceae)
Scrambling shrub with arching green shoots,

small divided leaves and fragrant yellow flowers borne in late winter. Height 30 cm (12 in) when prostrate, drought tolerance moderate, aspect sun to partial shade.

Species: *J. nudiflorum* can be grown as a trailer or to mound up against walls.

Juniperus (Pinaceae)

This genus contains several low-growing or prostrate species with potential. Examples include *J. communis* ssp. *alpina*, *J. communis* 'Repanda', *J. horozontalis*, and *J. procumbens*.

Knautia (Asteraceae)

Clump-forming perennials with pincushion flowers in shades of blue, purple, or red. Height 40–60 cm (16–24 in), drought tolerance moderate, aspect sun.

Species: *K. arvensis. K. macedonica* has crimson flowers.

Kniphofia (Liliaceae)

The red-hot pokers are clump-forming perennials with grassy foliage and upright flower spikes of yellow, orange, or red. The shorter species and hybrids make remarkably good green-roof plants in sheltered locations. Height 40–60 cm (16–24 in), drought tolerance high, aspect sun.

Species: Dwarf cultivars such as *K.* 'Border Ballet'.

Lavandula (Lamiaceae)

A group of subshrubs of major importance horticulturally. All are from drought-prone environments but may not thrive on very shallow substrates. Those available commercially vary considerably in frost-hardiness. Undoubtedly, one of the most important genera for green roofs. Height 20–50 cm (8–20 in), drought tolerance high, aspect sun.

Species: A wide range of species and cultivars are worth experimentation.

Libertia (Iridaceae)

Clump-forming perennials with evergreen grassy foliage and white flowers in early summer. Height 30–50 cm (12–20 in), drought tolerance moderate–high, aspect sun. A useful group for sheltered locations.

Species: *L. formosa.*

Lonicera (Caprifoliaceae)

Climbers or trailers that can be used to cover extensive areas of roof if used as trailer or as a climber over adjacent walls.

Species: Several are suitable, including *L.* ×*heckrottii.*

Omphalodes (Boraginaceae)

Mat-forming stoloniferous perennial with blue flowers in spring. Height 20 cm (8 in), drought tolerance moderate–low, aspect partial shade.

Species: *O. linifolia, O. verna.*

Perovskia (Labiatae)

Upright grey-leaved subshrubs with spikes of blue flowers in late summer. Excellent for naturalistic perennial mixtures. Height 50 cm (20 in), drought tolerance moderate, aspect sun.

Species: *P. atriplicifolia.*

Phlomis (Lamiaceae)
Aromatic perennials and shrubs with downy
leaves and pink, purple, or yellow flowers.
Height 30–60 cm (12–24 in), drought tolerance
high, aspect sun.
Species: *P. fruticosa* is a shrubby species.
P. samia, P. tuberosa, P. viscosa.

Pinus (Pinaceae)
Dwarf species and forms are useful evergreen
woody plants. Height 1–2 m (40–80 in),
drought tolerance moderate, aspect sun.
Species: *P. mugo* var. *pumilio, P. nigra* 'Helga'

Potentilla (Rosaceae)
Twiggy shrubs with small fresh green leaves
and flowers in various shades or yellow and
orange together with white. Height 40–60 cm
(16–24 in), drought tolerance high, aspect sun.
Species: *P. fruticosa*, inumerable hybrids

Prunus (Rosaceae)
Low-growing suckering shrubs with glossy
dark green leaves and bright pink cherry
flowers in spring. Height 1 m (40 in), drought
tolerance moderate, aspect sun.
Species: *P. pumila* var. *depressa. P. tenella* 'Fire
Hill' (1 m) has very dark pink flowers.

Rosa (Rosaceae)
Species from free-draining and sandy substrates
offer potential as green-roof species. Height
1–1.5 m (40–60 in), drought tolerance
moderate, aspect sun.
Species: *R. multiflora* has proven successful on
roofs. Others may include *R. rugosa* and
R. pimpinellifolia. Modern ground-cover

roses may also be worth trying.

Rosemarinus (Lamiaceae)
Aromatic subshrub with narrow shiny foliage
and blue flowers intermittently throughout the
year. Height 60 cm (24 in), drought tolerance
high, aspect sun.
Species: *R. officinalis.* Compact cultivars available.

Rumex (Polygonaceae)
Rhizomatous spreading perennial with small
grey-green leaves and tiny red-brown flowers
in upright heads. Found on acidic substrates.
Height 40 cm (16 in), drought tolerance
moderate–low, aspect sun.
Species: *R. acetosella* is hated as a weed when
in the garden, but useful as a resilient
ingredient on acidic substrates.

Salix (Saliaceae)
Dwarf ground-covering willows provide low
ground cover, while the more upright forms
make useful accent plants, particularly if cut
back hard periodically.
Species: *S. apoda, S. hastata* 'Wehrhahnii',
S. helvetica, S. lanata, S. purpurea 'Nana', *S. repens.*

Salvia (Lamiaceae)
Aromatic branching perennials and subshrubs
with blue flowers in early summer. Height
20–40+ cm (8–16+ in), drought tolerance
moderate–high, aspect sun.
Species: *S. nemorosa*; many cultivars and
hybrids with related species have been raised,
some are classified under *S.* ×*superba. S.
officinalis. S. pratensis* is short-lived but self-
sows; it does not compete well with grasses.

Santolina (Asteraceae)
Subshrubs with reduced green or grey leaves and bright yellow button flowers in summer. Height 40 cm (16 in), drought tolerance high, aspect sun.
Species: *S. chamaecyparissus*; pale yellow-flowered 'Lemon Queen' is 60 × 60 cm (24 × 24 in), 'Little Ness' is only 20 × 20 cm (8 × 8 in), while 'Weston' is only 15 × 20 cm (6 × 8 in) with intense silver foliage. *S. pinnata* is similar.

Sorbus (Rosaceae)
Suckering shrub with pinnate, dark purple-bronze foliage in autumn and white flowers in spring, red berries in autumn. Height 1 m (3.3 ft), drought tolerance moderate, aspect sun.
Species: *S. reducta.*

Spiraea (Rosaceae)
Compact much-branched shrubs with flat heads of pink flowers in early summer. Height 1 m (3.3 ft), drought tolerance moderate, aspect sun to partial shade.
Species: S. decumbens is a white-flowered species whose dimensions (30 × 50 cm, 13 × 20 in) make it potentially useful. *S. japonica*; there are many cultivars and hybrids available, including many with yellow- or bronze-tinted foliage. Dwarf cultivars such as 'Little Princess' (50 × 100 cm, 20 × 40 in) or 'Nana' (50 × 60 cm, 20 × 24 in) are particularly useful.

Stephanandra (Rosaceae)
Thicket-forming shrub with deeply lobed, toothed leaves and small white flowers in clusters borne in early summer. Height 60 cm (24 in), drought tolerance moderate, aspect sun to partial shade.
Species: *S. incisa* 'Crispa'.

Tellima (Saxifragaceae)
Clump-forming semi-evergreen perennial with rounded, lobed, pale hairy leaves and greenish flowers on upright stems in late spring. Height 20–40 cm (8–16 in), drought tolerance moderate, aspect partial shade.
Species: *T. grandiflora*. Forms are available with red- or purple-toned foliage.

Tradescantia (Commelinaceae)
A group of low-growing perennials, many with a creeping or trailing habit and attractive flowers. Many also have ornamental foliage and are thus commonly used as ground cover in the humid subtropical and tropical regions. They have considerable potential. Height 30 cm (12 in), drought tolerance moderate–low, aspect sun.

Trifolium (Fabaceae)
Creeping perennials with three-lobed leaves and rounded flower-heads. They root from the stems. Height 15 cm (6 in), drought tolerance low–moderate, aspect sun.
Species: *T. repens* has white flower-heads and is an aggressive species suitable for combining with grasses, for which it will provide nitrogen. There are an increasing number of cultivars of this and other clovers with highly decorative foliage, often marked with silver or red.

Zauschneria (Onagraceae)
Subshrubs from seasonally dry habitats in western North America. Ornamental and with high potential.

GRASSES AND GRASSLIKE PLANTS

Extensive: 4–6 cm (1.6–2.4 in) substrate depth

Carex (Cyperaceae)
The sedges are generally tough evergreen species that are useful for ground cover or binding together flowering green-roof plantings. Although most are usually associated with moist shady habitats, some will withstand dry conditions in full sun, although performance will be enhanced with increased humus in the substrate. Height 10 cm (4 in), drought tolerance high–moderate, aspect sun. **Species:** *C. caryophylla* is a glaucous-leaved sedge of nutrient-poor grasslands (10 cm, 4 in).

Corynephorus (Poaceae)
Short grass from sandy habitats with grey threadlike foliage and purplish flower spikes. Height 20 cm (8 in), drought tolerance high, aspect sun.
Species: *C. canescens.*

Festuca (Poaceae)
A very useful group of stress-tolerant grasses. The smaller species are tough and resilient but can be short-lived. Height 10–15 cm (4–6 in), drought tolerance high, aspect sun.
Species: *F. punctoria, F. vivipara.*

Extensive: 6–10 cm (2.4–4 in) substrate depth

Bouteloua (Poaceae)
Adaptable prairie grasses with one-sided flower spikes. Drought tolerance high, aspect sun. **Species:** *B. curtipendula* (40–50 cm, 16–20 in), *B. gracilis* (30–50 cm, 12–20 in); both grasses colour well in the autumn.

Buchloë (Poaceae)
Buffalo grass is a tough, short prairie grass; it is warm-season and therefore brown in winter, green in summer. Drought tolerance moderate, aspect sun.
Species: *B. dactyloides* (15 cm, 6 in).

Carex (Cyperaceae)
Height 10–20 cm (4–8 in), drought tolerance high–moderate, aspect sun to partial shade.
Species: *C. firma, C. montana, C. umbrosa.*

Festuca (Poaceae)
A group of stress-tolerant grasses, generally clump-forming, often with narrow wiry foliage. Height 20 cm (8 in), drought tolerance high, aspect sun.
Species: *F. cinerea* (syn. *F. glauca*) has blue-grey foliage, heightened in a range of cultivars. *F. ovina. F. rupicaprina, F. rupicola, F. valesiaca.*

Koeleria (Poaceae)
Blue-green clump-forming grass, found naturally on poor free-draining soils. Height 20 cm (8 in), drought tolerance high, aspect sun.
Species: *K. macrantha.*

Melica (Poaceae)
Clump-forming deciduous grass, naturally found on calcareous substrates. The flower spikes are white in appearance and radiate out from the clump. Particularly effective when viewed against a low sun. Height 30 cm (12 in), drought tolerance moderate, aspect sun.
Species: *M. ciliata.*

Extensive/semi-extensive: 10–15 cm (4–6 in) substrate depth

Briza (Poaceae)
Clump-forming grasses with nodding heads borne in early summer, found on calcareous substrates. Height 40 cm (16 in), drought tolerance moderate, aspect sun.
Species: *B. media. B. minor* is an important component of limestone meadows.

Carex (Cyperaceae)
Height 10 cm (4 in), drought tolerance high–moderate, aspect sun to partial shade.
Species: *C. digitata. C. flacca* has glaucous foliage.

Festuca (Poaceae)
Height 20 cm (8 in), drought tolerance high, aspect sun.
Species: *F. amethystina*, glaucous leaves and mauve flower-heads (30 cm, 12 in). *F. mairei.*

Helictotrichon (Poaceae)
A superb blue-foliage grass with a fountain effect in full flower. Height 60 cm (24 in), drought tolerance high, aspect sun.
Species: *H. sempervirens.*

Koeleria (Poaceae)
Clump-forming grasses, often with glaucous foliage, found naturally on poor free-draining soils. Height 20 cm (8 in), drought tolerance high, aspect sun.
Species: *K. glauca* is similar to *Festuca cinerea* (syn. *F. glauca*) but with more substantial foliage; can be short-lived. *K. pyramadalis*, *K. valesiana.*

Sesleria (Poaceae)
The Moor grasses are evergreen mat-forming grasses which will not be successful if exposed to prolonged summer drought.
Species: *S. albicans, S. autumnalis, S. caerulea.*

Stipa (Poaceae)
A choice group of clump- and tuft-forming grasses with highly ornamental characteristics. Delicate flower spikes with long awns respond to the slightest breeze. Height 30–60 cm (12–24 in), drought tolerance moderate–high, aspect sun.
Species: *S. capillata* and *S. pennata* are similar species with feathery panicles (60 cm, 24 in). *S. tenuissima* is a very beautiful species with wispy flower and seed-heads over a long summer to winter season, creating a lovely meadow effect; short-lived but readily self-sows. *S. cernua* is similar. *S. pulchra*. Many other species are worth a try.

Semi-extensive: 15–20+ cm (6–8 in) substrate depth

Calamagrostis (Gramineae)
A genus of very attractive grasses with substantial panicles that make effective late summer, autumn, and winter displays. Height 60 cm (24 in), drought tolerance moderate–high, aspect sun.
Species: *C. brachytricha* is a beautiful grass with arching foliage and flowers.

Carex (Cyperaceae)
Height 10 cm (4 in), drought tolerance high–moderate, aspect sun to partial shade.
Species: *C. morrowii* 'Variegata' is a good ground cover for shady roofs or full sun in moist substrate, but will not tolerate dryness.

Deschampsia (Poaceae)
Evergreen grasses making bold foliage clumps and a hazy flowering mass that ripens to golden yellow in late summer. Height 90 cm (36 in), drought tolerance low–moderate, aspect partial shade.
Species: *D. caespitosa*.

Festuca (Poaceae)
Species: *F. scoparia* (syn. *F. gautieri*) is a highly textural grass with mounds of very fine, deep green foliage reaching a height of 15 cm (6 in). Will not tolerate drought.

Luzula (Juncaceae)
The wood-rushes are clump-forming evergreens with attractive foliage rosettes from which arise flowering panicles that remain in good condition for many months. Height 30–40 cm (12–16 in), drought tolerance moderate, aspect partial shade to shade.
Species: *L. nivea* has creamy white panicles and makes a bold effect if planted en masse. *L. sylvatica* is an effective ground cover for shade.

Sporobolus (Poaceae)
The dropseeds are highly ornamental drought-tolerant prairie grasses that form mounded clumps of fine foliage and turn golden orange in autumn. Height 60 cm (24 in), drought tolerance moderate, aspect sun.
Species: *S. airoides*. *S. heterolepis* (60 cm, 24 in).

Stipa (Poaceae)
Height 30–60 cm (12–24 in), drought tolerance moderate–high, aspect sun.
Species: *S. calamagrostis* flowers late in the year with bottlebrush-like panicles.

Festuca cinerea

BULBS

Extensive: 4–6 cm (1.6–2.4 in) substrate depth

Allium (Liliaceae)
An extremely useful group with grassy leaves and globular flower-heads. Height 20–30+ cm (8–12+ in), drought tolerance high, aspect sun.
Species: *A. atropurpureum*, *A. caeruleum*, *A. carinatum*. *A. flavum* is a variable species; it is self-sowing, as are many others. *A. insubricum* is similar but pink or red. *A. cyaneum* is blue. *A. schoenoprasum* (chives) [illustrated on page 190] has mauve-purple flowers and is tolerant of moist conditions as well as dry. There are many other small alliums which are potentially good roof-greening plants.

Extensive: 6–10 cm (2.4–4 in) substrate depth

Allium (Liliaceae)
An extremely useful group with grassy leaves and globular flower-heads. Height 20–30+ cm (8–12+ in), drought tolerance high, aspect sun.
Species: *A. cernuum*, *A. moly*, *A. strictum*, *A. vineale*.

Muscari (Hyacinthaceae)
The grape hyacinths have intense blue flower-heads. Height 10–15 cm (4–6 in).
Species: *M. armeniacum*, *M. botryoides*. A range

of other species. All can self-sow to form extensive communities.

Extensive/semi-extensive: 10–15 cm (4–6 in) substrate depth

Allium (Liliaceae)
An extremely useful group with grassy leaves and globular flower-heads. Height 20–30+ cm (8–12+ in), drought tolerance high, aspect sun.
Species: *A. christophii*, *A. karatviense*.

Anemone (Ranunculaceae)
Star-shaped flowers in spring and early summer. Height 20 cm (8 in), drought tolerance low, aspect partial shade.
Species: *A. apennina*, *A. blanda*.

Crocus (Iridaceae)
A large genus of early-flowering bulbs, which are all dormant in summer. Height 5–10 cm (2–4 in), drought tolerance moderate, aspect sun to partial shade.
Species: *C. chrysanthus* has showy yellow flowers in late winter, early spring. *C. tommasinianus* has purple flowers and self-seeds freely.

Hyacinthoides (Liliacea)
Height 20 cm (8 in), drought tolerance low, aspect shade.
Species: *H. non-scripta*, bluebell, has blue flowers (pink and white hybrids); it can be used in partial shade in substrates that are not susceptible to prolonged summer drought. *H. hispanica* is a larger version.

Ixia (Iridaceae)

An extensive genus of South African geophytes often with highly coloured flowers in spring and early summer, becoming dormant in midsummer. Suitable for frost-free regions. Height 20 cm (8 in), drought tolerance high.

Narcissus (Amaryllidaceae)

The quintessential spring bulb. Dwarf species or varieties are potentially very useful for bringing colour to green roofs in spring, but they do not have the tolerance of high summer temperatures or drought that many bulbs do. Height 20 cm (8 in), drought tolerance low, aspect light shade.

Species: Many smaller species are worth experimentation.

Nerine (Amaryllidaceae)

An extensive genus of South African geophytes often with highly coloured flowers in spring and early summer, becoming dormant in midsummer. Suitable for frost-free regions. Height 30 cm (12 in), drought tolerance moderate–high, aspect sun.

Ornithogalum (Liliaceae)

White and green-striped flowers in spring. Height 30 cm (12 in), drought tolerance low, aspect partial shade.

Species: *O. nutans. O. umbellatum* grows to 30 cm (12 in) in height.

Scilla (Liliaceae)

Useful blue spring-flowering small bulbs. Height 10 cm (4 in), drought tolerance moderate, aspect partial shade.

Species: *S. bifolia, S. mischtschenkoana, S. siberica.*

Tulipa (Liliaceae)

An extensive genus of summer-dormant bulbs from the Mediterranean basin and Central Asia. While the tall garden hybrids may look out of place on roofs, the species or dwarf hybrids may be regarded as a valuable source of spring colour. Height 10–30 cm (4–12 in), drought tolerance moderate–high, aspect sun.

Species: *T. tarda, T. urumiensis.* Many others.

Façade-Greening Plant Directory

Size: refers primarily to height, but also potential spread if support mechanisms allow
Aspect: this is somewhat dependent on latitude, as with any plant
Optimum width of support: where trellis is used
Distance from wall: the distance the support needs to be from the wall, especially at the base, to allow for trunk thickening

Actinidia arguta (Actinidiaceae)
Cultivars and related species: 'Isai' is self-fertile. Several other species are worth trying.
Size: 9 m (29.7 ft)
Profile: maximum of 60 cm (2 ft)
Zone: 4
Foliage: ovate, bristly leaves, good yellow in autumn
Flowers, season: fragrant white, early summer
Fruit: yellow-green fruit on female plants
Origin: eastern Asia
Aspect: light shade to sun
Climbing mechanism: twining
Vigour: strong
Weight: medium, maximum of 20 kg per square metre (1.8 lb per square foot)

Support: vertical supports, round cross-section, trellis with right-angle mesh and widely spaced members
Minimum height of support: 5 m (16.5 ft)
Optimum width of support: 3 m (9.9 ft)
Distance from wall: 15 cm (6 in)

Actinidia deliciosa (Actinidiaceae)
kiwi fruit, Chinese gooseberry
Cultivars and related species: various female cultivars including 'Blake' which is self-fertile, males include 'Matua' and 'Tomuri'
Size: 12 m (39.6 ft)
Profile: maximum of 90 cm (3 ft)
Zone: 7
Foliage: 20-cm (8-in) long ovate leaves
Flowers, season: cream-coloured, early summer
Fruit: kiwi fruit of commerce
Origin: China
Aspect: full sun
Climbing mechanism: twining
Vigour: very strong
Weight: heavy, maximum of 25 kg per square metre (2.25 lb per square foot)
Support: vertical supports, round cross-

section, trellis with right-angle mesh
Minimum height of support: 6 m (19.8 ft)
Optimum width of support: 4 m (13.2 ft)
Distance from wall: at least 15 cm (6 in), with
the possibility of a sizeable trunk developing
in later years at the base

Actinidia kolomikta (Actinidiaceae)
Cultivars and related species: *Actinidia
polygama* (zone 4) is similar with silver areas on
leaves.
Size: 6 m (19.8 ft)
Profile: maximum of 90 cm (3 ft)
Zone: 4
Foliage: ovate leaves with dramatic white and
pink splashes
Flowers, season: fragrant white, early summer
Fruit: yellow-green fruit on female plants
Origin: eastern Asia
Aspect: full sun, dislikes exposure
Climbing mechanism: twining
Vigour: medium
Weight: medium, maximum of 20 kg per
square metre (1.8 lb per square foot)
Support: vertical supports, round cross-
section, trellis with right-angle mesh
Minimum height of support: 3 m (9.9 ft)
Optimum width of support: 2 m (6.6 ft)
Distance from wall: 8 cm (3.2 in)
Notes: Slow to establish, possibly faster in
continental climates.

Akebia quinata (Lardizabalaceae)
Cultivars and related species: *Akebia trifoliata*
is very similar with racemes of purple flowers.
Size: 10 m (33 ft)
Profile: maximum of 60 cm (2 ft)

Zone: 5
Foliage: palmate, rounded leaflets, evergreen or
semi-evergreen
Flowers, season: spicy-scented maroon flowers
in early spring, beautiful when backlit
Fruit: 9 cm (3.6 in) sausage-shaped violet fruit
Origin: eastern Asia
Aspect: very light shade
Climbing mechanism: twining
Vigour: strong
Weight: light, maximum of 15 kg per square
metre (1.4 lb per square foot)
Support: vertical supports, round cross-
section, trellis with right-angle mesh
Minimum height of support: 7 m (23.1 ft)
Optimum width of support: 2 m (6.6 ft)
Distance from wall: 10 cm (4 in)

Ampelopsis brevipedunculata (Vitaceae)
Cultivars and related species: *Ampelopsis
cordata* (zone 4) is similar, a native to the
south-eastern United States, growing to 10 m
(33 ft). *Ampelopsis tomentosa*, a native of the
south-eastern United States, is similar.
Size: 6 m (19.8 ft)
Profile: maximum of 60 cm (2 ft)
Zone: 9
Foliage: vine-shaped, yellow or orange in
autumn
Flowers, season: small green, summer
Fruit: purple, then blue berrylike fruit
Origin: north-eastern Asia
Aspect: light shade to sun
Climbing mechanism: tendrils
Vigour: medium
Weight: light, maximum of 15 kg per square
metre (1.4 lb per square foot)

Support: vertical supports, preferably angled cross-section with a maximum perimeter of 70 mm (2.8 in), trellis with right-angle mesh
Minimum height of support: 3 m (9.9 ft)
Optimum width of support: 2 m (6.6 ft)
Distance from wall: 10 cm (4 in)

Ampelopsis megalophylla (Vitaceae)
Cultivars and related species: *Ampelopsis aconitifolia* (zone 4) grows to 12 m (39.6 ft), with palmate leaves.
Size: 10 m (33 ft)
Profile: maximum of 90 cm (3 ft)
Zone: 5
Foliage: 60-cm (24-in) doubly pinnate leaves
Fruit: black fruit
Origin: western China
Aspect: light shade to sun
Climbing mechanism: tendrils
Vigour: strong
Weight: medium, maximum 20 kg per square metre (1.8 lb per square foot).
Support: vertical supports, with angled edges, with a maximum perimeter of 70 mm (2.8 in), trellis with right-angled mesh
Minimum height of support: 5 m (16.5 ft)
Optimum width of support: 3 m (9.9 ft)
Distance from wall: 15 cm (6 in)

Araujia sericifera (Asclepiadaceae)
cruel plant
Size: 10 m (33 ft)
Profile: maximum of 60 cm (2 ft)
Zone: 9
Foliage: 10-cm (4-in) lance-shaped leaves, evergreen
Flowers, season: bell-shaped fragrant white flowers, summer
Origin: South America
Aspect: light shade to sun
Climbing mechanism: twining
Vigour: medium
Weight: light, maximum 15 kg per square metre (1.4 lb per square foot)
Support: vertical supports, round cross-section, trellis with right-angle mesh
Minimum height of support: 5 m (16.5 ft)
Distance from wall: 8 cm (3.2 in)

Aristolochia macrophylla (Aristolochiaceae)
Dutchman's pipe
Cultivars and related species: *Aristolochia tomentosa* (zone 8), a native of the south-eastern United States, is similar. There are a great many tropical species.
Size: 10 m (33 ft)
Profile: maximum of 60 cm (2 ft)
Zone: 7
Foliage: heart-shaped leaves up to 30 cm (12 in) across
Flowers, season: small mottled flowers hidden in leaves, summer
Origin: eastern North America
Aspect: light shade
Climbing mechanism: twining
Vigour: strong
Weight: light, maximum of 15 kg per square metre (1.4 lb per square foot)
Support: vertical supports, round cross-section, trellis with right-angle mesh
Minimum height of support: 8 m (26.4 ft)
Optimum width of support: 3 m (9.9 ft)
Distance from wall: 10 cm (4 in)
Notes: Particularly needs soil moisture.

Bignonia capreolata (Bignoniaceae)
trumpet flower, cross vine
Size: 10–20 m (33–66 ft)
Profile: maximum of 90 cm (3 ft)
Zone: 10
Foliage: 18-cm (7.2-in) leaves with tendrils, evergreen but can lose leaves in cold weather
Flowers, season: orange-red, summer
Fruit: flat, beanlike.
Origin: south-eastern United States
Aspect: light shade to sun
Climbing mechanism: leaf tendrils
Vigour: very strong
Weight: medium, maximum 20 kg per square metre (1.8 lb per square foot).
Support: vertical supports, angled cross-section, trellis with right-angle mesh
Minimum height of support: 6 m (19.8 ft)
Distance from wall: 10 cm (4 in)

Bougainvillea spectabilis (Nyctaginaceae)
bougainvillea
Cultivars and related species: A vast range of cultivars and hybrids with other species in the genus: magenta, pink, red, dull orange, salmon, old gold, cream
Size: 8 m (26.4 ft)
Profile: maximum of 90 cm (3 ft)
Zone: 10
Foliage: light green oval leaves, evergreen
Flowers, season: small flowers surrounded by brilliantly colourful bracts, season is climate dependent
Origin: Brazil
Aspect: sun
Climbing mechanism: thorns
Vigour: strong

Weight: medium, maximum of 20 kg per square metre (1.8 lb per square foot)
Support: horizontal supports, trellis
Minimum height of support: 4 m (13.2 ft)
Optimum width of support: 4 m (13.2 ft)
Distance from wall: 15 cm (6 in)
Notes: Scandent stems may need training or pruning (take care to avoid the thorns).

Campsis radicans (Bignoniaceae)
trumpet vine
Cultivars and related species: *Campsis radicans* f. *flava* (syn. 'Yellow Trumpet') has yellow flowers. *Campsis grandiflora* (zone 7) is similar but produces few aerial roots and so needs support. *Campsis ×tagliabuana* 'Mme Galen' (zone 4) is particularly showy.
Size: 10 m (33 ft)
Profile: maximum of 90 cm (3 ft)
Zone: 4
Foliage: 10-cm (4-in) pinnate leaves, turning yellow in autumn
Flowers, season: trumpet-shaped orange-red, late summer to autumn
Origin: China
Aspect: full sun vital
Climbing mechanism: aerial roots
Vigour: strong
Weight: light, maximum of 15 kg per square metre (1.4 lb per square foot)
Support: horizontal supports, trellis with right-angle or diagonal mesh
Minimum height of support: 6 m (19.8 ft)
Optimum width of support: 4 m (13.2 ft)
Distance from wall: at least 15 cm (6 in), with the possibility of a sizeable trunk developing in later years at the base

Notes: Despite having aerial roots, some support is recommended.

Celastrus scandens (Celastraceae)
American bittersweet
Cultivars and related species: Many other similar species of which the eastern Asian *Celastrus orbiculatus* (zone 4) is best known, but it is notoriously invasive.
Size: 10 m (33 ft)
Profile: maximum of 1.2 m (4 ft)
Zone: 2
Foliage: 10-cm (4-in) ovate leaves, clear yellow in autumn
Flowers, season: small yellow-green, summer
Fruit: female plants have bright orange seeds
Origin: eastern North America
Aspect: light shade to sun
Climbing mechanism: twining
Vigour: strong
Weight: light, maximum of 15 kg per square metre (1.4 lb per square foot)
Support: vertical supports, round cross-section, trellis with right-angle mesh
Minimum height of support: 7 m (23.1 ft)
Optimum width of support: 2 m (6.6 ft)
Distance from wall: at least 15 cm (6 in), with the possibility of a sizeable trunk developing in later years at the base

Clematis
There are more than 200 species of clematis, varying greatly in size, along with well over 1000 hybrids. With the exception of the evergreen *C. armandii*, they tend to look untidy during the winter, but more than make up for this during their flowering season. The popular large-flowered hybrids rarely reach more than 15 m (49 ft) in height, and the more modern the variety, the smaller growing it is likely to be. For façade greening, introductions of species new to cultivation and new large-growing forms of well-known species could well greatly expand opportunities for work with this genus. There is also scope for hybridizing work, crossing evergreen *C. armandii* with other species, for example.

Clematis armandii (Ranunculaceae)
Size: 8 m (26.4 ft)
Profile: maximum of 60 cm (2 ft)
Zone: 8
Foliage: trifoliate, dark glossy evergreen ovate-lanceolate leaves
Flowers, season: profuse white flowers in early spring
Origin: China
Aspect: light shade to sun, shelter
Climbing mechanism: leaf twiner
Vigour: strong
Support: trellis with right-angle or diagonal mesh, preferably with angled cross-section, maximum cross-section of perimeter 45 mm (1.8 in)
Minimum height of support: 4 m (13.2 ft)
Optimum width of support: 3 m (9.9 ft)
Notes: Medium to fast growing, few lower branches produced.

Clematis montana (Ranunculaceae)
Cultivars and related species: Very popular with many cultivars now available. 'Elizabeth' is one of the most popular, with soft pink flowers and bronze foliage. Not all cultivars are as

vigorous as the species, so advice should be
sought when buying.
Size: 12 m (39.6 ft)
Profile: maximum of 90 cm (3 ft)
Zone: 6
Foliage: trifoliate leaf, green or purple-bronze
flushed
Flowers, season: pink or white, 5–8 cm
(2–3.2 in) across depending on variety, early
summer
Origin: central and western China, Himalayas
Aspect: light shade to sun
Climbing mechanism: leaf tendrils
Vigour: very strong
Weight: light, maximum of 15 kg per square
metre (1.4 lb per square foot)
Support: trellis with right-angle or diagonal
mesh, preferably with angled cross-section,
maximum cross-section of perimeter 45 mm
(1.8 in)
Minimum height of support: 5 m (16.5 ft)
Optimum width of support: 3 m (9.9 ft)
Distance from wall: 8 cm (3.2 in).

Clematis orientalis (Ranunculaceae)
lemon-peel clematis
Cultivars and related species: Several cultivars
and hybrids are now available, not all of which
may have the vigour of the parent. 'Bill
MacKenzie' is particularly good. *Clematis
tangutica* (zone 5) is a similar, slightly smaller
species.
Size: 5 m (16.5 ft)
Profile: maximum of 60 cm (2 ft)
Zone: 6
Foliage: small trifoliate leaves, fresh green
Flowers, season: nodding golden-yellow bells

with thick petals, midsummer to autumn
Fruit: fluffy seed heads
Origin: northern and central Asia
Aspect: light shade to sun
Climbing mechanism: leaf tendrils
Vigour: strong
Weight: very light, maximum of 10 kg per
square metre (0.9 lb per square foot)
Support: trellis with right-angle or diagonal
mesh, preferably with angled cross-section,
maximum cross-section of perimeter 30 mm
(1.2 in)
Minimum height of support: 5 m (16.5 ft)
Optimum width of support: 3 m (9.9 ft)
Distance from wall: 8 cm (3.2 in)

Clematis rehderiana (Ranunculaceae)
Size: 6 m (19.8 ft)
Profile: maximum of 90 cm (3 ft)
Zone: 6
Foliage: pinnate leaves, attractive dense growth
Flowers, season: masses of tiny fragrant
cream-coloured bells, mid to late summer
Origin: China
Aspect: sun, shelter
Climbing mechanism: leaf tendrils
Vigour: strong
Weight: light, maximum of 15 kg per square
metre (1.4 lb per square foot)
Support: trellis with right-angle or diagonal
mesh, preferably with angled cross-section,
maximum cross-section of perimeter 30 mm
(1.2 in)
Minimum height of support: 4 m (13.2 ft)
Optimum width of support: 3 m (9.9 ft)
Distance from wall: 8 cm (3.2 in)
Notes: Can be slow to establish.

Clematis terniflora (Ranunculaceae)

Size: 10 m (33 ft)

Profile: maximum of 90 cm (3 ft)

Zone: 6

Foliage: trifoliate, dark green

Flowers, season: small, white, slightly scented, autumn

Origin: eastern Asia

Aspect: sun, shelter

Climbing mechanism: leaf tendrils

Vigour: strong

Weight: light, maximum of 15 kg per square metre (1.4 lb per square foot)

Support: trellis with right-angle or diagonal mesh, preferably with angled cross-section, maximum cross-section of perimeter 45 mm (1.8 in)

Minimum height of support: 6 m (19.8 ft)

Optimum width of support: 3 m (9.9 ft)

Distance from wall: 5 cm (2 in)

Notes: Magnificent but can become tangled with age.

Clematis vitalba (Ranunculaceae)

old man's beard

Size: 15 m (49.5 ft)

Profile: maximum of 90 cm (3 ft)

Zone: 4

Foliage: multiple leaflets

Flowers, season: small, white, mid to late summer

Fruit: masses of fluffy seed heads

Origin: Europe

Aspect: light shade to sun

Climbing mechanism: leaf tendrils

Vigour: very strong

Weight: light, maximum of 15 kg per square metre (1.4 lb per square foot)

Support: trellis with right-angle or diagonal mesh, preferably with angled cross-section, maximum cross-section of perimeter 40 mm (1.6 in)

Minimum height of support: 8 m (26.4 ft)

Optimum width of support: 4 m (13.2 ft)

Distance from wall: 15 cm (6 in)

Notes: Relatively uninteresting but useful as one of the few large native climbers in much of northern Europe.

Cobaea scandens (Polemoniaceae)

cup and saucer vine

Size: 20 m (66 ft) in suitable climates

Profile: maximum of 30 cm (1 ft)

Zone: 10

Foliage: divided leaves, with tendrils

Flowers, season: large cup-shaped purple flowers, summer

Origin: Mexico

Aspect: sun

Climbing mechanism: tendrils

Vigour: strong

Weight: light, maximum of 15 kg per square metre (1.4 lb per square foot)

Support: trellis with right-angle or diagonal mesh, preferably with angled cross-section, maximum cross-section of perimeter 45 mm (1.8 in)

Minimum height of support: 2 m (6.6 ft) if grown as an annual

Optimum width of support: 2 m (6.6 ft)

Distance from wall: 8 cm (3.2 in)

Notes: Can be grown as a half-hardy annual, short-lived when grown as a perennial.

Cocculus carolinus (Menispermaceae)
Carolina moonseed
Size: 5 m (16.5 ft)
Profile: not measured
Zone: 7
Foliage: 13-cm long oval or heart-shaped leaves
Flowers, season: white flowers, summer
Fruit: red fruit in clusters
Origin: south-eastern United States
Aspect: light shade to sun
Climbing mechanism: twining
Vigour: not measured
Weight: not measured
Support: vertical supports, round cross-section, trellis with right-angle mesh
Minimum height of support: 3 m (9.9 ft)
Distance from wall: 10 cm (4 in)

Decumaria barbara (Hydrangeaceae)
Size: 9 m (29.7 ft)
Profile: maximum of 60 cm (2 ft)
Zone: 8
Foliage: 13-cm ovate leaves, evergreen or semi-evergreen
Flowers, season: fragrant white flowers in an 8 cm (3.2 in) wide head, summer
Origin: south-eastern United States
Aspect: light shade to sun
Climbing mechanism: aerial roots
Vigour: medium
Weight: light, maximum of 15 kg per square metre (1.4 lb per square foot)
Support: self-clinging
Minimum height of support: 4 m (13.2 ft)
Optimum width of support: 2 m (6.6 ft)
Distance from wall: 10 cm (4 in)
Notes: Bury stems when planting for more rapid growth in early years.

Euonymus fortunei var. *radicans* (Celastraceae)
Cultivars and related species: A number of cultivars exist. These are normally grown as shrubs, the climbing habit being optional. White-variegated 'Silver Queen' will climb to 6 m (19.8 ft), 'Emerald 'n' Gold' is strongly golden variegated. Compact varieties such as 'Golden Prince' are not suitable as climbers.
Size: 5 m (16.5 ft) as a climber
Profile: maximum of 60 cm (2 ft)
Zone: 5
Foliage: dark green evergreen, cultivars with silver or gold variegation
Fruit: white fruit, opening orange
Origin: eastern Asia
Aspect: light shade to sun
Climbing mechanism: aerial roots
Vigour: medium
Weight: heavy, with possible arborescent growth making possible 20–25 kg per square metre (2.3–2.7 lb per square foot)
Support: self-clinging, but mesh (cross or diagonal) or horizontal supports recommended
Minimum height of support: 4 m (13.2 ft)
Optimum width of support: 2 m (6.6 ft)
Distance from wall: 10 cm (4 in)
Notes: Like ivy, a mature phase has more bushy foliage.

Fallopia baldschuanica (Polygonaceae)
Russian vine, mile-a-minute vine
Cultivars and related species: *Fallopia aubertii* (zone 4) is very similar but with flowers in midsummer.

Size: 18 m (59.4 ft)
Profile: maximum of 60 cm (2 ft)
Zone: 4
Foliage: heart-shaped fresh green leaves
Flowers, season: white flowers massed in heads, late summer to autumn
Origin: central Asia
Aspect: light shade to sun
Climbing mechanism: twining
Vigour: very strong
Weight: light, maximum of 15 kg per square metre (1.4 lb per square foot)
Support: vertical supports, round cross-section, trellis with right-angle mesh
Minimum height of support: 8 m (26.4 ft)
Optimum width of support: 3 m (9.9 ft)
Distance from wall: 8 cm (3.2 in)
Notes: Very useful but only if a very large fast-growing plant is needed. Removal of unsightly tangled growth is occasionally necessary.

×Fatshedera lizei (Araliaceae)
Cultivars and related species: Several cultivars with variegated foliage are available.
Size: 6 × 4 m (19.8 × 13.2 ft)
Profile: maximum of 90 cm (3 ft)
Zone: 7
Foliage: glossy dark green lobed leaves, to 25 cm (10 in) across
Origin: garden origin
Aspect: shade, dislikes full sun
Climbing mechanism: rambler
Vigour: medium
Weight: light, maximum of 15 kg per square metre (1.4 lb per square foot)
Support: trellis with right-angle mesh or horizontal supports

Minimum height of support: 3 m (9.9 ft)
Optimum width of support: 2 m (6.6 ft)
Distance from wall: 10 cm (4 in)

Ficus pumila (Moraceae)
climbing fig, creeping fig
Size: 4 m (13.2 ft)
Profile: less than 15 cm (6 in)
Zone: 9
Foliage: 2- to 7-cm (0.8- to 2.8-in) long, tough, dark green
Origin: eastern Asia
Aspect: light shade
Climbing mechanism: aerial roots
Vigour: medium
Weight: very light, maximum of 10 kg per square metre (0.9 lb per square foot)
Support: self-clinging
Notes: Very useful in warmer climates.

Hedera helix (Araliaceae)
English ivy
Cultivars and related species: There are a vast number of cultivars of *H. helix* and a great many of other Hedera species, differing in leaf shape, colour, and level of variegation. Unfortunately, variegated varieties tend to lose their colour in shade and are less vigorous than the species. *Hedera hibernica* is a vigorous close relative to *H. helix* but is not recommended for façade greening as it does not produce many aerial roots. While most species ivies can grow to 30 m (90 ft), making them ideal for covering large areas of wall, many of the cultivars, the variegated ones especially, are less vigorous, which may make them ideal for smaller walls. However, we unfortunately have no idea of the

ultimate sizes of virtually all medium- or strong-growing cultivars, as they have never been grown to their full extent. 'Obovata', with oval-shaped leaves, is one that has been recommended for covering extensive areas (Rose 1996), while of the variegated forms 'Buttercup' is one of the more vigorous (Wassmann 2003). *Hedera canariensis* (zone 8) has larger leaves (to 20 cm, 8 in) and grows vigorously to 9 m (30 ft). It has several variegated forms. *Hedera colchica* 'Dentata' (zone 5) has large, highly decorative, foliage and is very vigorous. All ivies are essentially plants of maritime-influenced climates, making them less than ideal for areas with severe winter cold. Hardier than the type *H. helix* are 'Bulgaria', 'Romania', '238th St', 'Thorndale', and 'Wilson', all of which can be grown in the American Midwest. 'Baltica' is not suitable, apparently, despite the name. Those which develop a purple coloration in the winter, such as 'Woernerii' and 'Atropurpurea', are also very hardy. 'Goldheart' is very hardy but grows slowly (Wassmann 2003). In regions where ivy is hardy, any vigorous variety may be used. It should be noted that all *Hedera* species make extremely strong ground cover and their thick growth is capable of smothering native woodland flora in some areas where they have been introduced, notably the Pacific Northwest. Their use in some such areas is now forbidden. In areas where this is not a problem or where they are native, ivies are regarded as an excellent wildlife resource, a place for insect hibernation and bird nesting, and a late nectar source.

Size: 10 m (33 ft)
Profile: maximum of 30 cm (1 ft), but can eventually form bushy arborescent growth projecting to 90 cm (3 ft)
Zone: 4
Foliage: dark green, arrow-shaped, evergreen, extremely variable
Flowers, season: green, autumn
Fruit: black fruit in spherical clusters
Origin: Europe, western Asia
Aspect: sun or shade
Climbing mechanism: aerial roots
Vigour: strong
Weight: heavy, with possible arborescent growth making possible 20–25 kg per square metre (2.3–2.7 lb per square foot)
Support: self-clinging
Notes: Produces shrubby arborescent growth at the top of its support.

Holboellia coriacea (Lardizabalaceae)
Size: 7 m (23.1 ft)
Profile: maximum of 60 cm (2 ft)
Zone: 7
Foliage: 15-cm (6-in) trifoliate leaflets, evergreen
Flowers, season: green-white and pinkish fragrant flowers in clusters, spring
Origin: central China
Aspect: sun and shelter
Climbing mechanism: twining
Vigour: strong
Weight: light, max, 15 kg per square metre (1.4 lb per square foot)
Support: vertical supports, round cross-section, trellis with right-angle mesh
Minimum height of support: 3 m (9.9 ft)
Distance from wall: 10 cm (4 in)

Humulus lupulus (Cannabinaceae)

hop

Cultivars and related species: *Humulus lupulus* 'Aureus' has yellow foliage and seems almost as vigorous as the species.

Size: 7 m (23.1 ft)

Profile: maximum of 90 cm (3 ft)

Zone: 3

Foliage: lobed light green leaves, herbaceous

Fruit: greenish, papery, decorative

Origin: Northern Hemisphere

Aspect: light shade to sun

Climbing mechanism: twining

Vigour: very strong

Weight: very light, maximum of 10 kg per square metre (0.9 lb per square foot)

Support: vertical supports, round cross-section, trellis with right-angle mesh

Minimum height of support: 6 m (19.8 ft)

Optimum width of support: 2 m (6.6 ft)

Distance from wall: 5 cm (2 in)

Notes: Dead foliage in winter may need to be cleared away if unsightly.

Hydrangea petiolaris (Hydrangeaceae)

Cultivars and related species: *Hydrangea serratifolia* (syn. *H. integerrima*; zone 8) has evergreen leaves, but is less conspicuous.

Size: 15 m (49.5 ft)

Profile: maximum of 90 cm (3 ft)

Zone: 5

Foliage: 11-cm (4.4-in) long ovate leaves

Flowers, season: 25-cm (10-in) wide heads, outer florets creamy white and showy, midsummer

Origin: Far East

Aspect: semi-shade to shade

Climbing mechanism: aerial roots

Vigour: medium

Weight: light, maximum of 15 kg per square metre (1.4 lb per square foot)

Support: self-clinging, but mesh (cross or diagonal) or horizontal supports recommended for establishment

Minimum height of support: 4 m (13.2 ft)

Optimum width of support: 5 m (16.5 ft)

Distance from wall: 10 cm (4 in)

Notes: Bury stem on planting for more rapid growth in early years.

Ipomoea hederacea (Convolvulaceae)

morning glory

Size: 3–5 m (9.9–16.5 ft)

Profile: maximum of 30 cm (1 ft)

Zone: 8

Foliage: three-lobed leaves

Flowers, season: intense blue flowers throughout summer

Origin: Japan

Aspect: sun

Climbing mechanism: twining

Vigour: strong

Weight: very light, maximum of 10 kg per square metre (0.9 lb per square foot)

Support: vertical supports, round cross-section, trellis with right-angle or diagonal mesh

Minimum height of support: 2 m (6.6 ft)

Optimum width of support: 2 m (6.6 ft)

Distance from wall: 5 cm (2 in)

Notes: Half-hardy annual which is useful for summer screening.

Jasminum officianale (Oleaceae)
common jasmine

Cultivars and related species: In a genus of 200 species, there are a great many potential plants for warmer zones. Most are strong-growing twiners. Scent is always a valuable feature.

Size: 12 m (39.6 ft)
Profile: maximum of 1.2 m (4 ft)
Zone: 7
Foliage: small pinnate leaves
Flowers, season: fragrant white flowers, late summer to autumn.
Origin: mountains of western Asia
Aspect: sun
Climbing mechanism: twining
Vigour: medium
Weight: light, maximum of 15 kg per square metre (1.4 lb per square foot)
Support: trellis with right-angle or diagonal mesh, horizontal supports
Minimum height of support: 4 m (13.2 ft)
Optimum width of support: 3 m (9.9 ft)
Distance from wall: 5 cm (2 in)

Lonicera japonica (Caprifoliaceae)
evergreen honeysuckle

Size: 10 m (33 ft)
Profile: maximum of 90 cm (3 ft)
Zone: 4
Foliage: ovate leaves
Flowers, season: fragrant white flowers, summer
Origin: Japan
Aspect: light shade to sun
Climbing mechanism: twining
Vigour: strong

Weight: very light, maximum of 10 kg per square metre (0.9 lb per square foot)
Support: vertical supports, round cross-section, trellis with right-angle or diagonal mesh
Minimum height of support: 5 m (16.5 ft)
Optimum width of support: 3 m (9.9 ft)
Distance from wall: 5 cm (2 in)
Notes: Dangerously invasive in North America and southern Europe, but no reported problems in northern Europe.

Lonicera periclymenum (Caprifoliaceae)
common honeysuckle

Cultivars and related species: A wide variety is available, but given that some are chosen for compact growth, it is advisable to be sure eventual height is known when selecting.

Size: 7 m (23.1 ft)
Profile: maximum of 60 cm (2 ft)
Zone: 4
Foliage: slightly glaucous ovate leaves
Flowers, season: yellowish white intensely fragrant flowers, summer
Fruit: red berries, but not a major feature
Origin: Europe, Mediterranean basin
Aspect: light shade to sun
Climbing mechanism: twining
Vigour: medium
Weight: very light, maximum of 10 kg per square metre (0.9 lb per square foot)
Support: vertical supports, round cross-section, trellis with right-angle or diagonal mesh
Minimum height of support: 4 m (13.2 ft)
Optimum width of support: 2 m (6.6 ft)
Distance from wall: 5 cm (2 in)

Lonicera tragophylla (Caprifoliaceae)
Cultivars and related species: *Lonicera hildebrandtiana* (giant Burmese honeysuckle) grows to 10 m (33 ft), but is hardy only to zone 9.
Size: 12 m (39.6 ft)
Profile: maximum of 60 cm (2 ft)
Zone: 6
Foliage: 12-cm (4.8-in) long ovate leaves
Flowers, season: yellowish orange long-tubed flowers to 8 cm (3.2 in) long, summer
Fruit: red berries
Origin: central China
Aspect: shade or sun
Climbing mechanism: twining
Vigour: medium
Weight: very light, maximum of 10 kg per square metre (0.9 lb per square foot)
Support: vertical supports, round cross-section, trellis with right-angle or diagonal mesh
Minimum height of support: 6 m (19.8 ft)
Optimum width of support: 3 m (9.9 ft)
Distance from wall: 5 cm (2 in)

Menispermum canadense (Menispermaceae)
Canada moonseed
Size: 5 m (16.5 ft)
Profile: not measured
Zone: 5
Foliage: ovate leaves
Fruit: glossy black fruit
Origin: eastern North America
Aspect: sun
Climbing mechanism: twining
Vigour: strong
Weight: very light, maximum of 10 kg per square metre (0.9 lb per square foot)
Support: vertical supports, round cross-section, trellis with right-angle or diagonal mesh
Minimum height of support: 4 m (13.2 ft)
Optimum width of support: 2 m (6.6 ft)
Distance from wall: 5 cm (2 in)
Notes: Can sucker, which may be undesirable. Tangled growth may develop after a few years, necessitating a hard cut-back.

Muehlenbeckia complexa (Polygonaceae)
maidenhair vine
Size: 3 m (9.9 ft)
Profile: maximum of 60 cm (2 ft)
Zone: 8, possibly 7
Foliage: tiny leaves on dark wiry stems, forming a unique, dense, and intricate bushy habit
Origin: New Zealand
Aspect: light shade to sun, shelter
Climbing mechanism: twining
Vigour: medium
Weight: very light, maximum of 10 kg per square metre (0.9 lb per square foot)
Support: vertical, trellis with right-angle or diagonal mesh
Minimum height of support: 2 m (6.6 ft)
Optimum width of support: 2 m (6.6 ft)
Distance from wall: 5 cm (2 in)
Notes: Can be clipped into relatively geometric shapes.

Parthenocissus henryana (Vitaceae)
Cultivars and related species: *Parthenocissus thomsonii* is very similar.
Size: 10 m (33 ft)
Profile: maximum of 30 cm (1 ft)
Zone: 7
Foliage: white-veined leaves divided into three

to five leaflets, red in autumn
Origin: China
Aspect: best in light or medium shade
Climbing mechanism: suckers
Vigour: strong
Weight: light, maximum of 15 kg per square metre (1.4 lb per square foot)
Support: self-clinging

Parthenocissus quinquefolia (Vitaceae)
Virginia creeper (true)
Cultivars and related species: *Parthenocissus quinquefolia* 'Engelmannii' is the most reliable for self-clinging without support.
Size: 15 m (49.5 ft)
Profile: maximum of 30 cm (1 ft)
Zone: 3
Foliage: palmate leaves with five leaflets, fiery red in autumn
Origin: eastern North America
Aspect: light shade to sun
Climbing mechanism: suckers, but not always reliable
Vigour: strong
Weight: light, maximum of 15 kg per square metre (1.4 lb per square foot)
Support: self-clinging, but some supporting trellis (preferably diagonal mesh) advisable
Notes: Very widely grown and frequently confused with *Parthenocissus tricuspidata*.

Parthenocissus tricuspidata (Vitaceae)
Boston ivy, Japanese creeper, Virginia creeper (incorrectly)
Cultivars and related species: *Parthenocissus tricuspidata* 'Beverley Brook' has purple-tinged foliage.

Size: 20 m (66 ft)
Profile: less than 15 cm (6 in)
Zone: 4
Foliage: glossy leaves with three lobes, fiery red autumn colour
Origin: eastern Asia
Aspect: light shade to sun
Climbing mechanism: suckers
Vigour: strong
Weight: very light, maximum of 10 kg per square metre (0.9 lb per square foot)
Support: self-clinging
Notes: A shallow profile makes this an extremely useful species.

Passiflora caerulea (Passifloraceae)
passion flower
Cultivars and related species: With more than 400 species, *Passiflora* is one of the most important warm-climate genera of climbers.
Size: 10 m (33 ft)
Profile: maximum of 30 cm (1 ft)
Zone: 7
Foliage: deep green leaves, three- to nine-lobed
Flowers, season: complex pale green, blue, violet flowers, mid to late summer
Fruit: 6-cm orange fruit
Origin: southern Brazil
Aspect: sun, shelter
Climbing mechanism: tendrils
Vigour: strong
Weight: light, maximum of 15 kg per square metre (1.4 lb per square foot)
Support: trellis with right-angle or diagonal mesh, preferably with angled cross-section, maximum cross-section of perimeter 50 mm (2 in)

Minimum height of support: 5 m (16.5 ft)
Optimum width of support: 3 m (9.9 ft)
Distance from wall: 8 cm (3.2 in)

Periploca graeca (Asclepiadaceae)
silk vine
Size: 9 m (29.7 ft)
Profile: not measured
Zone: 6
Foliage: ovate glossy leaves
Flowers, season: purple-brown and greenish
  flowers, summer
Fruit: 12-cm (4.8-in) pods open to reveal silky
  tassels
Origin: south-eastern Europe, western Asia
Aspect: sun
Climbing mechanism: twining
Vigour: strong
Weight: not measured
Support: trellis with right-angle or diagonal
  mesh
Minimum height of support: 8 m (26.4 ft)
Optimum width of support: 3 m (9.9 ft)
Distance from wall: 8 cm (3.2 in)

Plumbago auriculata (Plumbaginaceae)
plumbago
Size: 6 m (19.8 ft)
Profile: maximum of 90 cm (3 ft)
Zone: 10
Foliage: light green leaves, evergreen
Flowers, season: profuse light blue flowers
  throughout growing season
Origin: South Africa
Aspect: light shade to sun
Climbing mechanism: lax rambler
Vigour: strong

Weight: medium, maximum of 20 kg per
  square metre (1.8 lb per square foot)
Support: horizontal or right-angled mesh
Minimum height of support: 3 m (9.9 ft)
Optimum width of support: 2.5 m (8.3 ft)
Distance from wall: 10 cm (4 in)
Notes: One of the finest, easiest, and most
  reliable plants for warm temperate climates.
  No real climbing mechanism, so it needs to
  be tied onto supports. Annual hard cut-back
  of wayward stems is often necessary.

Pyrostegia venusta (Bignoniaceae)
flame vine
Size: 25 m (82.5 ft)
Profile: maximum of 90 cm (3 ft)
Zone: 10
Foliage: pointed leaves, evergreen.
Flowers, season: narrow bright orange
  trumpets, summer
Origin: southern South America
Aspect: sun
Climbing mechanism: twining stems and
  tendrils
Vigour: strong
Weight: light, maximum 15 kg per square
  metre (1.4 lb per square foot)
Support: vertical supports, round cross-
  section, trellis with right-angle mesh
Minimum height of support: 10 m (33 ft)
Distance from wall: 10 cm (4 in)
Notes: Prefers acid soil.

Rosa (Rosaceae)
rose
Size: up to 9 m (29.7 ft) depending on variety
Profile: up to 1–2 m (40–80 in)

Foliage: rarely a feature in its own right

Flowers, season: flowers vary depending on species or cultivar, summer

Fruit: red hips can be attractive

Aspect: light shade to sun

Climbing mechanism: thorns

Weight: very light, maximum of 10 kg per square metre (0.9 lb per square foot)

Support: horizontal supports or trellis with right-angle or diagonal mesh, preferably with angled cross-section

Distance from wall: 10 cm (4 in)

Notes: Frequent tying-in of stray stems is vital, and annual pruning may be needed to control wayward downward-pointing stems. Climbing and rambling roses have only limited use for façade greening, as their lax habit means that frequent tying-in to supports is vital and their sometimes-vicious thorns can be a hazard.

Schisandra chinensis (Schisandraceae)

Cultivars and related species: Several similar species, all with spectacular fruit.

Size: 9 m (29.7 ft)

Profile: maximum of 90 cm (3 ft)

Zone: 8–9

Foliage: good-sized oval leaves

Flowers, season: cream, waxy, heavily scented, early summer

Fruit: striking red fruits, on female plants

Origin: Far East

Aspect: light shade best

Climbing mechanism: twining

Vigour: medium

Weight: medium, maximum 20 kg per square metre (1.8 lb per square foot)

Support: vertical supports with a round cross-section

Minimum height of support: 6 m (20 ft)

Optimum width of support: 3 m (10 ft)

Distance from wall: 15 cm (6 in)

Notes: Can be slow to start, but strong-growing eventually. Males and females must be grown together for fruit.

Schizophragma hydrangeoides (Hydrangeaceae)

Cultivars and related species: *Schizophragma integrifolium* is similar; *S. hydrangeoides* 'Rosea' has pink flowers.

Size: 12 m (39.6 ft)

Profile: maximum of 60 cm (2 ft)

Zone: 6

Foliage: dark, oval leaves

Flowers, season: lacecap hydrangea-like, showy, early summer

Origin: Japan

Aspect: light shade, or top in sun

Climbing mechanism: aerial roots

Vigour: medium

Weight: light, maximum of 15 kg per square metre (1.4 lb per square foot)

Support: self-clinging, but a trellis or horizontal supports will help in the initial stages

Minimum height of support: 4 m (13 ft)

Optimum width of support: 5 m (16 ft)

Distance from wall: 10 cm (4 in)

Notes: Bury stems when planting for more vigorous initial growth.

Sinofranchetia chinensis (Lardizabalaceae)

Size: 15 m (49.5 ft)

Profile: maximum of 60 cm (2 ft)

Zone: 6

Foliage: elegant trifoliate leaflets, to 15 cm
(6 in), bluish-green undersides
Fruit: pale purple, grapelike
Origin: China
Aspect: light shade
Climbing mechanism: twining
Vigour: strong
Weight: light, maximum of 15 kg per square
metre (1.4 lb per square foot)
Support: vertical supports, round cross-
section, trellis with right-angle mesh
Minimum height of support: 8 m (26.4 ft)
Distance from wall: 10 cm (4 in)

Solanum jasminoides (Solanaceae)
potato vine
Cultivars and related species: *Solanum
jasminoides* 'Album' has white flowers. *Solanum
crispum* is similar, but somewhat hardier;
S. c. 'Glasnevin' is a good selected form.
Size: 6 m (19.8 ft)
Profile: maximum of 60 cm (2 ft)
Zone: 8
Foliage: pointed dark green leaves, evergreen
Flowers, season: mauve-violet with central
yellow boss, summer
Origin: South America
Aspect: sun, shelter
Climbing mechanism: scrambler
Vigour: strong
Weight: light, maximum of 15 kg per square
metre (1.4 lb per square foot)
Support: vertical supports, round cross-
section, trellis with right-angled or diagonal
mesh
Minimum height of support: 3 m (9.9 ft)
Optimum width of support: 3 m (9.9 ft)

Distance from wall: 5 cm (2 in)
Notes: Initial tying-in necessary.

Stauntonia hexaphylla (Lardizabalaceae)
Size: 10 m (33 ft)
Profile: maximum of 30 cm (1 ft)
Zone: 8
Foliage: divided leaves with three to seven
leaflets, evergreen
Flowers, season: fragrant, violet-flushed white
flowers, spring
Fruit: dark greenish purple plumlike fruit,
edible
Origin: eastern Asia
Aspect: sun, shelter
Climbing mechanism: twining
Vigour: strong
Weight: light, max, 15 kg per square metre
(1.4 lb per square foot)
Support: vertical supports, round cross-
section, trellis with right-angle mesh
Minimum height of support: 5 m (16.5 ft)
Distance from wall: 10 cm (4 in)

Thunbergia grandiflora (Acanthaceae)
Bengal vine
Cultivars and related species: A large genus
with many showy climbers for warm regions,
of which *Thunbergia mysorensis*, with its long
pendant flower spikes, is most frequently seen.
Size: 6 m (19.8 ft), 2–3 m (6.6–9.9 ft) if grown
as an annual
Profile: maximum of 60 cm (2 ft)
Zone: 10
Foliage: elliptic leaves
Flowers, season: blue-mauve trumpet-shaped
flowers, summer to autumn

Origin: northern India

Aspect: sun, shelter

Climbing mechanism: twining

Vigour: strong

Weight: light, maximum of 15 kg per square metre (1.4 lb per square foot)

Support: vertical supports, round cross-section, trellis with right-angle mesh

Minimum height of support: 2 m (6.6 ft) if grown as an annual

Optimum width of support: 2 m (6.6 ft)

Distance from wall: 8 cm (3.2 in)

Notes: Sometimes grown as an annual, from cuttings taken from stock plants.

Trachelospermum jasminoides (Apocynaceae)

Cultivars and related species: *Trachelospermum asiaticum* is very similar but smaller.

Size: 9 m (29.7 ft)

Profile: maximum of 30 cm (1 ft)

Zone: 8

Foliage: deep green glossy leaves, evergreen

Flowers, season: bunches of heavily fragrant cream-coloured flowers, summer

Origin: eastern Asia

Aspect: light shade to sun, shelter

Climbing mechanism: twining

Vigour: medium

Weight: light, maximum of 15 kg per square metre (1.4 lb per square foot)

Support: vertical supports, round cross-section, trellis with right-angle mesh

Minimum height of support: 4 m (13.2 ft)

Optimum width of support: 2 m (6.6 ft)

Distance from wall: 5 cm (2 in)

Notes: Can be slow to establish and then slow to grow in cooler climates, but very attractive.

Tropaeoleum ciliatum (Tropaeoloceae)

Cultivars and related species: Several other climbing members of the genus may be worth experimenting with.

Size: 10 m (33 ft)

Profile: less than 15 cm (6 in)

Zone: 8, but not thoroughly evaluated

Foliage: small, neat six-lobed leaves, herbaceous

Flowers, season: yellow flowers, midsummer

Fruit: small purple fruit

Origin: Chile

Aspect: top growth best in sun or light shade

Climbing mechanism: twining

Vigour: strong

Weight: very light, max, 10 kg per square metre (0.9 lb per square foot)

Support: trellis

Minimum height of support: 5 m (16 ft)

Optimum width of support: 3 m (10 ft)

Distance from wall: 5 cm (2 in)

Notes: Potentially one of the most useful and effective herbaceous climbers for screening.

Vitis aestivalis (Vitaceae)

summer grape

Cultivars and related species: From central and eastern North America, *Vitis argentifolia* (zone 3) is similar with attractive white blooms on young shoots, to 10 m (33 ft). West coast *Vitis californica* (zone 7) grows to 10 m (33 ft), with crimson autumn colour. Other North American natives in the 10 m (33 ft) range include *Vitis labrusca* (zone 5).

Size: 15 m (49.5 ft)

Profile: maximum of 90 cm (3 ft)

Zone: 3

Foliage: dull green leaves to 30 cm (12 in) across

Fruit: black fruit

Origin: central and eastern North America

Aspect: sun or light shade

Climbing mechanism: tendrils

Vigour: strong

Weight: light, maximum of 15 kg per square metre (1.4 lb per square foot), although this may be exceeded by weight of trunk at lower levels, which carries much of its own weight

Support: trellis with right-angle or diagonal mesh, preferably with angled cross-section, maximum cross-section of perimeter 70 mm (2.8 in)

Minimum height of support: 8 m (26.4 ft)

Optimum width of support: 3 m (9.9 ft)

Distance from wall: at least 15 cm (6 in), with the possibility of a sizeable trunk developing in later years at the base

Notes: very vigorous

Vitis coignetiae (Vitaceae)

crimson glory vine

Cultivars and related species: *Vitis amurensis* (zone 4) grows to 9 m (29.7 ft), also has good autumn colour.

Size: 15 m (49.5 ft)

Profile: maximum of 90 cm (3 ft)

Zone: 5

Foliage: rough-textured leaves to 30 cm (12 in), crimson and scarlet autumn colour

Fruit: black, grapelike

Origin: Japan

Aspect: sun or light shade

Climbing mechanism: tendrils

Vigour: strong

Weight: light, maximum of 15 kg per square metre (1.4 lb per square foot), although this may be exceeded by weight of trunk at lower levels, which carries much of its own weight

Support: trellis with right-angle or diagonal mesh, preferably with angled cross-section, maximum cross-section of perimeter 70 mm (2.8 in)

Minimum height of support: 8 m (26.4 ft)

Optimum width of support: 3 m (9.9 ft)

Distance from wall: at least 15 cm (6 in), with the possibility of a sizeable trunk developing in later years at the base

Notes: One of the most magnificent climbers, very vigorous. This plant is a traditional subject for painting in Japan.

Vitis vinifera (Vitaceae)

grape vine

Cultivars and related species: *Vitis vinifera* 'Purpurea' has deep red leaves, turning purple in autumn. *Vitis vinifera* 'Brant' has light green leaves turning striking orange and red shades in autumn. Also a great many cultivars for dessert grape and wine production.

Size: 9 m (29.7 ft)

Profile: maximum of 60 cm (2 ft)

Zone: 6

Foliage: familiar lobed leaves

Fruit: luscious and edible

Origin: Caucasus

Aspect: sun

Climbing mechanism: tendrils

Vigour: strong

Weight: light, maximum of 15 kg per square metre (1.4 lb per square foot), although this may be exceeded by weight of trunk at lower levels, which carries much of its own weight

Support: trellis with right-angle or diagonal mesh, preferably with angled cross-section, maximum cross-section of perimeter 70 mm (2.8 in)

Minimum height of support: 5 m (16.5 ft)

Optimum width of support: 3 m (9.9 ft)

Distance from wall: at least 15 cm (6 in), with the possibility of a sizeable trunk developing in later years at the base

Notes: Façade greening allows the plant to run free, which may reduce grape production. Traditionally used for shading in Mediterranean climates.

Wisteria sinensis (Fabaceae)
wisteria

Cultivars and related species: A wide range of cultivars exists, mostly selected on the basis of flower colour. *Wisteria floribunda* (zone 4) is smaller (10 m, 33 ft). *Wisteria floribunda* 'Macrobotrys' has 1-m (40-in) long racemes of flowers.

Size: 30 m (99 ft)

Profile: maximum of 1.2 m (4 ft)

Zone: 5

Foliage: pinnate, up to 50 cm (20 in) long, attractive pale colour in spring

Flowers, season: fragrant, blue-mauve pendant, in racemes, early summer

Fruit: flattened beanlike pods

Origin: eastern Asia

Aspect: sun, shelter

Climbing mechanism: twining

Vigour: very strong

Weight: light, maximum of 15 kg per square metre (1.4 lb per square foot), although this

may be exceeded by weight of trunk at lower levels, which carries much of its own weight

Support: vertical supports, round cross-section, trellis with right-angle mesh

Minimum height of support: 15 m (16.5 ft)

Optimum width of support: 3 m (9.9 ft)

Distance from wall: at least 15 cm (6 in), with the possibility of a sizeable trunk developing in later years at the base

Notes: Traditionally pruning has been very hard to limit stem growth and to promote flowering. For façade greening, maximum growth is generally wanted. Owing to the plants size and strength, an annual inspection is recommended.

Suppliers

ROOF-GREENING COMPANIES

ZinCo GmbH
Grabenstrasse 33
D-72669 Unterensingen
Germany
Phone: +49 7022 6003 540
Fax: +49 7022 6003 541
E-mail: international@zinco.de
http://www.zinco.de

ZinCo Denmark I/S
Kildevangs Allé 1
DK-8260 Viby J
Denmark
Phone: +45 7012 1333
Fax: +45 8628 0466
E-mail: info@zinco.dk
http://www.zinco.dk

ZinCo Nederland BV
Postbus 9092
NL-1006 AB Amsterdam
The Netherlands
Phone: +31 20 6674852
Fax: +31 20 6673847
E-mail: daktuin@zinco.nl
http://www.zinco.nl

ZinCo Singapore Pte Ltd
170 Upper Bukit Timah Road
#15-03
SG-588179

Singapore
Phone: +65 6465 5648
Fax: +65 6465 5645
E-mail: admin@zinco.com.sg

ZinCo AG Dachbegrünungssysteme
Sägestrasse 7
CH-4104 Oberwil
Switzerland
Phone: +41 61 4015415
Fax: +41 61 4015416
E-mail: info@zinco.ch
http://www.zinco.ch

APP Dachgarten GmbH
Jurastrasse 21
D-85049 Ingolstadt
Germany
Phone: +49 841 3709496
Fax: +49 841 3709498
http://www.app.hu

GDT Gründach Technik GmbH
Dammstrasse 4
D-72669 Unterensingen
Germany
Phone: +49 7022 96320 0
Fax: +49 7022 96320 42
E-mail: gdt@gruendachtechnik.de
http://www.gruendachtechnik.de

Optigrün International AG
Am Birkenstock 19
D-72505 Krauchenwies-Göggingen
Germany
Phone: +49 0 7576 772 0
Fax: +49 0 7576 772 299
E-mail: info@optigruen.de
http://www.optigruen.de

Niederlassung Österreich
Landstraßer Hauptstraße 71/2
A-1030 Wien
Austria
Phone: +43 0 1 7172 8417
Fax: +43 0 1 7172 8110
http://www.optigruen.at

Erisco-Bauder Ltd
Broughton House
Broughton Road
Ipswich
Suffolk IP1 3QR
United Kingdom
Phone: +44 1473 257671
Fax: +44 1473 230761
E-mail: systems@erisco-bauder.co.uk
http://www.erisco-bauder.co.uk

American Hydrotech, Inc.
303 East Ohio Street
Chicago, Illinois 60611-3387
United States
Phone: +1 800 877 6125
Fax: +1 312 661 0731
http://www.hydrotechusa.com

Corus Building Systems
Kalzip Division
Haydock Lane
Haydock
St Helens
Merseyside WA11 9TY
United Kingdom
Phone: +44 0 1942 295500
Fax: +44 0 1942 272136
E-mail: kalzip-uk@corusgroup.com
http://www.kalzip.co.uk

Re-natur GmbH
Charles-Roß-Weg 24
24601 Ruhwinkel
Germany
Phone: +49 43 2390 10 0
Fax: + 49 43 2390 10 33
E-mail: info@re-natur.de
http://www.re-natur.de

Roofscapes, Inc.
7114 McCallum Street
Philadelphia, Pennsylvania 19119
United States
E-mail: cmiller@roofmeadow.com
http://www.roofmeadow.com

VegTech
Fagerås
SE-340 30 Vislanda
Sweden
Phone: 0046 472 303 16
Fax: 0046 472 300 23
http://www.vegtech.se

Alumasc Exterior Building Products Ltd
White House Works
Bold Road
Sutton
St Helens
Merseyside WA9 4JG
United Kingdom
Phone: +44 1744 648400
Fax: +44 1744 648401
E-mail: info@alumasc-exteriors.co.uk
http://www.alumasc-exteriors.co.uk

Blackdown Horticultural Consultants
Coombe St Nicholas
Taunton TA20 3HZ
United Kingdom
Phone: +44 1460 234582
E-mail: art@blackdownhortic.co.uk
http://www.greenroof.co.uk

MODULAR GREEN-ROOF SYSTEMS

GreenTech
1301 Macy Drive
Roswell, Georgia 30076
United States
Phone: +1 770 587 2522
http://www.greentechitm.com

FAÇADE-GREENING SUPPORT SYSTEMS

Jakob AG
Drahtseilfabrik
CH-3555 Trubschachen
Switzerland
Phone: +41 34 495 10 10
Fax: +41 34 495 10 25
E-mail: jakob@luewin.ch
http://www.jakob-inoxline.ch
Informative catalogue in English, affiliated
    companies in many other countries.

Jakob UK
Mendip Manufacturing Agency
Wells BA5 3ET
United Kingdom
Phone: +44 01761 241437
Fax: +44 01761 241437

Decorcable Innovations LLC
660 West Randolph Street
Chicago, Illinois 60661-2114
United States
Phone: +1 312 474 1100
Fax: +1 312 474 1789
E-mail: sales@decorcable.com

Schmitt/Abt. Ranktechnik
Gewerbegebiet Ommersheim
66399 Mandelbachtal
Germany
E-mail: info@schmitt-galabau.de
http://www.schmitt-galabau.de

SUPPLIERS

Hubert Waltermann GmbH & Co
D-58798 Balve-Garbeck
Postfach 1453
Germany
http://www.waltermann.de

Polygrün
Heerstraße 70
53894 Mechernich
Germany
E-mail: info@polygruen.de
http://www.polygruen.de

FAÇADE-GREENING CONSULTANCIES

Fritz Wassmann
Hofenstrasse 69
Hinterkappelen
CH 3032
Switzerland
Phone/Fax: +41 31 829 2755

BIOENGINEERING

Beat Scheuter
Zugerstrasse 76b
CH-6304 Baar
Switzerland
Phone: +41 41 767 28 23
Fax: +41 41 760 43 45
http://www.scheuter.ch

Beat Scheuter
5635 Shoeman Road
Hasslett, Michigan 48840-9723
United States
Phone: +1 517 655 2883

MODULAR WALL SYSTEMS

Soil Retention Systems
2501 State Street
Carlsbad, California 92008
United States
Phone: +1 760 966 6090
Fax: +1 760 966 6097
http://www.soilretention.com

Bibliography

Arbeitskreis Fassadenbegrünung. 2000. *Richtlinie für die Planung, Ausführung und Pflege von Fassadenbegrünung mit Kletterpflanzen.* Bonn, Germany: Forschungsgesellschaft Landschaftsentwicklung Landschaftsbau (FLL).

Barbour, M. C., and W. D. Billings. 1988. *North American Terrestrial Vegetation.* Cambridge, U.K.: University of Cambridge Press.

Bass, B. 2001. Reducing the urban heat island and its associated problems: Examining the role of green roof infrastructure. *Green Roofs Infrastructure Monitor* 3(1): 10–12.

Bass, B., R. Stull, S. Krayenjoff, and A. Martilli. 2002. Modelling the impact of green roof infrastructure on the urban heat island in Toronto. *Green Roofs Infrastructure Monitor* 4(1).

Bisgrove, R. 1992. *The Gardens of Gertrude Jekyll.* London: Frances Lincoln.

Boivin, M., M. Lamy, A. Gosselin, and B. Dansereau. 2001. Effect of artificial substrate depth on freezing injury of six herbaceous perennials grown in a green roof system. *HortTechnology* 11: 409–412.

Brandwein, T., and M. Köhler. 1993. In M. Köhler, ed. *Fassaden-und Dachbegrünung.* Stuttgart: Ulmer.

Brenneisen, S. 2003. The benefits of biodiversity from green roofs: key design consequences. *Greening Rooftops for Sustainable Communities*, Proceedings of the First North American Green Roofs Conference, Chicago, May 2003. Toronto: The Cardinal Group.

Broili, M. 2002. Eco-roofs as a stormwater management tool. *Newsletter of Living Systems Design Guild* April.

Burke, K. 2003. Green roofs and regenerative design strategies: The Gap's 901 Cherry Project. *Greening Rooftops for Sustainable Communities*, Proceedings of the First North American Green Roofs Conference, Chicago, May 2003. Toronto: The Cardinal Group.

Cheney, C. 2002. Greening Gotham's rooftops. *Green Roofs Infrastructure Monitor*, 4 (2).

Crûg Farm Nursery Catalogue. 2003. Wales: Crûg Farm.

Cushman, R. 1988. *Shortgrass Prairie.* Boulder, Colorado: Pruett.

Dunnett, N. 2002. Up on the roof. *The Garden* May: 380–383.

Dunnett, N., and A. Nolan. 2004. The effect of substrate depth and supplementary watering on the growth of nine herbaceous perennials in a semi-extensive green roof. *International Journal of Horticultural Science.* In press.

Emilsson, T. 2003. The influence of establishment method and species mix on plant cover. *Greening Rooftops for Sustainable Communities*, Proceedings of the First North American Green Roofs Conference, Chicago, May 2003. Toronto: The Cardinal Group.

English Nature. 2003. *Green Roofs: Their Existing Status and Potential for Conserving Biodiversity in Urban Areas.* English Nature Report no. 498. Peterborough, U.K.: English Nature.

Ferguson, B. K. 1998. *Introduction to Stormwater: Concept, Purpose, Design.* New York: John Wiley and Sons, Inc.

Garnett, T. 1997. Digging for change: The potential of urban food production. *Urban Nature Magazine* Summer: 62–65.

Gedge, D. 2003. From rubble to redstarts. *Greening Rooftops for Sustainable Communities*, Proceedings of the First North American Green Roofs Conference, Chicago, May 2003. Toronto: The Cardinal Group.

Green Roofs Infrastructure Monitor. 2001a. Vol. 2, no. 3.

Green Roofs Infrastructure Monitor. 2001b. Vol. 3, no. 2.

Grime, J. P. 2002. *Plant Strategies, Vegetation Processes and Ecosystem Properties.* Chichester, U.K.: John Wiley.

Hauth, E., and T. Liptan. 2003. Plant survival findings in the Pacific Northwest. *Greening Rooftops for Sustainable Communities*, Proceedings of the First North American Green Roofs Conference, Chicago, May 2003. Toronto: The Cardinal Group.

Herman, R. 2003. Green roofs in Germany: Yesterday, today and tomorrow. *Greening Rooftops for Sustainable Communities*, Proceedings of the First North American Green Roofs Conference, Chicago, May 2003. Toronto: The Cardinal Group.

Hewitt, T. 2003. *Garden Succulents.* RHS Wisley Handbook. London: Cassell Illustrated Publications.

Hill, P. 2001. Vertical thinking. *The Garden* April: 280–283.

Hitchmough, J. 1994. *Urban Landscape Management.* Sydney: Incata Press.

Hutchinson, D., P. Abrams, R. Retzlaff, and T. Liptan. 2003. Stormwater monitoring of two ecoroofs in Portland, Oregon, USA. *Greening Rooftops for Sustainable Communities*, Proceedings of the First North American Green Roofs Conference, Chicago, May 2003. Toronto: The Cardinal Group.

Jakob. 2002. Catalogue. Trubschachen, Switzerland: Jakob AG.

Jekyll, G. 1901. *Wall and Water Gardens.* New York: C. Scribner's Sons.

Johnson, J., and J. Newton. 1993. *Building Green: A Guide to Using Plants on Roofs, Walls and Pavements.* London: London Ecology Unit.

Kendle A. D., and J. E. Rose. 2000. The aliens have landed! What are the justifications for 'native only' policies in landscape plantings? *Landscape and Urban Planning* 47: 19–31.

Kingsbury, N. 2001. Roofing veldt. *The Garden* June: 446–449.

Köhler, M. 1993. *Fassaden-und Dachbegrünung.* Stuttgart: Ulmer.

Köhler, M., M. Schmidt, F. W. Grimme, M. Laar, and F. Gusmao. 2001. Urban water retention by greened roofs in temperate and tropical climates. *Proceedings of the 38th World Congress of the International Federation of Landscape Architects, Singapore.* Versailles: IFLA.

Kolb, W., 1988. Direktaussaat von Stauden und Graesern zur Extensivebegrünung von *Flachdaechern. Rasen-Turf-Gazon* 3. Republished in Veitshoechheimer Berichte, Heft 39, Dachbegrünung.

Kolb, W., 1995. *Dachbegrünung—Versuchsergebnisse Neue Landschaft* 10. Republished in Veitshoechheimer Berichte, Heft 39, Dachbegrünung.

Kolb, W., and T. Schwarz. 1986a. Zum Klimatisierungseffekt von Pflanzenbeständen auf Dächern, Teil I. *Zeitschrift für Vegetationstechnik* 9. Republished in Veitshoechheimer Berichte, Heft 39, Dachbegrünung.

Kolb, W., and T. Schwarz. 1986b. Zum Klimatisierungseffekt von Pflanzenbeständen auf Dächern, Teil II. *Zeitschrift für Vegetationstechnik* 9. Republished in Veitshoechheimer Berichte, Heft 39, Dachbegrünung.

Kolb, W., and T. Schwarz. 1999. *Dachbegrünung intensive und extensiv.* Stuttgart: Ulmer.

Kolb, W., T. Schwarz, R. Trunk, and H. Zott. 1989. Extensivbegrünung mit System? *Rasen-Turf-Gazon* 4: 91–97.

Kolb, W., and R. Trunk. 1993. *Allium ergänzen Sedum hervorragend Tagungband Landespflegetage.* Republished in Veitshoechheimer Berichte, Heft 39, Dachbegrünung.

Liptan, T. 2002. Author interview, Bureau of Environmental Services, Portland, Oregon, 26 October 2002.

Liptan, T., and R. Murase. 2002. Water gardens as stormwater infrastructure (Portland, Oregon). In R. France, ed. *Handbook of Water-Sensitive Planning and Design.* Boca Raton, Florida: Lewis Publishers.

Liu, K., and B. Baskaran. 2003. Thermal performance of green roofs through field evaluation. *Greening Rooftops for Sustainable Communities,* Proceedings of the First North American Green Roofs Conference, Chicago, May 2003. Toronto: The Cardinal Group.

Meiss, M. 1979. The climate of cities. In Iain Laurie, ed. *Nature in Cities.* Chichester, U.K.: John Wiley & Sons.

Mentens, J., D. Raes, and M. Hermy. 2003. Effect of orientation on the water balance of green roofs. *Greening Rooftops for Sustainable Communities,* Proceedings of the First North American Green Roofs Conference, Chicago, May 2003. Toronto: The Cardinal Group.

Miller, C. 2002. Mathematical simulation methods: A foundation for a developing general-purpose green roof simulation models. Unpublished conference notes, 8 December 2002.

Miller, C. 2003. Moisture management in green roofs. *Greening Rooftops for Sustainable Communities,* Proceedings of the First North American Green Roofs Conference, Chicago, May 2003. Toronto: The Cardinal Group.

Oberlander, C., E. Whitelaw, and E. Matsuzaki. 2002. *Introductory Manual for Greening Roofs for Public Works and Government Services in Canada.* Toronto: Public Works and Government Services.

Optigrün. 2002. Catalogue. Krauchenwies-Goggingen, Germany: Optigrün.

Osmundson, T. 1999. *Roof Gardens, History, Design, Construction.* New York: W. W. Norton and Co.

Peck, S. P. 2003a. Private benefits, public benefits. Available via http://www.peck.ca/grhcc/

Peck, S. 2003b. Towards an integrated green roof infrastructure evaluation for Toronto. *Green Roofs Infrastructure Monitor* 5(1): 4–5.

Peck, S., and M. Kuhn. 2000. *Design Guidelines for Green Roofs.* Toronto: Environment Canada.

Peck, S. P., C. Callaghan, M. E. Kuhn, and B. Bass. 1999. *Greenbacks from Greenroofs: Forging a New Industry in Canada.* Toronto: Canada Mortgage and Housing Corp.

Randall, D. 2003. Conversation with author, Bristol, U.K., 6 March 2003.

Rose, P. Q. 1996. *The Gardeners Guide to Growing Ivies.* Newton Abbot, U.K.: David and Charles.

Rowe, D., R. Clayton, N. Van Woert, M. Monterusso, and D. Russell. 2003. Green roof slope, substrate depth and vegetation influence runoff. *Greening Rooftops for Sustainable Communities*, Proceedings of the First North American Green Roofs Conference, Chicago, May 2003. Toronto: The Cardinal Group.

Schillander, P., and S. Hultengren. 1998. *Plants and Animals on the Alvars of Öland*. Kälmar, Sweden: Länsstyrelsen Kälmar Län.

Scholz-Barth, K. 2001. Green roofs: Stormwater management from the top down. *Environmental Design & Construction* January/February.

Spronken-Smith, R. A., and T. R. Oke. 1998. The thermal regime of urban parts in two cities with different summer temperatures. *International Journal of Remote Sensing* 19(11): 2085–2104.

Stein, S. 1993. *Restoring the Ecology of Our Own Backyards*. Boston: Houghton Mifflin.

Stender, I. 2002. Policy incentives for green roofs in Germany. *Green Roofs Infrastructure Monitor* 4(1).

Stephenson, R. 1994. *Sedum: Cultivated stonecrops*. Portland, Oregon: Timber Press.

Tan, P., N. Wong, Y. Chen, C. Ong, and A. Sia. 2003. Thermal benefits of rooftop gardens in Singapore. *Greening Rooftops for Sustainable Communities*, Proceedings of the First North American Green Roofs Conference, Chicago, May 2003. Toronto: The Cardinal Group.

Ulrich, R. 1984. View through a window may influence recovery from surgery. *Science* 224: 420–421.

Ulrich, R. 1986. Human responses to vegetation and landscapes. *Landscape and Urban Planning* 13: 29–44.

Ulrich, R. S., and R. Simons. 1986. Recovery from stress during exposure to everyday outdoor environments. In J. Wineman, R. Barnes, and C. Zimring, eds. *The Costs of Not Knowing*, Proceedings of the 17th Annual Conference of the Environmental Research Association. Washington, D.C.: Environmental Research Association.

Valazquez, L. 2003. Modular green roof technology: An overview of two systems. *Greening Rooftops for Sustainable Communities*, Proceedings of the First North American Green Roofs Conference, Chicago, May 2003. Toronto: The Cardinal Group.

Von Stulpnagel, A., M. Horbert, and H. Sukopp. 1990. The importance of vegetation for the urban climate. In H. Sukopp, ed. *Urban Ecology*. The Hague, The Netherlands: Academic Publishing.

Wassmann, F. 2003. Interview with Noël Kingsbury, April 10, 2003, Hinterkappelen, Switzerland.

White, J. W. 2001. Green roof infrastructure and preventing fire hazards. *Green Roofs Infrastructure Monitor* 3(1).

White, J. W., and E. Snodgrass. 2003. Extensive green roof plant selection and characteristics. *Greening Rooftops for Sustainable Communities*, Proceedings of the First North American Green Roofs Conference, Chicago, May 2003. Toronto: The Cardinal Group.

Wieditz, I. 2003. Urban biodiversity: An oxymoron? *Green Roofs Infrastructure Monitor* 5(1): 8–9.

FURTHER READING

Façade greening

There is virtually nothing on façade greening written in English. The following sources are in German and between them are very comprehensive.

Brandwein, T. www.biotekt.de.

Köhler. M. 1997. *Fassaden-und Dachbegrünung*. Stuttgart: Ulmer.

Richtlinie für die Planung, Ausführung und Pflege von Fassadenbegrünung mit Kletterpflanzen. 2000. Bonn: Forschungsgesellschaft Landschaftsentwicklung Landschaftsbau (FLL).

Roof greening

Virtually all English-language material is available on the web, much of which duplicates the German and other European research. To date, the two major books in English have been:

Johnson, J., and J. Newton. 1993. *Building Green: A Guide to Using Plants on Roofs, Walls and Pavements*. London: London Ecology Unit. This provides a very useful overview of the use of plants on buildings.

Osmundson, T. 1999. *Roof Gardens: History, Design, Construction*. New York: W. W. Norton and Co. This comprehensive book concentrates mainly on intensive roof gardens.

For readers of German, there are several books which are very useful on techniques and plants:

Kolb, W., and T. Schwarz. 1999. *Dachbegrünung, intensiv und extensiv*. Stuttgart: Ulmer. This is the most useful all-round book.

Richtlinie für die Planung, Ausführung und Pflege von Dachbegrünung. 1995. Bonn: Forschungsgesellschaft Landschaftsentwicklung Landschaftsbau (FLL).

Technical specifications for planning, implementation, and maintenance:

Ernst, W. 2002. *Dachabdichtung–Dachbegrünung 1. Fehler. Ursachen, Auswirkungen und Vermeidung*. Stuttgart: IRB Verlag. This provides a study of failures of roof sealing and roof greening as well as their causes, effects, and prevention.

Ernst, W., and H.-J. Liesecke. 2002. *Dachabdichtung–Dachbegrünung. Fachbuchpaket*. Stuttgart: IRB Verlag. This gives detailed technical information on roof protection and sealing and greening.

Index

Plates are indicated with bold page numbers.
Plants described only in the appendices, pages
191–242, are not included here.